2017

THE BEST OF
COUNTRY COOKING

Taste of Home

For other *Taste of Home* books and products,
visit ShopTasteofHome.com.

THE BEST FIXIN'S

When it comes to feeding your family, you don't have to sacrifice flavor for ease! In *The Best of Country Cooking*, you'll find 319 recipes that are big on flavor and comfort—and just like Mom made. What's not to love?

Look inside for:

Contest Winner

Blue-Ribbon Recipes

On the hunt for recipes with the highest praise? Look for the blue-ribbon recipes featured in each chapter—they've all placed in a *Taste of Home* contest, meaning you can trust they'll shine at your next meal.

Meals in Minutes

Need a home-cooked meal quick? We've got you covered! Flip to p. 96 for no-fuss recipes you can have table-ready in a half hour...or less! It doesn't get much easier than that.

Cookies, Bars & Candies

Sometimes you just need to bake up some homemade love. Look no further than the Cookies, Bars & Candies chapter (p. 146) for dozens of the most gooey, decadently yummy treats to wow at your next potluck or party.

Try a new meal tonight from *The Best of Country Cooking*, then sit back and wait for the compliments to roll in! Since all the recipes come from home cooks just like you, you can count on them for down-home goodness. All you have to do now is enjoy the delicious results!

■ EDITORIAL

Editor-in-Chief **Catherine Cassidy**
Vice President, Content Operations **Kerri Balliet**
Creative Director **Howard Greenberg**

Managing Editor/Print & Digital Books **Mark Hagen**
Associate Creative Director **Edwin Robles Jr.**

Associate Editor **Molly Jasinski**
Art Director **Raeann Thompson**
Layout Designer **Nancy Novak**
Editorial Services Manager **Dena Ahlers**
Editorial Production Coordinator **Jill Banks**
Copy Chief **Deb Warlaumont Mulvey**
Copy Editors **Dulcie Shoener (senior), Ronald Kovach, Chris McLaughlin, Ellie Piper**

Content Director **Julie Blume Benedict**
Food Editors **Gina Nistico; James Schend; Peggy Woodward, RDN**
Recipe Editors **Sue Ryon (lead); Irene Yeh**
Editorial Services Administrator **Marie Brannon**

Culinary Director **Sarah Thompson**
Test Cooks **Nicholas Iverson (lead), Matthew Hass**
Food Stylists **Kathryn Conrad (lead), Lauren Knoelke, Shannon Roum**
Prep Cooks **Bethany Van Jacobson (lead), Melissa Hansen, Aria C. Thornton**
Culinary Team Assistant **Maria Petrella**

Photography Director **Stephanie Marchese**
Photographers **Dan Roberts, Jim Wieland**
Photographer/Set Stylist **Grace Natoli Sheldon**
Set Stylists **Melissa Franco (lead), Stacey Genaw, Dee Dee Schaefer**
Set Stylist Assistant **Stephanie Chojnacki**

Business Architect, Publishing Technologies **Amanda Harmatys**
Business Analyst, Publishing Technologies **Kate Unger**
Junior Business Analyst, Publishing Technologies **Shannon Stroud**

Editorial Business Manager **Kristy Martin**
Rights & Permissions Associate **Samantha Lea Stoeger**
Editorial Business Associate **Andrea Meiers**

Editor, *Taste of Home* **Emily Betz Tyra**
Art Director, *Taste of Home* **Kristin Bowker**

■ BUSINESS

Vice President, Group Publisher **Kirsten Marchioli**
Publisher, *Taste of Home* **Donna Lindskog**
Business Development Director, Taste of Home Live **Laurel Osman**
Strategic Partnerships Manager, Taste of Home Live **Jamie Piette Andrzejewski**

■ TRUSTED MEDIA BRANDS, INC.

President & Chief Executive Officer **Bonnie Kintzer**
Chief Financial Officer **Dean Durbin**
Chief Marketing Officer **C. Alec Casey**
Chief Revenue Officer **Richard Sutton**
Chief Digital Officer **Vince Errico**
Senior Vice President, Global HR & Communications **Phyllis E. Gebhardt, SPHR; SHRM-SCP**
General Counsel **Mark Sirota**
Vice President, Magazine Marketing **Christopher Gaydos**
Vice President, Product Marketing **Brian Kennedy**
Vice President, Operations **Michael Garzone**
Vice President, Consumer Marketing Planning **Jim Woods**
Vice President, Digital Product & Technology **Nick Contardo**
Vice President, Financial Planning & Analysis **William Houston**

PICTURED ON THE FRONT COVER Balsamic Three-Bean Salad (p. 47), Bacon Cheeseburger Slider Bake (p. 13), Oregon's Best Marionberry Pie (p. 174) and Buffalo Chicken Lasagna (p. 77).

PICTURED ON THE BACK COVER Maryland-Style Crab Soup (p. 143), Ultimate Pot Roast (p. 95) and Bacon & Mushroom Omelets (p. 116).

CONTENTS

SNACKS & BEVERAGES

Host a party, head to a tailgate, offer an after-school snack, or savor a fun time at home with family—you can do it all with the tasty eats and sweet sippers in this chapter. There's something for everyone here!

Mocha Cappuccino Punch

Coffee, meet ice cream. An inventive way to indulge a crowd, this luscious java punch will quench the urgent chocolate cravings for you and your friends.
—**FANCHEON RESLER** ALBION, IN

PREP: 15 MIN. + CHILLING
MAKES: 13 SERVINGS (¾ CUP EACH)

- 1 cup hot water
- 2 tablespoons instant coffee granules
- ¼ teaspoon ground cinnamon
- 1 can (14 ounces) fat-free sweetened condensed milk
- ½ cup chocolate syrup
- 1 quart half-and-half cream
- 1 quart chocolate ice cream
- 2 cups club soda, chilled
  Baking cocoa

1. In a small bowl, whisk the water, coffee granules and cinnamon until coffee granules are dissolved. Stir in milk and chocolate syrup. Cover and refrigerate until chilled.
2. Transfer milk mixture to a punch bowl; stir in half-and-half cream. Add scoops of ice cream; gradually pour in club soda. Dust top with cocoa. Serve immediately.

Contest Winner

Five-Spice Chicken Wings

These wings are baked to a perfect golden brown and shine with mild Asian spices. Thanks to an overnight marinade, the chicken inside stays tender while the skin maintains that signature crunch.
—**CRYSTAL JO BRUNS** ILIFF, CO

PREP: 20 MIN. + MARINATING • **BAKE:** 25 MIN.
MAKES: ABOUT 3 DOZEN

- 3½ pounds chicken wings
- 3 green onions, chopped
- 2 tablespoons sweet chili sauce
- 2 tablespoons reduced-sodium soy sauce
- 2 tablespoons fish sauce or additional soy sauce
- 4 garlic cloves, minced
- 1 tablespoon sugar
- 1 tablespoon Chinese five-spice powder
- 2 medium limes, cut into wedges

1. Cut chicken wings into three sections; discard wing tip sections. Combine the onions, chili sauce, soy sauce, fish sauce, garlic, sugar and five-spice powder in a large resealable plastic bag. Add wings; seal bag and toss to coat. Refrigerate 8 hours or overnight.
2. Drain the chicken, discarding marinade. Place wings in a greased 15x10x1-in. baking pan.
3. Bake at 425° for 25-30 minutes or until no longer pink, turning every 10 minutes. Squeeze lime wedges over the wings.
NOTE *Uncooked chicken wing sections (wingettes) may be substituted for whole chicken wings.*

Jalapeno Poppers with Lime Cilantro Dip

Crispy with a creamy filling, these little pepper bites always earn rave reviews. They're fit for any event, from a cocktail soiree to a simple party.

—TANA ROGERS NEW YORK, NY

PREP: 30 MIN. • **BAKE:** 20 MIN.
MAKES: 2 DOZEN (2 CUPS DIP)

- 12 jalapeno peppers
- 1 package (8 ounces) cream cheese, softened
- 1¼ cups shredded sharp cheddar cheese
- 4 green onions, finely chopped
- ⅓ cup all-purpose flour
- 6 large egg whites, lightly beaten
- 1½ cups panko (Japanese) bread crumbs
- ½ teaspoon salt
- ½ teaspoon pepper

LIME CILANTRO DIP

- 2 cups (16 ounces) sour cream
- 4 green onions, finely chopped
- ¼ cup lime juice
- 2 tablespoons minced fresh cilantro
- ½ teaspoon garlic salt

1. Cut jalapenos in half lengthwise and remove seeds. Place jalapenos on an ungreased baking sheet. Broil 4 in. from the heat for 4-6 minutes on each side or until lightly blistered. Cool slightly.

2. In a small bowl, beat cream cheese and cheddar cheese until blended. Stir in onions. Spoon into pepper halves.

3. Place the flour, egg whites and bread crumbs in separate shallow bowls. Coat jalapenos with flour, then dip in egg whites and coat with crumbs. Place on a greased baking sheet; sprinkle with salt and pepper. Bake at 350° for 18-20 minutes or until lightly browned.

4. For dip, combine all ingredients in a small bowl. Serve with poppers.

NOTE *Wear disposable gloves when cutting hot peppers; the oils can burn skin. Avoid touching your face.*

Black Forest Ham Roll-Ups

I love to entertain at both home and the office. Ham and cheese rolled in tortillas make a quick appetizer that is easy to transport.

—SUSAN ZUGEHOER HEBRON, KY

PREP: 25 MIN. + CHILLING
MAKES: ABOUT 6½ DOZEN

- 1 package (8 ounces) cream cheese, softened
- 2 teaspoons minced fresh parsley
- 2 teaspoons dried celery flakes
- 2 teaspoons Dijon mustard
- 1 teaspoon lemon juice
- ⅛ teaspoon salt
- ⅛ teaspoon pepper
- ½ cup dried cranberries, chopped
- 2 green onions, chopped
- 5 flour tortillas (10 inches), room temperature
- ½ pound thinly sliced Black Forest deli ham
- ½ pound thinly sliced Swiss cheese

1. In a small bowl, mix first seven ingredients until blended. Stir in cranberries and green onions; spread over tortillas. Layer with ham and cheese. Roll up tightly; wrap in plastic wrap. Refrigerate at least 1 hour.

2. Just before serving, unwrap and cut each tortilla crosswise into 16 slices.

Contest Winner

Contest Winner

3. Stir in cranberries, mushrooms, oil, lemon pepper, salt and paprika; cook and stir 2 minutes. Reduce heat. Stir in juice; cook and stir until mushrooms are tender, about 4 minutes.

4. On a parchment paper-lined baking sheet, unfold puff pastry sheet and form a 10-in. square, using a rolling pin if necessary. With a ruler, cut a 10x2-in. rectangle with a long sharp knife or pastry wheel. From the 10x2-in. strip, cut two 10x½-in. strips and two 7x½-in. strips. Remove and discard trimmings. Prick the remaining 10x8-in. pastry base all over with a fork. Brush water ½ in. around edges of pastry base. Place the 10x½-in. and 7x½-in. strips along edges to form sides. Press lightly.

5. Spread cranberry mixture to edges; sprinkle with bacon. Bake 18-22 minutes or until pastry is golden brown. Cool 10 minutes. Sprinkle with basil. Serve warm with topping.

Moscow Mule

Here's an old-time cocktail that was popular in the 1940s and '50s. It's traditionally served in a copper mug with plenty of ice.
—*TASTE OF HOME* TEST KITCHEN

START TO FINISH: 5 MIN. • **MAKES:** 6 SERVINGS

- 2 **cups ginger ale, chilled**
- 2 **cups ginger beer, chilled**
- ⅔ **cup lime juice**
- 1¼ **cups vodka**
   Ice cubes
   Lime slices, optional

Combine the ginger ale, ginger beer, lime juice and vodka in a pitcher. Serve over ice. If desired, serve with lime slices.

Cranberry Bacon Galette

Sweet, smoky, tangy, fresh—the flavors in this distinctive appetizer are sure to perk up taste buds. I sprinkle the warm squares with basil and add a dollop or two of a mascarpone cheese topping.
—**MERRY GRAHAM** NEWHALL, CA

PREP: 25 MIN. • **BAKE:** 20 MIN. + COOLING • **MAKES:** 9 SERVINGS

- 1 **carton (8 ounces) mascarpone cheese**
- 1 **tablespoon orange marmalade**
- 1 **tablespoon jellied cranberry sauce**
- 2 **tablespoons sugar**
- 1 **cup chopped red onion**
- 1 **cup dried cranberries**
- ¾ **cup chopped fresh mushrooms**
- 1 **tablespoon olive oil**
- ½ **teaspoon lemon-pepper seasoning**
- ¼ **teaspoon salt**
- ¼ **teaspoon smoked paprika**
- 3 **tablespoons cranberry-tangerine juice**
- 1 **sheet frozen puff pastry, thawed**
- 5 **cooked bacon strips, crumbled**
- ¼ **cup minced fresh basil**

1. Preheat oven to 400°. For topping, in a small bowl, combine the cheese, marmalade and cranberry sauce. Refrigerate until serving.

2. In a large skillet, cook sugar over medium-high heat 1-2 minutes or until it just begins to melt. Add onion; cook and stir 2 minutes longer.

Reuben Rounds

Fans of the classic Reuben sandwich will go crazy for baked pastry spirals of corned beef, Swiss cheese and sauerkraut. They're a breeze to make, and bottled Thousand Island dressing makes the perfect dipping sauce.

—**CHERYL SNAVELY** HAGERSTOWN, MD

START TO FINISH: 30 MIN. • **MAKES:** 16 APPETIZERS

- 1 sheet frozen puff pastry, thawed
- 6 slices Swiss cheese
- 5 slices deli corned beef
- ½ cup sauerkraut, rinsed and well drained
- 1 teaspoon caraway seeds
- ¼ cup Thousand Island salad dressing

1. Preheat oven to 400°. Unfold puff pastry; layer with cheese, corned beef and sauerkraut to within ½ in. of edges. Roll up jelly-roll style. Trim ends and cut crosswise into 16 slices. Place on greased baking sheets, cut side down. Sprinkle with caraway seeds.
2. Bake 18-20 minutes or until golden brown. Serve with salad dressing.

Cranberry-Banana Smoothies

When the main meal is over, I make a fruit-filled smoothie for a sweet treat. Don't have a frozen banana? Just use a regular banana and add more ice.

—**GINA FENSLER** CINCINNATI, OH

START TO FINISH: 5 MIN. • **MAKES:** 2 SERVINGS

- 1 large banana, peeled, quartered and frozen
- ⅔ cup whole-berry cranberry sauce
- ½ cup fat-free vanilla yogurt
- ½ cup ice cubes

Place all ingredients in a blender; cover and process until smooth. Serve immediately.

Lemon-Herb Olives with Goat Cheese

Greek olives have a wonderful taste that comes into play when you mix them with lemon and fresh herbs. Spoon over goat cheese and tuck in crackers.

—**JEANNE AMBROSE** MILWAUKEE, WI

START TO FINISH: 15 MIN. • **MAKES:** 6 SERVINGS

- 3 tablespoons olive oil
- 2 teaspoons grated lemon peel
- 1 garlic clove, minced
- ½ teaspoon minced fresh oregano or rosemary
- ¼ teaspoon crushed red pepper flakes
- ½ cup assorted pitted Greek olives
- 1 package (5.3 ounces) fresh goat cheese
- 1 tablespoon minced fresh basil
  Assorted crackers

1. In a small skillet, combine the first five ingredients; heat over medium heat 2-3 minutes or just until fragrant, stirring occasionally. Stir in olives; heat through, allowing flavors to blend. Cool completely.
2. To serve, place cheese on a serving plate. Stir basil into olive mixture; spoon over cheese. Serve with crackers.

Rhubarb Mint Tea

A bumper crop of rhubarb and mint from my garden was the inspiration for this thirst-quenching pick-me-up. Raspberries deepen the tea's vibrant red color. A pitcherful will look so pretty on your table.

—**LAURIE BOCK** LYNDEN, WA

PREP: 15 MIN. • **COOK:** 45 MIN. + CHILLING
MAKES: 12 SERVINGS (1 CUP EACH)

- 4 **cups chopped fresh rhubarb**
- 2 **cups fresh raspberries**
- 2 **packages (¾ ounce each) fresh mint leaves**
- 3 **quarts water**
- 4 **black tea bags**
- 2 **cups sugar**
   Ice cubes
- 12 **mint sprigs**

In a 6-qt. stockpot, combine rhubarb, raspberries, mint and water; bring to a boil. Reduce heat; simmer, uncovered, 30 minutes. Remove from heat. Add tea bags; steep, covered, 3-5 minutes according to taste. Using a fine mesh strainer, strain tea, discarding tea bags and pulp. Stir in sugar until dissolved; cool slightly. Transfer to a pitcher; refrigerate until cooled completely. Serve over ice with mint sprigs.

Contest Winner

Stuffed Asiago-Basil Mushrooms

If you don't like mushrooms, you'll have to give them a second try with this recipe. These pretty appetizers taste divine. To turn the recipe into a main dish, double the filling and use large portobellos.

—**LORRAINE CALAND** SHUNIAH, ON

PREP: 25 MIN. • **BAKE:** 10 MIN.
MAKES: 2 DOZEN

- 24 **baby portobello mushrooms (about 1 pound), stems removed**
- ½ **cup reduced-fat mayonnaise**
- ¾ **cup shredded Asiago cheese**
- ½ **cup loosely packed basil leaves, stems removed**
- ¼ **teaspoon white pepper**
- 12 **cherry tomatoes, halved**
   Grated Parmesan cheese, optional

1. Preheat the oven to 375°. Place the portobello caps in a greased 15x10x1-in. baking pan. Bake for 10 minutes. Meanwhile, place the mayonnaise, Asiago cheese, basil and pepper in a food processor; process until blended.

2. Drain juices from mushrooms. Fill each with 1 rounded teaspoon mayonnaise mixture; top each with a tomato half.

3. Bake 8-10 minutes or until lightly browned. If desired, top with grated Parmesan cheese.

ITALIAN SAUSAGE MUSHROOMS
Omit filling. Prepare mushrooms as directed. In a large skillet, cook 1 pound bulk Italian sausage over medium heat until no longer pink; drain. In a bowl, mix 6 ounces softened cream cheese, 3 tablespoons minced fresh parsley and sausage; spoon into mushroom caps. Bake as directed. Sprinkle with an additional 1 tablespoon minced fresh parsley.

Smoked Salmon Cheese Spread

Pretzels, chips and veggies would all make delicious dippers for this creamy salmon dip. It's wonderful with crackers and wine.

—**JILL CAMPBELL** HUNTSVILLE, TX

START TO FINISH: 15 MIN.
MAKES: 2½ CUPS

- 2 **packages (8 ounces each) cream cheese, softened**
- 1 **package (4 ounces) smoked salmon or lox**
- 3 **tablespoons horseradish sauce**
- 1 **tablespoon lemon juice**
- 1 **tablespoon Worcestershire sauce**
- ¼ **teaspoon Creole seasoning**
- ¼ **teaspoon coarsely ground pepper**
  Chopped walnuts and snipped fresh dill
  Assorted crackers

Place the first seven ingredients in a food processor; process until blended. Transfer the spread to a serving dish and sprinkle with walnuts and dill. Refrigerate, covered, until serving. Serve with crackers.

NOTE *The following spices may be substituted for 1 teaspoon Creole seasoning: ¼ teaspoon each salt, garlic powder and paprika; and a pinch each of dried thyme, ground cumin and cayenne pepper.*

Balsamic-Glazed Chicken Wings

Tired of the same ol' Buffalo and BBQ sauces? Try spreading your wings with a new balsamic-brown-sugar glaze. Sweet and mildly tangy, these have a taste that'll appeal to any crowd.

—**GRETCHEN WHELAN** SAN FRANCISCO, CA

PREP: 20 MIN. + MARINATING
BAKE: 25 MIN. • **MAKES:** ABOUT 1½ DOZEN

- 2 **pounds chicken wings**
- 1½ **cups balsamic vinegar**
- 2 **garlic cloves, minced**
- 2 **teaspoons minced fresh rosemary or ½ teaspoon dried rosemary, crushed**
- ¼ **teaspoon salt**
- ¼ **teaspoon pepper**
- ¼ **cup packed brown sugar**

Contest Winner

1. Cut chicken wings into three sections; discard wing tip sections. In a small bowl, combine the vinegar, garlic, rosemary, salt and pepper. Pour ½ cup marinade into a large resealable plastic bag. Add the chicken; seal bag and turn to coat. Refrigerate for 1 hour. Cover and refrigerate remaining marinade.
2. Drain chicken wings and discard the marinade; place in a greased 15x10x1-in. baking pan. Bake at 375° for 25-30 minutes or until no longer pink, turning every 10 minutes.
3. Meanwhile, combine brown sugar and reserved marinade in a small saucepan. Bring to a boil; cook until liquid is reduced by half.
4. Place wings in a large bowl. Pour glaze over wings and toss to coat.
FREEZE OPTION *Cover and freeze cooled wings in freezer containers. To use, partially thaw in the refrigerator overnight. Reheat wings in a foil-lined 15x10x1-in. baking pan in a preheated 325° oven until they are heated through, covering them if necessary to prevent excess browning.*
NOTE *Uncooked chicken wing sections (wingettes) may be substituted for whole chicken wings.*

MAKE TASTY BROTHS

Instead of discarding wing tips when cutting whole chicken wings into pieces, I add the tips to broths and gravy for flavor.
—**MARGARET M.**
ST. JOHN, NB

KID-FRIENDLY EATS

Get everyone together and watch the smiles appear when you serve these four delightful recipes. You'll win over folks who are both the young and young at heart.

Cherry Cobbler Smoothies

I created this fruity and refreshing smoothie packed with good-for-you cherries and vanilla yogurt.
—**SHERRY MOTE** MARIETTA, GA

START TO FINISH: 10 MIN.
MAKES: 5 SERVINGS

- 2 **cups vanilla yogurt**
- ½ **cup orange juice**
- ¼ **cup honey**
- 1 **teaspoon vanilla extract**
- 1 **teaspoon almond extract**
- 2 **cups ice cubes**
- 2 **cups frozen pitted dark sweet cherries**
- 2 **teaspoons ground cinnamon**

In a blender, combine all ingredients; cover and process for 30 seconds or until smooth. Pour into chilled glasses; serve immediately.

Ravioli Appetizer Pops

Ravioli on a stick will have everyone talking. You can use packaged dipping sauces, or make your own.
—**ERIKA MONROE-WILLIAMS** SCOTTSDALE, AZ

PREP: 25 MIN. • **COOK:** 5 MIN./BATCH
MAKES: 3½ DOZEN

- ½ **cup dry bread crumbs**
- 2 **teaspoons pepper**
- 1½ **teaspoons dried oregano**
- 1½ **teaspoons dried parsley flakes**
- 1 **teaspoon salt**
- 1 **teaspoon crushed red pepper flakes**
- ⅓ **cup all-purpose flour**
- 2 **large eggs, lightly beaten**
- 1 **package (9 ounces) refrigerated cheese ravioli**
  Oil for frying
  Grated Parmesan cheese, optional
- 42 **lollipop sticks**
  Warm marinara sauce and prepared pesto

1. In a shallow bowl, mix bread crumbs and seasonings. Place flour and eggs in separate shallow bowls. Dip ravioli in flour to coat both sides; shake off excess. Dip in egg, then in crumb mixture, patting to help coating adhere.

2. In an electric or large skillet, heat ½ in. of oil to 375°. Fry ravioli, a few at a time, 1-2 minutes on each side or until golden brown. Drain on paper towels. If desired, immediately sprinkle with cheese. Carefully insert a lollipop stick into back of each ravioli. Serve warm with marinara sauce and pesto.

Bacon Cheeseburger Slider Bake

I created this dish to fill two pans because these sliders disappear fast. Just cut the recipe in half if you want to make only one pan's worth.

—**NICK IVERSON** MILWAUKEE, WI

PREP: 20 MIN. • **BAKE:** 25 MIN.
MAKES: 2 DOZEN

- 2 packages (18 ounces each) Hawaiian sweet rolls
- 4 cups (16 ounces) shredded cheddar cheese, divided
- 2 pounds ground beef
- 1 cup chopped onion
- 1 can (14½ ounces) diced tomatoes with garlic and onion, drained
- 1 tablespoon Dijon mustard
- 1 tablespoon Worcestershire sauce
- ¾ teaspoon salt
- ¾ teaspoon pepper
- 24 bacon strips, cooked and crumbled

GLAZE

- 1 cup butter, cubed
- ¼ cup packed brown sugar
- 4 teaspoons Worcestershire sauce
- 2 tablespoons Dijon mustard
- 2 tablespoons sesame seeds

1. Preheat oven to 350°. Without separating rolls, cut each package of rolls horizontally in half; arrange the bottom halves in two greased 13x9-in. baking pans. Sprinkle each pan of rolls with 1 cup cheese. Bake 3-5 minutes or until cheese is melted.

2. In a large skillet, cook beef and onion over medium heat 6-8 minutes or until beef is no longer pink and onion is tender, breaking up beef into crumbles; drain. Stir in tomatoes, mustard, Worcestershire sauce, salt and pepper. Cook and stir 1-2 minutes or until combined.

3. Spoon beef mixture evenly over rolls; sprinkle with remaining cheese. Top with bacon. Replace tops. For glaze, in a microwave-safe bowl combine the butter, brown sugar, Worcestershire sauce and mustard. Microwave, covered, on high until the butter is melted, stirring occasionally. Pour over the rolls; sprinkle with sesame seeds. Bake rolls, uncovered, 20-25 minutes or until golden brown and heated through.

FREEZE OPTION *Cover and freeze unbaked sandwiches; prepare and freeze glaze. To use, partially thaw in refrigerator overnight. Remove from refrigerator 30 minutes before baking. Preheat oven to 350°. Pour the glaze over buns and sprinkle with sesame seeds. Bake sandwiches as directed, increasing time to 10-15 minutes or until cheese is melted and a thermometer inserted in center reads 165°.*

Brownie Batter Dip

I'm all about the sweeter side of dips, and this brownie-batter one pretty much fits in with my life's philosophy: Chocolate makes anything better. Grab some fruit, cookies or salty snacks and start dunking.

—**MEL GUNNELL** BOISE, ID

START TO FINISH: 10 MIN.
MAKES: 20 SERVINGS
(2 TABLESPOONS EACH)

- 1 package (8 ounces) cream cheese, softened
- ¼ cup butter, softened
- 2 cups confectioners' sugar
- ⅓ cup baking cocoa
- ¼ cup 2% milk
- 2 tablespoons brown sugar
- 1 teaspoon vanilla extract
- ¼ cup M&M's minis, optional Animal crackers, pretzels and/or sliced apples

In a large bowl, beat cream cheese and butter until smooth. Beat in the confectioners' sugar, cocoa, milk, brown sugar and vanilla until smooth. If desired, sprinkle with M&M's minis. Serve with dippers of your choice.

Crumb-Topped Clams

In my family, it wouldn't be Christmas Eve without baked clams. However, they make a special bite for any occasion and are always a hit.

—**ANNMARIE LUCENTE** MONROE, NY

PREP: 35 MIN. • **BROIL:** 10 MIN.
MAKES: 2 DOZEN

    2   pounds kosher salt
    2   dozen fresh littleneck clams
    ½   cup dry bread crumbs
    ¼   cup chicken broth
    1   tablespoon minced fresh parsley
    2   tablespoons olive oil
    2   garlic cloves, minced
    ¼   teaspoon dried oregano
        Dash pepper
    1   tablespoon panko (Japanese)
        bread crumbs
        Lemon wedges

1. Spread salt into an ovenproof metal serving platter or a 15x10x1-in. baking pan. Shuck clams, leaving clams and juices in bottom shells. Arrange in prepared platter; divide the juices among shells.
2. In a small bowl, mix dry bread crumbs, chicken broth, parsley, oil, garlic, oregano and pepper; spoon over clams. Sprinkle with bread crumbs.
3. Broil 4-6 in. from heat 6-8 minutes or until the clams are firm and the crumb mixture is crisp and golden brown. Serve dish immediately with lemon wedges.

Blue Cheese & Bacon Stuffed Peppers

Grilling is a huge summer highlight for my family, which is one reason we're such fans of this recipe. Whenever I put out a plate of these cute little appetizers, people come flocking.

—**TARA CRUZ** KERSEY, CO

START TO FINISH: 20 MIN.
MAKES: 1 DOZEN

    3   medium sweet yellow, orange or
        red peppers
    4   ounces cream cheese, softened
    ½   cup crumbled blue cheese
    3   bacon strips, cooked and crumbled
    1   green onion, thinly sliced

1. Cut the peppers into quarters. Remove and discard stems and seeds. In a small bowl, mix cream cheese, blue cheese, bacon and green onion until blended.
2. Grill the peppers, covered, over medium-high heat or broil 4 in. from heat 2-3 minutes on each side or until slightly charred.
3. Remove peppers from grill; fill each with about 1 tablespoon cheese mixture. Grill 2-3 minutes longer or until cheese is melted.

Cheesy Snack Mix

Our love for Mexican food inspired me to add taco seasoning in my party mix. The flavor is so mild that it's even kid-friendly.

—**ELIZABETH WYNNE** AZTEC, NM

PREP: 10 MIN. • **COOK:** 5 MIN. + COOLING
MAKES: 2½ QUARTS

- 3 **cups Corn Chex**
- 3 **cups Rice Chex**
- 3 **cups cheddar miniature pretzels**
- ¼ **cup butter, melted**
- 1 **envelope cheesy taco seasoning**
- 2 **cups white cheddar popcorn**

1. In a large microwave-safe bowl, combine cereal and pretzels. In a small bowl, mix melted butter and taco seasoning; drizzle over cereal mixture and toss to coat.

2. Microwave, uncovered, on high for 3-3½ minutes or until heated through, stirring once every minute. Stir in popcorn. Transfer to a baking sheet to cool completely. Store in an airtight container.

NOTE *This recipe was tested in a 1,100-watt microwave.*

Steamed Turkey Dumplings

This snack tastes wonderful but will not make you feel as though you've eaten an entire meal. The dumplings are easy to make and a joy to serve—try them at your next party!

—**DONNA BARDOCZ** HOWELL, MI

PREP: 30 MIN. • **COOK:** 10 MIN./BATCH
MAKES: 20 APPETIZERS (⅓ CUP SAUCE)

- 2 **green onions, thinly sliced**
- 2 **tablespoons cornstarch**
- 2 **tablespoons minced fresh gingerroot**

- 1 **tablespoon reduced-sodium soy sauce**
- 1 **teaspoon sesame oil**
- ½ **pound lean ground turkey**
- 20 **wonton wrappers**
- 9 **lettuce leaves**

DIPPING SAUCE
- ¼ **cup reduced-sodium soy sauce**
- 1½ **teaspoons finely chopped green onion**
- 1½ **teaspoons sesame oil**
- 1 **garlic clove, minced**

1. In a large bowl, combine onions, cornstarch, ginger, soy sauce and oil. Crumble turkey over the mixture and mix well.

2. Place 1 tablespoon turkey mixture in the center of a wonton wrapper. (Keep remaining wrappers covered with a damp paper towel until ready to use.) Moisten edges with water. Fold one corner diagonally over filling and press edges to seal.

3. Line a steamer basket with three lettuce leaves. Arrange a third of the dumplings 1 in. apart over lettuce; place in a large saucepan over 1 in. of water. Bring to a boil; cover and steam for 10-12 minutes or until a thermometer reads 165°. Discard lettuce. Repeat twice.

4. Combine sauce ingredients; serve with dumplings.

Roast Beef Finger Sandwiches

These simple sandwiches are ideal for a bridal shower, brunch or high tea, when the menu is a bit more substantial. The mustard adds a nice kick without being overly spicy.
—**ANNDREA BAILEY** HUNTINGTON BEACH, CA

START TO FINISH: 15 MIN. • **MAKES:** 1½ DOZEN

- ½ cup butter, softened
- ½ cup chopped pitted Greek olives
- ¼ cup spicy brown mustard
- ¼ teaspoon pepper
- 6 slices whole wheat bread, crusts removed
- 6 ounces thinly sliced deli roast beef
- 6 slices white bread, crusts removed

Place butter, olives, mustard and pepper in a food processor; pulse until chopped. Spread butter mixture over wheat bread; top with roast beef and white bread. Cut each sandwich crosswise into thirds.

SOFTEN BUTTER IN A FLASH

Waiting for butter to come to room temperature is like waiting for water to boil. To soften ½ cup cold butter quickly, place an unwrapped stick on a microwave-safe plate. In a 1,100-watt microwave, heat at 30 percent power for 15-20 seconds or until softened.

Loaded Pulled Pork Cups

Potato nests are simple to make and surprisingly handy for pulled pork, cheese, sour cream and other toppings. Make, bake and collect the compliments.
—**MELISSA SPERKA** GREENSBORO, NC

PREP: 40 MIN. • **BAKE:** 25 MIN. • **MAKES:** 1½ DOZEN

- 1 package (20 ounces) refrigerated shredded hash brown potatoes
- ¾ cup shredded Parmesan cheese
- 2 large egg whites, beaten
- 1 teaspoon garlic salt
- ½ teaspoon onion powder
- ¼ teaspoon pepper
- 1 carton (16 ounces) refrigerated fully cooked barbecued shredded pork
- 1 cup (4 ounces) shredded Colby-Monterey Jack cheese
- ½ cup sour cream
- 5 bacon strips, cooked and crumbled
  Minced chives

1. Preheat oven to 450°. In a large bowl, mix hash browns, Parmesan cheese, egg whites and seasonings until blended. Divide potatoes among 18 well-greased muffin cups; press onto bottoms and up sides to form cups.
2. Bake 22-25 minutes or until the edges are dark golden brown. Carefully run a knife around the sides of each cup. Cool for 5 minutes before removing from the pans to a serving platter. Meanwhile, heat the barbecued pork according to package directions.
3. Sprinkle cheese into cups. Top with pork, sour cream and bacon; sprinkle with chives. Serve warm.

Warm & Cozy Spiced Cider

We take winter seriously in Minnesota. This comforting cider flavored with cinnamon, cloves and fruit juices helps warm and brace our spirits.

—**CHRIS RUNYAN** MONTEVIDEO, MN

START TO FINISH: 30 MIN. • **MAKES:** 10 SERVINGS (¾ CUP EACH)

- 2 quarts unsweetened apple cider
- 1 cup orange juice
- 1 can (5½ ounces) apricot nectar
- 1 teaspoon ground cinnamon
- ⅛ teaspoon ground cloves

In a 6-qt. stockpot, combine all ingredients. Bring to a boil. Reduce heat; simmer, uncovered, 15 minutes to allow flavors to blend. Serve warm.

Rosemary Lemonade

A friend suggested I add a sprig of rosemary to lemonade. The herb makes the drink taste fresh and light.

—**DIXIE GRAHAM** RANCHO CUCAMONGA, CA

PREP: 10 MIN. • **COOK:** 15 MIN. + CHILLING
MAKES: 8 SERVINGS (1 CUP EACH)

- 2 cups water
- 2 fresh rosemary sprigs
- ½ cup sugar
- ½ cup honey
- 1¼ cups fresh lemon juice
- 6 cups cold water
    Ice cubes
    Additional lemon slices and fresh rosemary sprigs, optional

1. In a small saucepan, bring 2 cups water to a boil; add rosemary sprigs. Reduce heat; simmer, covered, 10 minutes.
2. Strain water; discarding rosemary. Stir in sugar and honey until dissolved. Transfer to a pitcher; refrigerate 15 minutes.
3. Add lemon juice; stir in cold water. Serve over ice. If desired, top with additional lemon slices and rosemary sprigs.

Warm Feta Cheese Dip

We're huge fans of appetizers, and this super-easy baked dip is a mashup of some of our favorite ingredients. It goes so well with a basket of crunchy tortilla chips or slices of a French bread baguette.

—**ASHLEY LECKER** GREEN BAY, WI

START TO FINISH: 30 MIN. • **MAKES:** 2 CUPS

- 1 package (8 ounces) cream cheese, softened
- 1½ cups (6 ounces) crumbled feta cheese
- ½ cup chopped roasted sweet red peppers
- 3 tablespoons minced fresh basil or 2 teaspoons dried basil
    Sliced French bread baguette or tortilla chips

Preheat oven to 400°. In a small bowl, beat cream cheese, feta cheese, peppers and basil until blended. Transfer to a greased 3-cup baking dish. Bake 25-30 minutes or until bubbly. Serve with baguette slices or chips.

NOTE *To prepare in a slow cooker, mix ingredients as directed. Pour into a greased 1½-qt. slow cooker; cook, covered, on low 2-3 hours or until heated through.*

Contest Winner

Contest Winner

Roasted Grape Crostini

A trip to Spain introduced me to its culinary treasures, like manchego cheese and sherry. This appetizer always impresses folks who've never tasted roasted grapes. They're amazing!

—JANICE ELDER CHARLOTTE, NC

PREP: 35 MIN. • **BROIL:** 5 MIN.
MAKES: 2 DOZEN

- **3** cups seedless red or green grapes, halved lengthwise
- **2** tablespoons sherry vinegar or rice vinegar
- **2** tablespoons olive oil
- ½ teaspoon salt
- ¼ teaspoon freshly ground pepper
- **1** teaspoon grated orange peel
- **24** slices French bread baguette (cut diagonally ½ inch thick)
- ½ cup shaved manchego cheese or Romano cheese
  Thinly sliced fresh basil leaves

1. Preheat oven to 400°. Toss the first five ingredients; spread in a greased 15x10x1-in. pan. Roast until the grapes are lightly browned and softened, 30-35 minutes. Stir in orange peel.
2. Preheat broiler. Arrange bread slices on an ungreased baking sheet. Broil 3-4 in. from heat until lightly browned, 1-2 minutes per side. Top with warm grape mixture; sprinkle with cheese and basil.

FREEZE, THEN GRATE

Grating fresh orange peel is a lot easier when you place the orange in the freezer the night before.

—JENNIFER B. SHEBOYGAN, WI

Grilled Guacamole

If you're a guacamole lover, try this fun grilled version that gives it a smoky edge. The veggies tend to darken a bit when heated, so stir the guacamole gently to prevent further discoloration.
—**LINDSAY SPRUNK** NOBLESVILLE, IN

PREP: 10 MIN. • **GRILL:** 10 MIN. + COOLING
MAKES: 12 SERVINGS

- 1 medium red onion, cut into ½-inch slices
- 2 plum tomatoes, halved and seeded
- 1 jalapeno pepper, halved and seeded
- 2 tablespoons canola oil, divided
- 3 medium ripe avocados, halved and pitted
- ¼ cup fresh cilantro leaves, chopped
- 2 tablespoons lime juice
- 2 teaspoons ground cumin
- ¾ teaspoon salt
  Tortilla chips

1. In a large bowl, combine onion, tomatoes, pepper and 1 tablespoon oil; gently toss to coat. Grill, covered, over medium-high heat or broil 4 in. from heat 6-8 minutes or until tender and charred, turning occasionally. Brush avocados with the remaining oil. Grill or broil the avocados, cut side down, 4-6 minutes longer or until charred. Cool vegetables completely.

2. Chop onion, tomatoes and pepper; set aside. Peel avocados; transfer to a large bowl and mash with a fork. Stir in vegetables, cilantro, lime juice, cumin and salt. Serve immediately with chips.

NOTE *Wear disposable gloves when cutting hot peppers; the oils can burn skin. Avoid touching your face.*

Spiked Orange Refresher

My two-tone drink will impress party guests, with or without the rum. You can use another citrus fruit in place of the orange if you like.
—**MARYBETH MANK** MESQUITE, TX

PREP: 15 MIN. • **COOK:** 15 MIN. + COOLING
MAKES: 10 SERVINGS

- 3 medium oranges
- 1½ cups turbinado (washed raw) sugar
- 1½ cups water
- 1 cup fresh mint leaves
- 8 slices fresh gingerroot
  Crushed ice
- 5 ounces spiced rum, optional
- 1 bottle (1 liter) club soda, chilled

1. Using a vegetable peeler, remove colored layer of peel from oranges in strips, leaving the white pith. Cut oranges crosswise in half; squeeze juice from oranges.

2. In a small saucepan, combine sugar, water and orange juice; bring to a boil. Stir in mint, ginger and orange peel; return to a boil. Reduce heat; simmer, uncovered, 10 minutes. Cool syrup mixture completely.

3. Strain syrup, discarding solids. To serve, fill 10 highball glasses halfway with ice. Add 2 ounces syrup and, if desired, ½ ounce rum to each glass; top with soda.

SIDE DISHES & CONDIMENTS

Whether you're in the mood for grilling, roasting, baking or stovetop cooking, these spectacular sides are here to help. In addition, who knew homemade jam and salsa could be so easy to make? You'll be amazed!

Roasted Brussels Sprouts with Cranberries

The preparation and cooking are so quick, there's practically nothing to this recipe! I throw in dried cranberries, but you can let your imagination take over. Add a handful of raisins or walnuts at the end, even sliced oranges. If your Brussels sprouts are large, cut them in half.

—**ELLEN RUZINSKY** YORKTOWN HEIGHTS, NY

PREP: 15 MIN. • **BAKE:** 20 MIN.
MAKES: 12 SERVINGS (½ CUP EACH)

- 3 **pounds fresh Brussels sprouts, trimmed and halved**
- 3 **tablespoons olive oil**
- 1 **teaspoon kosher salt**
- ½ **teaspoon pepper**
- ½ **cup dried cranberries**

Preheat the oven to 425°. Divide the Brussels sprouts between two greased 15x10x1-in. baking pans. Drizzle with oil; sprinkle with salt and pepper. Toss to coat. Roast 20-25 minutes or until tender, stirring occasionally. Transfer to a large bowl; stir in cranberries.

No-Cook Fresh Tomato Sauce

Go for this sauce when you have a box of pasta or a store-bought pizza shell and need a surefire topping. When you need only 15 minutes for prep work and there's no cooking involved, you can't go wrong!

—**JULIANNE SCHNUCK** MILWAUKEE, WI

PREP: 15 MIN. + STANDING
MAKES: 3½ CUPS

- 1½ **pounds assorted fresh tomatoes, coarsely chopped (about 4½ cups)**
- ⅓ **cup minced fresh basil**
- 1 **tablespoon olive oil**
- 2 **garlic cloves, coarsely chopped**
  Salt and pepper to taste
  Hot cooked angel hair pasta or spaghetti
  Grated Parmesan cheese

1. In a large bowl, toss tomatoes with basil, oil and garlic; season with salt and pepper to taste. Let stand at room temperature 30-60 minutes or until juices are released from tomatoes, stirring occasionally.
2. Serve with hot pasta. Sprinkle with cheese.

Homemade Mayonnaise

Did you know America's top-selling condiment and go-to dressing for chicken, tuna and potato salad can be prepared right in your own kitchen with only a handful of everyday pantry items? It's a cinch with this handy recipe.

—**TASTE OF HOME** TEST KITCHEN

START TO FINISH: 25 MIN.
MAKES: 1¼ CUPS

- 2 **large egg yolks**
- 2 **tablespoons water**
- 2 **tablespoons lemon juice**
- ½ **teaspoon salt**
  Dash white pepper
- 1 **cup olive oil**

1. In a double boiler or metal bowl over simmering water, constantly whisk the egg yolks, water and lemon juice until mixture reaches 160° or is thick enough to coat the back of a spoon. While stirring, quickly place the bottom of the pan in a bowl of ice water; continue stirring for 2 minutes or until cooled.
2. Transfer to a blender. Add salt and pepper. While processing, gradually add oil in a steady stream. Transfer to a small bowl. Cover and refrigerate for up to 7 days.

Spicy Ketchup

When this zesty ketchup is bubbling on the stove, the aroma takes me back to my childhood. One taste and I'm home again.
—**KAREN NAIHE** KAMUELA, HI

PREP: 30 MIN. • **COOK:** 1½ HOURS + CHILLING
MAKES: 1 CUP

- 1 tablespoon olive oil
- 1 medium onion, chopped
- 3 pounds tomatoes (about 11 medium), coarsely chopped
- 1 cinnamon stick (3 inches)
- ¾ teaspoon celery seed
- ½ teaspoon mustard seed
- ¼ teaspoon whole allspice
- ⅓ cup sugar
- 1 teaspoon salt
- ¾ cup red wine vinegar
- 1½ teaspoons smoked paprika
- 1½ teaspoons Sriracha Asian hot chili sauce, optional

1. In a large saucepan, heat oil over medium-high heat. Add onion; cook and stir until tender. Stir in tomatoes; cook, uncovered, over medium heat 25-30 minutes or until the tomatoes are softened.

2. Press tomato mixture through a fine-mesh strainer; discard solids. Return mixture to pot; bring to a boil. Cook, uncovered, until liquid is reduced to 1½ cups, about 10 minutes.

3. Place cinnamon, celery seed, mustard seed and allspice on a double thickness of cheesecloth. Gather corners of cloth to enclose spices; tie securely with string. Add to tomatoes. Stir in sugar and salt; return to a boil. Reduce heat; simmer, uncovered, 20-25 minutes or until thickened.

4. Stir in remaining ingredients; bring to a boil. Simmer, uncovered, 10-15 minutes longer or until it reaches desired consistency, stirring occasionally. Discard spice bag.

5. Transfer to a covered container; cool slightly. Refrigerate until cold. Store in refrigerator for up to 1 week.

Parmesan Butternut Squash

Cubed butternut squash sprinkled with Parmesan and bread crumbs makes a superb side dish that I love to share. Using the microwave helps cut down on a long roasting time.
—**JACKIE O'CALLAGHAN** WEST LAFAYETTE, IN

START TO FINISH: 25 MIN.
MAKES: 8 SERVINGS

- 1 medium butternut squash (about 3 pounds), peeled and cut into 1-inch cubes
- 2 tablespoons water
- ½ cup panko (Japanese) bread crumbs
- ½ cup grated Parmesan cheese
- ¼ teaspoon salt
- ⅛ teaspoon pepper

1. Place squash and water in a large microwave-safe bowl. Microwave, covered, on high 15-17 minutes or until tender; drain.

2. Preheat broiler. Transfer squash to a greased 15x10x1-in. baking pan. Toss bread crumbs with cheese, salt and pepper; sprinkle over squash. Broil 3-4 in. from heat 1-2 minutes or until topping is golden brown.

NOTE *This recipe was tested in a 1,100-watt microwave.*

Cumin-Roasted Carrots

Carrots make a super side—big on flavor and a breeze to cook. Plus, I can actually get my husband to eat these spiced veggies.
—**TAYLOR KISER** BRANDON, FL

PREP: 20 MIN. • **COOK:** 35 MIN. • **MAKES:** 12 SERVINGS

- 2 tablespoons coriander seeds
- 2 tablespoons cumin seeds
- 3 pounds carrots, cut into 4x½-inch sticks
- 3 tablespoons coconut oil or butter, melted
- 8 garlic cloves, minced
- 1 teaspoon salt
- ½ teaspoon pepper
  Minced fresh cilantro, optional

1. Preheat oven to 400°. In a dry small skillet, toast the coriander and cumin seeds over medium heat 45-60 seconds or until aromatic, stirring frequently. Cool slightly. Grind in a spice grinder, or with a mortar and pestle, until finely crushed.
2. Place carrots in a large bowl. Add melted coconut oil, garlic, salt, pepper and crushed spices, and toss to coat. Divide carrots between two 15x10x1-in. baking pans coated with cooking spray, spreading evenly.
3. Roast 35-40 minutes or until crisp-tender and lightly browned, stirring and rotating pans halfway. Before serving, sprinkle with cilantro if desired.
NOTE *Two tablespoons each of ground coriander and ground cumin may be substituted for whole spices. Before using, toast the ground spices in a dry skillet until they are aromatic, stirring frequently.*

Lemon-Rosemary Marmalade

I love bringing lemon and rosemary together. This unique marmalade goes great with roast chicken, herbed pork roast, lamb chops or a savory biscuit.
—**BIRDIE SHANNON** ARLINGTON, VA

PREP: 2¼ HOURS • **PROCESS:** 10 MIN. • **MAKES:** 5 HALF-PINTS

- 7 medium lemons (about 2 pounds)
- ½ teaspoon baking soda, divided
- 7 cups water
- 4 cups sugar
- 4 teaspoons minced fresh rosemary
- 2 drops yellow food coloring, optional

1. Using a vegetable peeler, peel lemons into wide strips. With a sharp knife, carefully remove white pith from peels. Cut peels into ¼-in. strips. Set fruit aside.
2. Place lemon strips in a small saucepan; add water to cover and ¼ teaspoon baking soda. Bring to a boil. Reduce heat to medium. Cook, covered, 10 minutes; drain. Repeat with remaining baking soda.
3. Cut a thin slice from the top and bottom of lemons; stand lemons upright on a cutting board. With a knife, cut outer membrane from lemons. Working over a bowl to catch juices, cut along the membrane of each segment to remove fruit. Squeeze membrane to reserve additional juice.
4. Place lemon sections and reserved juices in a Dutch oven. Stir in 7 cups water and lemon peel. Bring to a boil. Reduce the heat; simmer, uncovered, 25 minutes. Add sugar. Bring to a boil. Reduce heat; simmer, uncovered, 40-50 minutes or until slightly thickened, stirring occasionally. Remove from heat; immediately stir in rosemary and, if desired, food coloring.
5. Ladle hot mixture into five hot half-pint jars, leaving ¼-in. headspace. Wipe rims. Center lids on jars; screw on bands until fingertip tight.
6. Place jars into canner with simmering water, ensuring that they are completely covered with water. Bring to a boil; process for 10 minutes. Remove jars and cool.
NOTE *The processing time listed is for altitudes of 1,000 feet or less. Add 1 minute to the processing time for each 1,000 feet of additional altitude.*

Roasted Potatoes with Garlic Butter

A platter of golden and orange potatoes serves double duty for your dinner centerpiece.
—**ELIZABETH KELLEY** CHICAGO, IL

PREP: 30 MIN. • **BAKE:** 20 MIN. • **MAKES:** 10 SERVINGS

- 8 medium Yukon Gold potatoes, peeled
- 3 medium sweet potatoes, peeled
- 2 tablespoons canola oil
- ½ teaspoon salt
- ¼ teaspoon pepper
- ¼ cup butter
- 3 garlic cloves, minced
- 1 tablespoon minced fresh thyme or 1 teaspoon dried thyme
- ½ cup shredded cheddar cheese
- ⅓ cup grated Parmesan cheese
  Additional minced fresh thyme, optional

1. Cut Yukon Gold and sweet potatoes into ⅛-in. slices; toss with oil and sprinkle with salt and pepper. Divide potatoes between two greased 15x10x1-in. baking pans. Roast at 425° for 17-20 minutes or until tender.
2. Meanwhile, in a small skillet, heat butter over medium heat. Add garlic and thyme; cook and stir for 1 minute. Transfer roasted potatoes to a large bowl. Drizzle with butter mixture; toss to coat. Sprinkle with cheeses and, if desired, additional thyme; toss to combine.

Sweet and Sour Zucchini Pickles

Is your garden overflowing with zucchini? To put all those ripe-and-ready beauties to good use, make these unexpected pickles. At Christmastime, you'll have jars of them to share as holiday gifts from your kitchen.
—**TINA BUTLER** ROYSE CITY, TX

PREP: 1 HOUR + SOAKING • **PROCESS:** 10 MIN.
MAKES: ABOUT 6 PINTS

- 11 cups thinly sliced zucchini (about 3 pounds)
- 1 large onion, halved and thinly sliced
- ⅓ cup canning salt
- 4½ cups white vinegar
- 3 cups sugar
- 1 tablespoon mustard seed
- 1½ teaspoons ground turmeric

1. Place zucchini and onion in a large nonreactive bowl. Sprinkle with salt; toss to coat. Add water to cover; let stand at room temperature 2 hours. Drain; rinse and drain thoroughly.
2. In a 6-qt. stockpot, combine remaining ingredients. Bring to a boil, stirring to dissolve sugar. Reduce heat; simmer 5 minutes to allow flavors to blend. Add zucchini mixture; return to a boil, stirring occasionally. Reduce heat; simmer, uncovered, 4-5 minutes or until heated through.
3. Carefully ladle hot mixture into six hot 1-pint jars, leaving ½-in. headspace. Remove air bubbles and, if necessary, adjust headspace by adding hot pickling liquid. Wipe rims. Center lids on jars; screw on bands until fingertip tight.
4. Place jars into canner with simmering water, ensuring that they are completely covered with water. Bring to a boil; process for 10 minutes. Remove jars and cool.
NOTE *The processing time listed is for altitudes of 1,000 feet or less. For altitudes up to 3,000 feet, add 5 minutes; 6,000 feet, add 10 minutes; 8,000 feet, add 15 minutes; 10,000 feet, add 20 minutes.*

Nanny's Parmesan Mashed Potatoes

My grandsons rave over these creamy potatoes loaded with Parmesan. That's all the endorsement I need! Sometimes I use golden or red potatoes, with skins on.

—KALLEE KRONG-MCCREERY
ESCONDIDO, CA

PREP: 20 MIN. • **COOK:** 20 MIN.
MAKES: 12 SERVINGS (¾ CUP EACH)

- 5 pounds potatoes, peeled and cut into 1-inch pieces
- ¾ cup butter, softened
- ¾ cup sour cream
- ½ cup grated Parmesan cheese
- 1¼ teaspoons garlic salt
- 1 teaspoon salt
- ½ teaspoon pepper
- ¾ to 1 cup 2% milk, warmed
- 2 tablespoons minced fresh parsley

1. Place potatoes in a 6-qt. stockpot; add water to cover. Bring to a boil. Reduce the heat; cook, uncovered, 10-15 minutes or until tender. Drain potatoes; return to pot and stir over low heat 1 minute to dry.
2. Coarsely mash potatoes, gradually adding butter, sour cream, cheese, seasonings and enough milk to reach desired consistency. Stir in parsley.

Sweet Potato & Carrot Casserole

This tangy and sweet casserole is full of flavor. We've served it at many celebrations over the years and it's always been a big hit!

—GLORIA MEZIKOFSKY WAKEFIELD, MA

PREP: 55 MIN. • **BAKE:** 25 MIN. + STANDING
MAKES: 12 SERVINGS

- ½ cup golden raisins
- 3½ pounds medium sweet potatoes (about 6 potatoes)
- 4 large carrots, cut into 1½-inch pieces
- ¼ cup butter or nondairy margarine
- 1½ cups packed brown sugar
- ⅓ cup orange juice

1. Preheat oven to 375°. In a small bowl, cover raisins with hot water; let stand 30 minutes.
2. Place potatoes in a 6-qt. stockpot; add water to cover. Bring to a boil. Reduce the heat; cook, uncovered, 15-20 minutes or just until tender. Remove potatoes and cool slightly. Add carrots to same pot of boiling water; cook, uncovered, 15-20 minutes or until tender; drain.
3. Peel the sweet potatoes and cut crosswise into 1½-in.-thick slices. Arrange potatoes and carrots in a greased 13x9-in. baking dish, cut sides down.
4. Drain raisins. In a small saucepan, melt butter over medium heat; stir in raisins. Add brown sugar and orange juice, stirring to dissolve sugar. Pour over vegetables.
5. Bake, uncovered, 25-30 minutes or until heated through and sauce is bubbly; if desired, baste occasionally with sauce. Let stand 10 minutes; toss before serving.

LEFTOVERS IN SALAD

Have leftover golden raisins and carrots? Throw together a quick salad by grating the carrots and adding a handful or two of golden raisins. Toss with the juice of one or two oranges.
—MARIE R. LAKE CHARLES, LA

Baked Three-Cheese Macaroni

My ultimate comfort food, and a must-have for family events, is a divine blend of cheddar, Gruyere and Parmesan cheeses.
—JOAN SULLIVAN GAMBRILLS, MD

PREP: 20 MIN. • **BAKE:** 30 MIN.
MAKES: 12 SERVINGS (¾ CUP EACH)

- 1 package (16 ounces) elbow macaroni or fusilli pasta
- 6 tablespoons butter, cubed
- ½ cup all-purpose flour
- 4 cups 2% milk, warmed
- 4 cups shredded Gruyere cheese
- 2 cups shredded extra-sharp cheddar cheese
- 2 teaspoons salt
- ¾ teaspoon freshly ground pepper
- ¼ teaspoon freshly ground nutmeg
- 1½ cups panko (Japanese) bread crumbs
- ½ cup grated Parmesan cheese
- 2 tablespoons butter, melted

1. Preheat oven to 350°. Cook the macaroni in a 6-qt. stockpot according to package directions for al dente. Drain; return to pot.

2. In a saucepan, melt 6 tablespoons butter over medium heat. Stir in flour until smooth; whisk in warmed milk. Bring to a boil, stirring constantly; cook and stir 2-3 minutes or until thickened.

3. Remove from the heat; stir in Gruyere and cheddar cheeses, salt, pepper and nutmeg. Add to macaroni, tossing to coat.

4. Transfer macaroni to a greased 13x9-in. baking dish. Toss bread crumbs with Parmesan cheese and melted butter; sprinkle over casserole. Bake, uncovered, 30-40 minutes or until bubbly and top is golden brown.

Contest Winner

Lemon Roasted Fingerlings and Brussels Sprouts

I've tried this recipe with other veggie combinations, too. The trick is choosing ones that roast in about the same amount of time. Try skinny green beans and thinly sliced onions, cauliflower florets and baby carrots, or okra and cherry tomatoes.
—COURTNEY GAYLORD COLUMBUS, IN

PREP: 15 MIN. • **BAKE:** 20 MIN.
MAKES: 8 SERVINGS

- 1 pound fingerling potatoes, halved
- 1 pound Brussels sprouts, trimmed and halved
- 6 tablespoons olive oil, divided
- ¾ teaspoon salt, divided
- ¼ teaspoon pepper
- 3 tablespoons lemon juice
- 1 garlic clove, minced
- 1 teaspoon Dijon mustard
- 1 teaspoon honey

1. Preheat the oven to 425°. Place the potatoes and Brussels sprouts in a greased 15x10x1-in. baking pan. Drizzle vegetables with 2 tablespoons oil; sprinkle with ½ teaspoon salt and pepper. Toss to coat. Roast 20-25 minutes or until tender, stirring once.

2. In a small bowl, whisk lemon juice, garlic, mustard, honey and remaining oil and salt until blended. Transfer vegetables to a large bowl; drizzle with vinaigrette and toss to coat. Serve warm.

FIRE UP THE GRILL

Don't let the warm weather months go by without giving these flame-kissed recipes a try!
Turn up the heat, throw these recipes on the grill, and you'll be eating before you know it.

Tarragon Asparagus

I grow purple asparagus, so I'm always looking for new ways to prepare it. Recently, my husband and I discovered how wonderful any color of asparagus tastes when it's grilled.

—SUE GRONHOLZ BEAVER DAM, WI

START TO FINISH: 15 MIN.
MAKES: 8 SERVINGS

- 2 **pounds fresh asparagus, trimmed**
- 2 **tablespoons olive oil**
- 1 **teaspoon salt**
- ½ **teaspoon pepper**
- ¼ **cup honey**
- 2 **to 4 tablespoons minced fresh tarragon**

On a large plate, toss asparagus with oil, salt and pepper. Grill, covered, over medium heat 6-8 minutes or until crisp-tender, turning the asparagus occasionally and basting frequently with honey during the last 3 minutes. Sprinkle with tarragon.

Corn with Cilantro-Lime Butter

I grow cilantro in my garden. When I created a lime butter for grilled corn, I made sure to include some fresh cilantro in the recipe.

—ANDREA REYNOLDS WESTLAKE, OH

PREP: 15 MIN. + CHILLING • **GRILL:** 15 MIN.
MAKES: 12 SERVINGS

- ½ **cup butter, softened**
- ¼ **cup minced fresh cilantro**
- 1 **tablespoon lime juice**
- 1½ **teaspoons grated lime peel**
- 12 **medium ears sweet corn, husks removed**
- **Grated cotija cheese, optional**

1. In a small bowl, mix the butter, cilantro, lime juice and lime peel. Shape into a log; wrap in plastic wrap. Refrigerate 30 minutes or until firm. Wrap each ear of corn with a piece of heavy-duty foil (about 14 in. square).
2. Grill corn, covered, over medium heat 15-20 minutes or until tender, turning occasionally. Meanwhile, cut lime butter into 12 slices. Remove corn from grill. Carefully open foil, allowing the steam to escape. Serve corn with butter and, if desired, cheese.

Sweet & Smoky Salsa

I love the roasted flavor that grilling gives food. If you can't use wood chip charcoal, you might try adding a little liquid smoke to the salsa while it cooks.

—SHELLY BEVINGTON HERMISTON, OR

PREP: 1 HOUR • **PROCESS:** 15 MIN.
MAKES: 4 PINTS

- 1 cup soaked mesquite wood chips
- 2 medium onions
- 12 garlic cloves, peeled
- 3 teaspoons barbecue seasoning, divided
- 2 pounds tomatillos, husks removed (about 12)
- 2 pounds plum tomatoes (about 8)
- 6 jalapeno peppers
- 1½ cups cider vinegar
- 1¼ cups packed brown sugar
- 1½ teaspoons salt
- ½ teaspoon pepper
- ⅓ cup minced fresh cilantro

1. Add wood chips to grill according to manufacturer's directions.
2. Cut onions in quarters; place in a bowl. Add garlic and 1½ teaspoons barbecue seasoning; toss to coat. Arrange on grilling grid; place on greased grill rack. Grill, covered, over medium heat 10-15 minutes or until tender, turning occasionally.

3. Meanwhile, cut the tomatillos, tomatoes and jalapenos in half; place in a large bowl. Add the remaining barbecue seasoning and toss to coat. Grill in batches, covered, over medium heat 4-6 minutes or until tender, turning occasionally.
4. When cool enough to handle, chop vegetables. Transfer to a Dutch oven; stir in vinegar, brown sugar, salt and pepper. Bring to a boil. Reduce heat; simmer, uncovered, 15-20 minutes or until slightly thickened. Immediately stir in cilantro.
5. Carefully ladle hot mixture into four hot 1-pint jars, leaving ½-in. headspace. Remove air bubbles and adjust headspace, if necessary, by adding hot mixture. Wipe rims. Center lids on jars; screw on bands until fingertip tight.
6. Place the jars into canner with simmering water, ensuring that they are completely covered with water. Bring to a boil; process for 15 minutes. Remove jars and cool.
NOTES *Wear disposable gloves when cutting hot peppers; the oils can burn skin. Avoid touching your face. If you do not have a grilling grid, use a disposable foil pan. Poke holes in the bottom of the pan with a meat fork to allow liquid to drain.*

Contest Winner

Grilled Balsamic-Lime Sweet Potatoes

For me, summer parties are about spending time together and preparing food that's good to grill. One of our favorites is sweet potatoes with lime and balsamic glaze.

—RAQUEL PERAZZO WEST NEW YORK, NJ

PREP: 15 MIN. • **GRILL:** 10 MIN./BATCH
MAKES: 8 SERVINGS

- 5 medium sweet potatoes (about 3 pounds)
- 2 tablespoons olive oil
- 1 teaspoon salt
- ¼ teaspoon pepper
- ¼ cup chopped fresh cilantro
- ¼ cup packed brown sugar
- ¼ cup lime juice
- 3 tablespoons white or regular balsamic glaze

1. Peel and cut each sweet potato lengthwise into eight wedges; place in a large bowl. Toss with oil, salt and pepper.
2. In batches, cook potatoes on a greased grill rack, covered, over medium heat 8-10 minutes or until tender, turning occasionally.
3. In a large bowl, mix remaining ingredients; add potatoes and toss to coat.

Spinach-Parm Casserole

For those who ignore Popeye and won't eat their spinach, I find that spinach with garlicky butter and cheese helps change their minds.

—JUDY BATSON TAMPA, FL

START TO FINISH: 25 MIN.
MAKES: 6 SERVINGS

- 5 cups water
- 2 pounds fresh baby spinach
- 5 tablespoons butter
- 3 tablespoons olive oil
- 3 garlic cloves, minced
- 1 tablespoon Italian seasoning
- ¾ teaspoon salt
- 1 cup grated Parmesan cheese

1. Preheat oven to 400°. In a stockpot, bring 5 cups water to a boil. Add the spinach; cook, covered, 1 minute or just until wilted. Drain well.
2. In a small skillet, heat butter and oil over medium-low heat. Add garlic, Italian seasoning and salt; cook and stir until garlic is tender, 1-2 minutes.
3. Spread spinach in a greased 8-in. square or 1½-qt. baking dish. Drizzle with butter mixture; sprinkle with cheese. Bake, uncovered, until cheese is lightly browned, 10-15 minutes.

Contest Winner

Heirloom Tomato Pie

My green-thumb neighbors like to share produce with me. I return the delicious favor by baking tomato pies for all.

—ANGELA BENEDICT DUNBAR, WV

PREP: 45 MIN. • **BAKE:** 35 MIN. + COOLING
MAKES: 8 SERVINGS

- 1¼ pounds heirloom tomatoes (about 4 medium), cut into ¼-inch slices
- ¾ teaspoon salt, divided
- 1½ cups shredded extra-sharp cheddar cheese
- ¾ cup all-purpose flour
- ¼ cup cold butter, cubed
- 1 to 2 tablespoons half-and-half cream
- 5 bacon strips, cooked and crumbled

FILLING
- 1 package (8 ounces) cream cheese, softened
- ½ cup loosely packed basil leaves, thinly sliced
- 2 tablespoons minced fresh marjoram
- 1½ teaspoons minced fresh thyme
- ½ teaspoon garlic powder
- ⅛ teaspoon coarsely ground pepper

1. Preheat oven to 350°. Place tomato slices in a single layer on paper towels; sprinkle with ½ teaspoon salt. Let stand 45 minutes. Pat dry.
2. Meanwhile, place cheese, flour and remaining salt in a food processor; pulse until blended. Add butter; pulse until butter is the size of peas. While pulsing, add just enough cream to form moist crumbs. Press dough onto bottom and up sides of an ungreased 9-in. fluted tart pan with removable bottom. Gently press bacon into dough. Bake 20-22 minutes or until light brown. Cool on a wire rack.
3. In a large bowl, beat the cream cheese, herbs and garlic powder until blended. Spread over crust. Top with tomato slices; sprinkle with pepper. Bake 35-40 minutes longer or until edges are golden brown and tomatoes are softened. Cool on a wire rack. Refrigerate leftovers.

Sweet Corn & Potato Gratin

Two popular vegetables are paired in this old-fashioned, down-home side. The garlic and onion flavors appeal to adults, and the crispy topping has kids looking for seconds.

—JENNIFER OLSON PLEASANTON, CA

PREP: 30 MIN. • **BAKE:** 45 MIN. + STANDING
MAKES: 8 SERVINGS

- 1 medium onion, thinly sliced
- 2 tablespoons butter
- 2 tablespoons all-purpose flour
- 2 garlic cloves, minced
- 1 teaspoon salt
- ½ teaspoon pepper
- 1 cup whole milk
- 2 pounds medium Yukon Gold potatoes, peeled and cut into ⅛-inch slices
- 2 cups fresh or frozen corn
- 1 can (8¼ ounces) cream-style corn
- ¾ cup panko (Japanese) bread crumbs
- 1 tablespoon butter, melted

1. Preheat oven to 350°. In a large saucepan, saute onion in butter until tender. Stir in flour, garlic, salt and pepper until blended; gradually add milk. Stir in potatoes. Bring to a boil. Reduce heat; cook and stir 8-10 minutes or until potatoes are crisp-tender.

2. Stir in corn and cream-style corn. Transfer to an 8-in. square baking dish coated with cooking spray.

3. In a small bowl, combine the bread crumbs and butter; sprinkle over the potatoes. Bake 45-50 minutes or until golden brown and potatoes are tender. Let stand 10 minutes before serving.

Grandma's Cranberry Stuff

What tastes better than turkey and cranberry together? This classic combo is even better with my grandma's classic recipe for cranberry stuffing. Your friends and family will love it.

—CATHERINE CASSIDY MILWAUKEE, WI

PREP: 10 MIN. • **MAKES:** 3 CUPS

- 1 medium navel orange
- 1 package (12 ounces) fresh or frozen cranberries, thawed
- 1 cup sugar
- 1 cup chopped walnuts, toasted

Cut unpeeled orange into wedges, removing any seeds, and place in a food processor. Add cranberries and sugar; pulse until chopped. Add the walnuts; pulse just until combined.
NOTE *To toast nuts, bake in a shallow pan in a 350° oven for 5-10 minutes or cook in a skillet over low heat until lightly browned, stirring occasionally.*

Berry-Basil Limeade Jam

My husband and I have fun picking fruit. We ended up with too many strawberries, so, inspired by a mojito recipe, it was time to make jam.

—ERICA INGRAM LAKEWOOD, OH

START TO FINISH: 25 MIN.
MAKES: 8½ CUPS

- 8 cups fresh strawberries, hulled
- 1 package (1¾ ounces) powdered fruit pectin
- ⅓ cup lime juice
- 1 teaspoon butter
- 7 cups sugar
- ¼ cup minced fresh basil
- 4 teaspoons grated lime peel

1. Rinse nine 1-cup plastic or freezer-safe containers and lids with boiling water. Dry thoroughly.

2. In a small bowl, thoroughly crush the strawberries, 1 cup at a time, to measure exactly 5 cups; transfer to a 6-qt. stockpot. Stir in pectin, lime juice and butter. Bring to a full rolling boil over high heat, stirring constantly. Stir in sugar; return to a full rolling boil. Boil and stir 1 minute. Immediately stir in basil and lime peel.

3. Immediately fill all containers to within ½ in. of tops. Wipe off top edges of containers; immediately cover with lids. Let stand at room temperature 24 hours.

4. The jam is now ready to use. Refrigerate up to 3 weeks or freeze up to 12 months. Thaw frozen jam in refrigerator before serving.

Beans, Bacon & Tomato Bake

On cold winter days, I pull out the bacon, tomatoes and lima beans for a veggie-packed side that nourishes the family.
—**KAREN KUMPULAINEN** FOREST CITY, NC

PREP: 10 MIN. • **BAKE:** 35 MIN. • **MAKES:** 12 SERVINGS (⅔ CUP EACH)

- 8 **bacon strips, cut into 1-inch pieces**
- 1 **cup finely chopped onion**
- ⅔ **cup finely chopped celery**
- ½ **cup finely chopped green pepper**
- 2 **garlic cloves, minced**
- 2 **teaspoons all-purpose flour**
- 2 **teaspoons sugar**
- 2 **teaspoons salt**
- ¼ **teaspoon pepper**
- 2 **cans (14½ ounces each) diced tomatoes, undrained**
- 8 **cups frozen lima beans (about 42 ounces), thawed**

1. Preheat oven to 325°. In a 6-qt. stockpot, cook bacon, onion, celery and green pepper over medium heat until bacon is crisp and vegetables are tender. Add garlic; cook 1 minute longer. Stir in flour, sugar, salt and pepper. Add tomatoes. Bring to a boil, stirring constantly; cook and stir 1-2 minutes or until thickened. Stir in beans.
2. Transfer to a greased 3-qt. baking dish. Bake, covered, 35-40 minutes or until beans are tender.

Thyme-Baked Apple Slices

I'll often make these apples as an alternative to potatoes when serving meat. My family asks for seconds often.
—**CONSTANCE HENRY** HIBBING, MN

PREP: 15 MIN. • **BAKE:** 25 MIN. • **MAKES:** 6 SERVINGS

- 4 **cups apple cider**
- ¼ **cup butter, cubed**
- 8 **large Braeburn apples (about 4 pounds)**
- 3½ **teaspoons minced fresh thyme, divided**

1. Place cider in a large saucepan. Bring to a boil; cook 18-20 minutes or until liquid is reduced to ⅔ cup. Remove from heat; stir in butter.
2. Peel and cut each apple into eight wedges. In a large bowl, toss apples with ¼ cup of the reduced cider and 3 teaspoons thyme. Transfer to a foil-lined 15x10x1-in. baking pan. Bake 10 minutes.
3. Drizzle apples with the remaining reduced cider. Bake 12-15 minutes longer or until tender. Sprinkle with the remaining thyme.

Mushroom & Peas Rice Pilaf

Anything goes in a rice pilaf, so add peas and baby portobello mushrooms for a burst of color and a variety of textures.
—**STACY MULLENS** GRESHAM, OR

START TO FINISH: 25 MIN. • **MAKES:** 6 SERVINGS

- 1 **package (6.6 ounces) rice pilaf mix with toasted almonds**
- 1 **tablespoon butter**
- 1½ **cups fresh or frozen peas**
- 1 **cup sliced baby portobello mushrooms**

1. Prepare pilaf according to package directions.
2. In a large skillet, heat butter over medium heat. Add peas and mushrooms; cook and stir 6-8 minutes or until tender. Stir in rice.

Loaded Stuffed Potato Pancakes

When I make mashed potatoes, I always cook some extra so I can prepare these over-the-top pancakes. Fill them with sour cream, ranch dressing, melted cheese—or all three.

—JANE WHITTAKER PENSACOLA, FL

PREP: 25 MIN. • **COOK:** 5 MIN./BATCH
MAKES: 8 POTATO PANCAKES

- 2 cups mashed potatoes (with added milk and butter)
- ⅔ cup shredded cheddar cheese
- ⅓ cup all-purpose flour
- 1 large egg, lightly beaten
- 1 tablespoon minced chives
- ½ teaspoon salt
- ½ teaspoon pepper
- ⅔ cup seasoned bread crumbs
- 1 teaspoon garlic powder
- 1 teaspoon onion powder
- ½ teaspoon cayenne pepper
- ⅓ cup cream cheese, softened
  Oil for deep-fat frying

1. In a large bowl, combine the first seven ingredients. In a shallow bowl, mix the bread crumbs, garlic powder, onion powder and cayenne.

2. Shape 2 teaspoons cream cheese into a ball. Wrap ¼ cup of potato mixture around cream cheese to cover completely. Drop into the crumb mixture. Gently coat and shape into a ½-in.-thick patty. Repeat with remaining cream cheese and potato mixture.

3. In an electric skillet or deep-fat fryer, heat oil to 375°. Fry stuffed pancakes, a few at a time, 1-2 minutes on each side or until golden brown. Drain on paper towels.

Roasted Cabbage & Onions

I roast veggies to bring out their sweetness, and it works wonders with onions and cabbage. The vinegar-mustard sauce makes this dish similar to a slaw.

—ANN SHEEHY LAWRENCE, MA

PREP: 10 MIN. • **COOK:** 30 MIN. + STANDING
MAKES: 6 SERVINGS

- 1 medium head cabbage (about 2 pounds), coarsely chopped
- 2 large onions, chopped
- ¼ cup olive oil
- ¾ teaspoon salt
- ¾ teaspoon pepper
- 3 tablespoons minced fresh chives
- 3 tablespoons minced fresh tarragon

DRESSING

- 2 tablespoons white balsamic vinegar or white wine vinegar
- 2 tablespoons olive oil
- 2 tablespoons Dijon mustard
- 1 tablespoon lemon juice
- ½ teaspoon salt
- ½ teaspoon pepper

1. Preheat oven to 450°. Place cabbage and onions in a large bowl. Drizzle with oil; sprinkle with salt and pepper and toss to coat. Transfer to a shallow roasting pan, spreading evenly. Roast 30-35 minutes or until the vegetables are tender and lightly browned, stirring halfway.

2. Transfer cabbage mixture to a large bowl. Add chives and tarragon; toss to combine. In a small bowl, whisk dressing ingredients until blended. Drizzle over cabbage mixture; toss to coat. Let stand 10 minutes to allow flavors to blend. Serve warm or at room temperature.

Refrigerator Jalapeno Dill Pickles

I'm passionate about making pickles. My husband is passionate about eating them. He's too impatient to let them cure on the shelf, so I found this quick recipe to make him happy. Add hotter peppers if you like.

—**ANNIE JENSEN** ROSEAU, MN

PREP: 20 MIN. + CHILLING
MAKES: ABOUT 4 DOZEN PICKLE SPEARS

- 3 pounds pickling cucumbers (about 12)
- 1 small onion, halved and sliced
- ¼ cup snipped fresh dill
- 1 to 2 jalapeno peppers, sliced
- 3 garlic cloves, minced
- 2½ cups water
- 2½ cups cider vinegar
- ⅓ cup canning salt
- ⅓ cup sugar

1. Cut each cucumber lengthwise into four spears. In a very large bowl, combine the cucumbers, onion, dill, jalapenos and garlic. In a big saucepan, combine water, vinegar, salt and sugar. Bring to a boil; cook and stir just until salt and sugar are dissolved. Pour over cucumber mixture; cool.

2. Cover tightly and refrigerate for at least 24 hours. Store in refrigerator for up to 2 months.

NOTE *Wear disposable gloves when cutting hot peppers; the oils can burn skin. Avoid touching your face.*

Contest Winner

Triple-Mushroom au Gratin Potatoes

When I first started cooking, the only mushrooms I used were the button variety. Now I love experimenting with different types. This is wonderful as a side dish to accompany a grilled steak, or even as a main dish with a salad of mixed greens.

—**NADINE MESCH** MOUNT HEALTHY, OH

PREP: 30 MIN. • **BAKE:** 1 HOUR + STANDING
MAKES: 10 SERVINGS

- 6 tablespoons butter, divided
- ½ pound each sliced fresh shiitake, baby portobello and button mushrooms
- 1 tablespoon sherry, optional
- 5 tablespoons all-purpose flour
- 3 cups half-and-half cream
- 3 tablespoons minced fresh rosemary
- 1½ teaspoons salt
- 1 teaspoon pepper
- 2 cups shredded Gruyere cheese
- 2 pounds red potatoes, thinly sliced
- ½ teaspoon paprika

1. Preheat oven to 350°. In a large skillet, heat 1 tablespoon butter over medium-high heat. Add mushrooms; cook and stir until tender. If desired, stir in sherry and cook 1-2 minutes longer or until evaporated. Remove mushrooms from pan.

2. In the same pan, melt remaining butter over medium heat. Stir in the flour until smooth; gradually whisk in the cream. Bring to a boil, stirring constantly; cook and stir 2 minutes or until thickened. Reduce heat to medium-low. Stir in rosemary, salt and pepper. Gradually add cheese, stirring until it is melted. Remove from the heat.

3. Arrange potatoes in an even layer in a greased 13x9-in. baking dish. Top with mushrooms and sauce mixture; sprinkle with paprika.

4. Bake, covered, 40 minutes. Bake, uncovered, 20-25 minutes longer or until golden brown and bubbly. Let stand 15 minutes before serving.

Browned Butter Roasted Cauliflower

When I was growing up, my mother always raved about how deliciously sweet and tender cauliflower can be. Here, the briny capers, lemon juice and sweet raisins together allow the caramelized, nutty cauliflower to shine.
—GINA MYERS SPOKANE, WA

PREP: 50 MIN. • **BAKE:** 15 MIN.
MAKES: 4 SERVINGS

- 6 garlic cloves, unpeeled
- 3 tablespoons unsalted butter
- 1 medium head cauliflower, broken into florets
- ¼ teaspoon salt
- ¼ teaspoon pepper
- ¼ cup golden raisins
- ¼ cup chopped fresh parsley
- 1 tablespoon capers, drained and coarsely chopped
- 2 teaspoons lemon juice

1. Preheat oven to 400°. Cut stem ends off unpeeled garlic cloves. Wrap cloves in a piece of foil. Bake 25-30 minutes or until cloves are soft. Unwrap and cool to room temperature. Squeeze garlic from skins. Mash with a fork.
2. Meanwhile, in a small heavy saucepan, melt butter over medium heat. Heat 5-7 minutes or until golden brown, stirring constantly. Remove from heat.
3. Place cauliflower in a greased 15x10x1-in. baking pan. Drizzle with browned butter; sprinkle with the salt and pepper. Toss to coat. Roast 15-20 minutes or until cauliflower is golden brown and tender.
4. Transfer cauliflower to a bowl. Add remaining ingredients and roasted garlic; toss to combine.

Roasted Pumpkin and Brussels Sprouts

While traveling to Taiwan, we visited a restaurant where fresh vegetables, including pumpkin, were served. That inspired me to roast pumpkin with Brussels sprouts for special occasions.
—PAM CORRELL BROCKPORT, PA

PREP: 15 MIN. • **BAKE:** 35 MIN.
MAKES: 8 SERVINGS

- 1 medium pie pumpkin (about 3 pounds), peeled and cut into ¾-inch cubes
- 1 pound fresh Brussels sprouts, trimmed and halved lengthwise
- 4 garlic cloves, thinly sliced
- ⅓ cup olive oil
- 2 tablespoons balsamic vinegar
- 1 teaspoon sea salt
- ½ teaspoon coarsely ground pepper
- 2 tablespoons minced fresh parsley

1. Preheat oven to 400°. In a large bowl, combine pumpkin, Brussels sprouts and garlic. In a bowl, whisk oil, vinegar, salt and pepper; drizzle over vegetables and toss to coat.
2. Transfer to a greased 15x10x1-in. baking pan. Roast 35-40 minutes or until tender, stirring once. Sprinkle with parsley.

Giardiniera

Sweet and tangy, this Italian condiment is packed with peppers, cauliflower, carrots and other crisp-tender veggies. Offer it alongside pickles or olives on a relish tray.

—**TASTE OF HOME** TEST KITCHEN

PREP: 1 HOUR • **PROCESS:** 10 MIN./BATCH • **MAKES:** 10 PINTS

- 6 cups white vinegar
- 3½ cups sugar
- 3 cups water
- 4½ teaspoons canning salt
- 1 tablespoon dried oregano
- 1 tablespoon fennel seed
- 2 small heads cauliflower, broken into small florets (about 12 cups)
- 4 large carrots, sliced
- 4 celery ribs, cut into ½-inch slices
- 48 pearl onions, peeled and trimmed (about 1¼ pounds)
- 4 large sweet red peppers, cut into ½-inch strips
- 4 serrano peppers, seeds removed and thinly sliced
- 10 bay leaves
- 20 whole peppercorns
- 10 garlic cloves, thinly sliced

1. In a large stockpot, combine vinegar, sugar, water, canning salt, oregano and fennel seed. Bring to a boil. Add cauliflower, carrots, celery, and onions; return to a boil. Remove from heat; add peppers.

2. Carefully ladle the hot mixture into 10 hot 1-pint jars, leaving ½- in. headspace. Add a bay leaf, 2 peppercorns and a few slices of garlic to each jar. Remove air bubbles and adjust headspace, if necessary, by adding hot mixture. Wipe rims. Center the lids on jars; screw on the bands until fingertip tight.

3. Place jars into canner with simmering water, ensuring that they are completely covered with water. Bring to a boil; process for 10 minutes. Remove jars and cool.

NOTE *The processing time listed is for altitudes of 1,000 feet or less. For altitudes up to 3,000 feet, add 5 minutes; 6,000 feet, add 10 minutes; 8,000 feet, add 15 minutes; 10,000 feet, add 20 minutes.*

Deluxe Hash Brown Casserole

My son-in-law gave me the recipe for this hash brown casserole, which my kids say is addictive. It's also an amazing make-ahead dish.

—**AMY OSWALT** BURR, NE

PREP: 10 MIN. • **BAKE:** 50 MIN. + COOLING
MAKES: 12 SERVINGS (⅔ CUP EACH)

- 1½ cups sour cream onion dip
- 1 can (10¾ ounces) condensed cream of chicken soup, undiluted
- 1 envelope ranch salad dressing mix
- 1 teaspoon onion powder
- 1 teaspoon garlic powder
- ½ teaspoon pepper
- 1 package (30 ounces) frozen shredded hash brown potatoes, thawed
- 2 cups (8 ounces) shredded cheddar cheese
- ½ cup crumbled cooked bacon

Preheat oven to 375°. In a large bowl, mix the first six ingredients; stir in potatoes, cheese and bacon. Transfer to a greased 13x9-in. baking dish. Bake 50-60 minutes or until golden brown.

FREEZE OPTION *Cover and freeze the unbaked casserole. To use, partially thaw in refrigerator overnight. Remove from the refrigerator 30 minutes before baking. Preheat oven to 375°. Bake the casserole as directed, increasing the time to 1¼-1½ hours or until the top is golden brown and a thermometer inserted in the center reads 165°.*

Dried Cherry & Sausage Dressing

Apples and dried cherries add a sweet-tart flavor to my homemade stuffing. It helps create a special dinner.
—**CONNIE BOLL** CHILTON, WI

PREP: 40 MIN. • **BAKE:** 45 MIN. • **MAKES:** 20 SERVINGS (¾ CUP EACH)

- 1 loaf (1 pound) unsliced Italian bread
- ¼ cup cherry juice blend or unsweetened apple juice
- 1 cup dried cherries
- 1 pound bulk Italian sausage
- 2 celery ribs, chopped
- 1 medium onion, chopped
- 2 medium Granny Smith apples, chopped
- ½ cup chopped fresh parsley
- ½ cup butter, melted
- 1 teaspoon Italian seasoning
- 1 teaspoon fennel seed
- 1 teaspoon rubbed sage
- ½ teaspoon salt
- ¼ teaspoon pepper
- 2 large eggs
- 2 cups chicken stock

1. Preheat oven to 375°. Cut bread into 1-in. cubes; transfer to two 15x10x1-in. baking pans. Bake 10-15 minutes or until toasted. Cool slightly. In a small saucepan, bring the juice blend to a boil. Stir in cherries. Remove from heat; let stand 10 minutes. Drain.

2. Meanwhile, in a large skillet, cook sausage, celery and onion over medium heat 8-10 minutes or until sausage is no longer pink and vegetables are tender, breaking up sausage

into crumbles; drain. Transfer to a large bowl; stir in the apples, parsley, butter, seasonings, bread cubes and drained cherries. In a small bowl, whisk eggs and stock; pour over bread mixture and toss to coat.

3. Transfer to a greased 13x9-in. baking dish (dish will be full). Bake, covered, 30 minutes. Bake, uncovered, 15-20 minutes or until golden brown.

Jasmine Rice with Coconut & Cherries

Our favorite rice deserves a bit of color and sweetness. We add cherries, peanuts, orange peel and coconut. That does the trick!
—**JOY ZACHARIA** CLEARWATER, FL

PREP: 10 MIN. • **COOK:** 20 MIN. + STANDING • **MAKES:** 4 SERVINGS

- 2½ cups water
- 1 tablespoon olive oil
- ¾ teaspoon salt
- 1½ cups uncooked jasmine rice
- ⅓ cup dried cherries
- ¼ cup chopped salted peanuts
- 1 teaspoon grated orange peel
- ¼ cup flaked coconut, toasted

1. In a large saucepan, bring water, oil and salt to a boil. Stir in rice; return to a boil, stirring once. Reduce heat; simmer, covered, 15-17 minutes or until water is absorbed.

2. Stir in cherries, peanuts and orange peel; let stand, covered, 10 minutes. Sprinkle with coconut.

NOTE *To toast coconut, bake in a shallow pan in a 350° oven for 5-10 minutes or cook in a skillet over low heat until golden brown, stirring occasionally.*

SOUPS, SALADS & SANDWICHES

Have your usual sandwich, salad or soup offerings gotten a little stale? Go for a menu switch-up! Choose from any of these deliciously easy options for winning lunchtime combos.

Salami & Provolone Pasta Salad

This quickly assembled pasta salad has all the flavors of an Italian sub. It's the perfect dish when you want something that's fast, light and cool.

—**JILL DONLEY** WARSAW, IN

PREP: 25 MIN. + CHILLING
MAKES: 8 SERVINGS

- 3 cups uncooked cellentani pasta or elbow macaroni
- 1 medium sweet red pepper, chopped
- 4 ounces provolone cheese, cubed (about 1 cup)
- 4 ounces hard salami, cubed (about 1 cup)
- ⅓ cup prepared Italian salad dressing
  Additional Italian salad dressing and minced fresh basil, optional

1. Cook pasta according to package directions. Meanwhile, in a large bowl, combine pepper, cheese and salami.
2. Drain pasta and rinse in cold water. Add to pepper mixture. Drizzle with ⅓ cup dressing and toss to coat. Refrigerate, covered, at least 1 hour. If desired, stir in additional dressing to moisten and sprinkle with basil before serving.

Contest Winner

Butternut Squash and Roasted Pepper Soup

Having a bowl of this sweet and savory soup brings back the warm feelings of home. The cilantro gives it just the right amount of punch.

—**STACEY PETERSON** NEW HAVEN, CT

PREP: 30 MIN. • **COOK:** 40 MIN.
MAKES: 9 SERVINGS (2¼ QUARTS)

- 2 large sweet red peppers
- 1 medium onion, coarsely chopped
- 1 tablespoon canola oil
- 2 garlic cloves, minced
- 1 medium butternut squash (3 to 3½ pounds), peeled and cubed
- 6 cups vegetable stock
- 1½ teaspoons curry powder
- ½ teaspoon salt
- ¼ teaspoon ground cinnamon
- ¼ teaspoon pepper
  Minced fresh cilantro, optional

1. Cut peppers in half; remove seeds. Broil peppers 4 in. from heat until skins blister, about 5 minutes. Immediately place peppers in a small bowl; cover and let stand for 20 minutes. Peel off and discard charred skin. Chop peppers.
2. In a large saucepan coated with cooking spray, saute onion in oil for 3 minutes. Add garlic; cook 1 minute longer. Add butternut squash; cook for 3 minutes. Stir in the stock, curry powder, salt, cinnamon, pepper and red peppers. Bring to a boil. Reduce heat; cover and simmer for 20-25 minutes or until squash is tender.
3. Cool slightly. In a blender, process 7 cups soup in batches until smooth. Return all to pan and heat through. Garnish with cilantro if desired.

GARLIC CLOVE SUB

When a recipe calls for a clove of garlic and you have no fresh bulbs, substitute ¼ teaspoon of garlic powder for each clove. You can also buy jars of fresh minced garlic at the store to save some time.

Burger Americana

Here's a good basic burger your family will love. Grill the patties and load them sky-high with all the best toppings. Cheese, lettuce and tomato are classics, of course, but consider giving bacon and blue cheese a try, too.

—SUSAN MAHANEY NEW HARTFORD, NY

START TO FINISH: 25 MIN.
MAKES: 4 SERVINGS

- ½ cup seasoned bread crumbs
- 1 large egg, lightly beaten
- ½ teaspoon salt
- ½ teaspoon pepper
- 1 pound ground beef
- 1 tablespoon olive oil
- 4 sesame seed hamburger buns, split
  Toppings of your choice

1. In a large bowl, combine bread crumbs, egg, salt and pepper. Add beef; mix lightly but thoroughly. Shape into four ½-in.-thick patties. Press a shallow indentation in the center of each with your thumb. Brush both sides of patties with oil.
2. Grill the burgers, covered, over medium heat or broil 4 in. from heat 4-5 minutes on each side or until a thermometer reads 160°. Serve on buns with toppings.

Grilled Beef & Blue Cheese Sandwiches

Roast beef, red onion and blue cheese really amp up this deluxe grilled sandwich. If you like a little bit of heat, mix some horseradish into the spread.

—BONNIE HAWKINS ELKHORN, WI

START TO FINISH: 25 MIN.
MAKES: 4 SERVINGS

- 2 ounces cream cheese, softened
- 2 ounces crumbled blue cheese
- 8 slices sourdough bread
- ¾ pound thinly sliced deli roast beef
- ½ small red onion, thinly sliced
- ¼ cup olive oil

1. In a small bowl, mix cream cheese and blue cheese until blended. Spread over bread slices. Layer four of the slices with roast beef and onion; top with remaining bread slices.
2. Brush outsides of sandwiches with oil. In a large skillet, toast sandwiches over medium heat 4-5 minutes on each side or until golden brown.

Smoked Gouda Veggie Melt

After a long day of teaching, I like to make these cheesy open-faced sandwiches. My 8-year-old daughter is a big fan, too.

—CHARLIE HERZOG WEST BROOKFIELD, VT

START TO FINISH: 25 MIN.
MAKES: 4 SERVINGS

- 1 cup chopped fresh mushrooms
- 1 cup chopped fresh broccoli
- 1 medium sweet red pepper, chopped
- 1 small onion, chopped
- 2 tablespoons olive oil
- 8 slices Italian bread (½ inch thick)
- ½ cup mayonnaise
- 1 garlic clove, minced
- 1 cup shredded smoked Gouda cheese

1. Preheat oven to 425°. Place the mushrooms, broccoli, pepper and onion in a greased 15x10x1-in. baking pan. Drizzle with oil; toss to coat. Roast 10-12 minutes or until tender.
2. Meanwhile, place bread slices on a baking sheet. Mix mayonnaise and garlic; spread over bread.
3. Change oven setting to broil. Spoon vegetables over bread slices; sprinkle with cheese. Broil 3-4 in. from heat 2-3 minutes or until cheese is melted.

Chicken & Caramelized Onion Grilled Cheese

My grilled cheese sandwich combines chicken with sweet caramelized onions, red peppers, Swiss cheese and sourdough bread. It's oh-my-goodness good.

—KADIJA BRIDGEWATER BOCA RATON, FL

PREP: 40 MIN. • **GRILL:** 15 MIN. • **MAKES:** 4 SERVINGS

- 2 tablespoons olive oil
- 2 large sweet onions, thinly sliced
- ¾ teaspoon salt, divided
- 1 teaspoon minced fresh rosemary or ¼ teaspoon dried rosemary, crushed
- 2 boneless skinless chicken breast halves (6 ounces each)
- 2 tablespoons lemon juice
- ¼ teaspoon pepper
- ¼ cup mayonnaise
- ⅓ cup finely chopped roasted sweet red peppers
- 8 slices sourdough bread
- 12 slices Swiss cheese
- 2 tablespoons butter, softened

1. In a large skillet, heat the oil over medium heat. Add the onions and a ¼ teaspoon salt; cook and stir 6-8 minutes or until they are softened. Reduce the heat to medium-low; cook 30-40 minutes or until deep golden brown, stirring occasionally. Stir in rosemary.

2. Meanwhile, pound chicken with a meat mallet to ½-in. thickness. Drizzle with lemon juice; sprinkle with pepper and remaining salt. Grill, covered, over medium heat or broil 4 in. from heat 5-7 minutes on each side or until no longer pink. Cut into strips.

3. In a small bowl, mix mayonnaise and red peppers. Spread half of the mayonnaise mixture over four slices of bread. Layer each with one slice cheese, chicken, onions and two slices of cheese. Spread remaining mayonnaise mixture over remaining bread; place over the top. Spread outsides of sandwiches with butter.

4. Grill the sandwiches, covered, over medium heat or broil 4 in. from heat 2-3 minutes on each side or until golden brown and cheese is melted.

Apple-Carrot Slaw with Pistachios

A vibrant slaw like this will be an all-star at your next tailgate. I julienne the carrots and apples because I love the way they look.

—LINDA SCHEND KENOSHA, WI

START TO FINISH: 20 MIN. • **MAKES:** 8 SERVINGS (1 CUP EACH)

- 6 cups julienned carrots (about 9 ounces)
- 4 medium Fuji, Gala or other sweet apples, julienned
- ¼ cup lemon juice
- 2 tablespoons sugar
- 1½ teaspoons ground cinnamon
- 1 cup chopped pistachios, divided
  Dash salt

In a large bowl, combine first five ingredients. Add ½ cup pistachios; toss to combine. Season with salt to taste. Refrigerate, covered, until serving. Just before serving, sprinkle with remaining pistachios.

Fresh Corn & Potato Chowder

This soup was one of my favorites as a child in upstate New York, and I still love it today. For extra depth, place the cob in the soup, simmer, then remove.

—TRACY BIVINS KNOB NOSTER, MO

PREP: 15 MIN. • **COOK:** 25 MIN. • **MAKES:** 6 SERVINGS

- 1 tablespoon butter
- 1 medium onion, chopped
- 1 pound red potatoes (about 3 medium), cubed
- 1½ cups fresh or frozen corn (about 7 ounces)
- 3 cups reduced-sodium chicken broth
- 1¼ cups half-and-half cream, divided
- 2 green onions, thinly sliced
- ½ teaspoon salt
- ¼ teaspoon freshly ground pepper
- 3 tablespoons all-purpose flour
- 1 tablespoon minced fresh parsley

1. In a large saucepan, heat butter over medium-high heat. Add onion; cook and stir 2-4 minutes or until tender. Add potatoes, corn, broth, 1 cup cream, green onions, salt and pepper; bring to a boil. Reduce heat; simmer, covered, for 12-15 minutes or until potatoes are tender.

2. In a small bowl, mix the flour and remaining cream until smooth; stir into soup. Return to a boil, stirring constantly; cook and stir 1-2 minutes or until slightly thickened. Stir in the parsley.

CLAM & CORN CHOWDER *Decrease broth to 2½ cups. Stir in 2 cans (6½ ounces each) undrained minced clams.*

Lemon Cranberry Quinoa Salad

As the cook of the family, I appreciate how simple this dish is to make on a busy weeknight, and it's versatile enough to include ingredients that you have on hand. My favorite variation is to substitute diced mango for cranberries.

—MARY SHENK DEKALB, IL

START TO FINISH: 30 MIN. • **MAKES:** 8 SERVINGS

- ¼ cup olive oil
- 2 teaspoons grated lemon peel
- 2 tablespoons lemon juice
- 2 teaspoons minced fresh gingerroot
- ¾ teaspoon salt

SALAD
- 2 cups reduced-sodium chicken broth
- 1 cup quinoa, rinsed
- 1 cup chopped peeled jicama or tart apple
- 1 cup chopped seeded cucumber
- ¾ cup dried cranberries
- ½ cup minced fresh parsley
- 1 green onion, thinly sliced
- 1 cup cubed avocado

1. For dressing, in a small bowl, whisk first five ingredients until blended.

2. In a small saucepan, bring broth to a boil. Add quinoa. Reduce heat; simmer, covered, 12-15 minutes or until liquid is absorbed. Remove from heat; fluff with a fork. Transfer to a large bowl.

3. Add jicama, cucumber, cranberries, parsley and green onion to quinoa. Drizzle with dressing and toss to coat. Serve warm, or refrigerate and serve cold. Gently stir in avocado before serving.

NOTE *Look for quinoa in the cereal, rice or organic food aisle at the grocery store.*

Contest Winner

FRUITFUL OFFERINGS

Who said salads had to be boring? With these creative recipes, eating well tastes great!
Embark on a new flavor adventure by adding a touch of sweetness to your veggie-filled plates.

Minty Watermelon Salad

My 4-year-old twin grandchildren love to cook in the kitchen with me. Last summer, the three of us were experimenting with watermelon and cheese, and that's where this recipe began. It's a tasty choice for picnics and neighborhood gatherings, or as a healthy snack on a hot summer day.

—**GWENDOLYN VETTER** ROGERS, MN

PREP: 20 MIN. + CHILLING
MAKES: 8 SERVINGS

- 6 cups cubed watermelon
- ½ cup thinly sliced fennel bulb
- ⅓ cup crumbled feta cheese
- 2 tablespoons minced fresh mint
- 2 tablespoons thinly sliced pickled onions
- ½ teaspoon pepper

In a large bowl, combine all the ingredients. Refrigerate, covered, for at least 1 hour.

Citrus Steak Salad

Your family will think you spent hours on this beautiful main-dish salad with its from-scratch dressing, but it's an absolute cinch!

—*TASTE OF HOME* TEST KITCHEN

START TO FINISH: 25 MIN.
MAKES: 4 SERVINGS (1 CUP VINAIGRETTE)

- 6 tablespoons olive oil
- ¼ cup cider vinegar
- ¼ cup orange juice
- 2 tablespoons minced fresh parsley
- 2 tablespoons honey
- 1 garlic clove, minced
- 1 teaspoon chili sauce
- ½ teaspoon salt
- 8 cups torn romaine
- ¾ pound cooked beef sirloin steak, sliced
- 2 cups sliced fresh strawberries
- 1 medium red onion, sliced
- 1 can (11 ounces) mandarin oranges, drained
- 1 cup pecan halves, toasted
- ½ cup fresh goat cheese, crumbled

In a small bowl, whisk the first eight ingredients; set aside. Divide romaine among four plates; top with steak, strawberries, onion, oranges, pecans and cheese. Serve with vinaigrette.

Roasted Apple Salad with Spicy Maple-Cider Vinaigrette

We bought loads of apples and needed to use them. To help the flavors come alive, I roasted the apples and tossed them with a sweet dressing.
—JANICE ELDER CHARLOTTE, NC

PREP: 15 MIN. • **BAKE:** 20 MIN. + COOLING
MAKES: 8 SERVINGS

- 4 medium Fuji, Gala or other firm apples, quartered
- 2 tablespoons olive oil

DRESSING
- 2 tablespoons cider vinegar
- 2 tablespoons olive oil
- 1 tablespoon maple syrup
- 1 teaspoon Sriracha Asian hot chili sauce
- ½ teaspoon salt
- ¼ teaspoon pepper

SALAD
- 1 package (5 ounces) spring mix salad greens
- 4 pitted dates, quartered
- 1 log (4 ounces) fresh goat cheese, crumbled
- ½ cup chopped pecans, toasted

1. Preheat oven to 375°. Place apples in a foil-lined 15x10x1-in. baking pan; drizzle with oil and toss to coat. Roast 20-30 minutes or until tender, stirring occasionally. Cool completely.

2. In a small bowl, whisk dressing ingredients until blended. In a large bowl, combine salad greens and dates. Drizzle dressing over salad and toss to coat.

3. Divide mixture among eight plates. Top with goat cheese and roasted apples; sprinkle with pecans. Serve immediately.

NOTE *To toast nuts, bake in a shallow pan in a 350° oven for 5-10 minutes or cook in a skillet over low heat until lightly browned, stirring occasionally.*

Cantaloupe Chicken Salad with Yogurt Chive Dressing

It's hard to find recipes that four children and my husband love. That's why this refreshing combo of melon and chicken is so special to our family.
—BETSY KING DULUTH, MN

START TO FINISH: 30 MIN.
MAKES: 5 SERVINGS

- ½ cup plain yogurt
- ½ cup reduced-fat mayonnaise
- 1 tablespoon minced chives
- 1 tablespoon lime juice
- ¼ teaspoon salt
- 5 cups cubed cantaloupe
- 2½ cups cubed cooked chicken breast
- 1 medium cucumber, seeded and chopped
- 1 cup green grapes, halved

In a large bowl, combine the first five ingredients. Add the cantaloupe, chicken, cucumber and grapes; toss gently to combine. Serve immediately.

CURRIED CHICKEN FRUIT SALAD
Cut dressing in half; substitute ¼ to ½ teaspoon curry powder for chives. Add the chicken, grapes, and a drained 8-ounce can of pineapple tidbits.

Mixed Greens with Bacon & Cranberries

When my menu calls for a green salad, I rely on this one loaded with crumbled bacon, dried cranberries and blue cheese. The homemade vinaigrette is full of zesty flavor.

—**TERESA RALSTON** NEW ALBANY, OH

START TO FINISH: 20 MIN.
MAKES: 8 SERVINGS (¾ CUP EACH)

- ½ cup orange juice
- ½ cup dried cranberries
- 4 cups fresh arugula or baby spinach
- 4 cups spring mix salad greens
- ½ cup crumbled blue cheese
- 6 thick-sliced peppered bacon strips, cooked and crumbled

VINAIGRETTE
- 2 tablespoons balsamic vinegar
- 2 tablespoons olive oil
- 1 tablespoon honey
- 1½ teaspoons orange juice
- 1½ teaspoons Dijon mustard
- 1 teaspoon grated orange peel
- ⅛ teaspoon salt
- ⅛ teaspoon pepper

1. In a small saucepan, bring orange juice to a boil; remove from heat. Stir in cranberries; let stand 5 minutes. Drain, discarding remaining juice or saving for another use.

2. In a large bowl, combine arugula and salad greens; top with cheese, bacon and cranberries. In a small bowl, whisk vinaigrette ingredients. Drizzle over salad; toss to coat. Serve immediately.

Contest Winner

Garden Turkey Burgers

These juicy burgers get plenty of color and pop from the onion, zucchini and red pepper. I often make the mixture ahead of time and refrigerate it. Later, I can put the burgers on the grill and then whip up a salad or side dish.

—**SANDY KITZMILLER** UNITYVILLE, PA

START TO FINISH: 25 MIN.
MAKES: 6 SERVINGS

- 1 cup old-fashioned oats
- ¾ cup chopped onion
- ¾ cup finely chopped sweet red or green pepper
- ½ cup shredded zucchini
- ¼ cup ketchup
- 2 garlic cloves, minced
- ¼ teaspoon salt, optional
- 1 pound ground turkey
- 6 whole wheat hamburger buns, split and toasted

1. In a large bowl, combine the first seven ingredients. Crumble turkey over mixture and mix well. Shape into six ½-in.-thick patties.

2. Moisten a paper towel with cooking oil; using long-handled tongs, rub on grill rack to coat lightly. Grill burgers, covered, over medium heat or broil 4 in. from heat for 4-6 minutes on each side or until a thermometer reads 165° and juices run clear. Serve on buns.

FREEZE OPTION *Place patties on a plastic wrap-lined baking sheet; wrap and freeze until firm. Remove from pan and transfer to a resealable plastic freezer bag; return to freezer. To use, grill frozen patties as directed, increasing time as necessary for a thermometer to read 165°.*

Creamy Root Veggie Soup

For chilly nights, we fill the pot with parsnips and celery root for a smooth, creamy soup that is flavored with garlic, bacon and thyme.

—**SALLY SIBTHORPE** SHELBY TOWNSHIP, MI

PREP: 15 MIN. • **COOK:** 1 HOUR
MAKES: 8 SERVINGS

- 4 **bacon strips, chopped**
- 1 **large onion, chopped**
- 3 **garlic cloves, minced**
- 1 **large celery root, peeled and cubed (about 5 cups)**
- 6 **medium parsnips, peeled and cubed (about 4 cups)**
- 6 **cups chicken stock**
- 1 **bay leaf**
- 1 **cup heavy whipping cream**
- 2 **teaspoons minced fresh thyme**
- 1 **teaspoon salt**
- ¼ **teaspoon white pepper**
- ¼ **teaspoon ground nutmeg**
  Additional minced fresh thyme

1. In a Dutch oven, cook bacon over medium heat until crisp, stirring occasionally. Remove with a slotted spoon; drain on paper towels. Cook and stir onion in bacon drippings 6-8 minutes or until tender. Add garlic; cook 1 minute longer.

2. Add celery root, parsnips, stock and bay leaf. Bring to a boil. Reduce heat; cook, uncovered, 30-40 minutes or until vegetables are tender. Remove the bay leaf.

3. Puree soup using an immersion blender. Or, cool slightly and puree in batches in a blender; return to pan. Stir in the cream, 2 teaspoons thyme, salt, pepper and nutmeg; heat soup through. Top servings with bacon and additional thyme.

Balsamic Three-Bean Salad

Here's my little girl's favorite salad. She eats it just about as fast as I can make it. Prepare it ahead so the flavors have plenty of time to get to know each other.

—**STACEY FEATHER** JAY, OK

PREP: 25 MIN. + CHILLING
MAKES: 12 SERVINGS (¾ CUP EACH)

- 2 **pounds fresh green beans, trimmed and cut into 2-inch pieces**
- ½ **cup balsamic vinaigrette**
- ¼ **cup sugar**
- 1 **garlic clove, minced**
- ¾ **teaspoon salt**
- 2 **cans (16 ounces each) kidney beans, rinsed and drained**
- 2 **cans (15 ounces each) cannellini beans, rinsed and drained**
- 4 **fresh basil leaves, torn**

1. Fill a Dutch oven three-fourths full with water; bring to a boil. Add the green beans; cook them uncovered for 3-6 minutes or until crisp-tender. Drain and immediately drop into ice water. Drain and pat dry.

2. In a large bowl, whisk vinaigrette, sugar, garlic and salt until the sugar is dissolved. Add the canned beans and green beans; toss to coat. Refrigerate, covered, at least 4 hours. Stir in basil just before serving.

Contest Winner

Antipasto Braid

We're fans of Mediterranean food, so this play on antipasto is a winner in my family.

—PATRICIA HARMON BADEN, PA

PREP: 25 MIN. • **BAKE:** 30 MIN. + STANDING
MAKES: 12 SERVINGS

- ⅓ **cup pitted Greek olives, chopped**
- ¼ **cup marinated quartered artichoke hearts, drained and chopped**
- ¼ **cup julienned oil-packed sun-dried tomatoes**
- 2 **tablespoons plus 2 teaspoons grated Parmesan cheese, divided**
- 3 **tablespoons olive oil, divided**
- 1 **tablespoon chopped fresh basil or 1 teaspoon dried basil**
- 1 **tube (11 ounces) refrigerated crusty French loaf**
- 6 **thin slices prosciutto or deli ham**
- 4 **slices provolone cheese**
- ¾ **cup julienned roasted sweet red peppers**

1. Preheat oven to 350°. In a bowl, toss olives, artichokes, tomatoes, 2 tablespoons Parmesan cheese, 2 tablespoons oil and basil until combined.

2. On a lightly floured surface, carefully unroll French loaf dough; roll into a 15x10-in. rectangle. Transfer to a greased 15x10x1-in. baking pan. Layer prosciutto, provolone cheese and red peppers lengthwise down center third of rectangle. Top with olive mixture.

3. On each long side, cut 10 strips about 3½ in. into the center. Starting at one end, fold alternating strips at an angle across filling, pinching ends to seal. Brush with remaining oil and sprinkle with remaining Parmesan cheese.

4. Bake 30-35 minutes or until golden brown. Let braid stand 10 minutes before cutting. Serve warm.

Hearty Steak & Barley Soup

My entire family digs into this delicious and comforting soup. Loaded with chunks of tender beef, the rich broth also includes plenty of fresh mushrooms, sliced carrots and wholesome barley.

—**BARBARA BEATTIE** GLEN ALLEN, VA

PREP: 10 MIN. • **COOK:** 30 MIN. • **MAKES:** 4 SERVINGS

- 2 tablespoons all-purpose flour
- ½ teaspoon salt
- ¼ teaspoon pepper, divided
- 1 pound lean beef top sirloin steak, cut into ½-inch cubes
- 1 tablespoon canola oil
- 2 cups sliced fresh mushrooms
- 2 cans (14½ ounces each) reduced-sodium beef broth
- 2 medium carrots, sliced
- ¼ teaspoon garlic powder
- ¼ teaspoon dried thyme
- ½ cup quick-cooking barley

1. In a large resealable plastic bag, combine the flour, salt and ⅛ teaspoon pepper. Add beef and shake to coat. In a Dutch oven, brown beef in oil over medium heat or until the meat is no longer pink. Remove beef and set aside.

2. In the same pan, saute mushrooms until tender. Add the broth, carrots, garlic powder, thyme and remaining pepper; bring to a boil. Add barley and beef. Reduce heat; cover and simmer for 20-25 minutes until the meat, vegetables and barley are tender.

Contest Winner

Red & Green Salad with Toasted Almonds

During a long Midwest winter, I crave greens and tomatoes from the garden. This salad has a fantastic out-of-the-garden taste. Thank goodness I can get the ingredients year-round.

—**JASMINE ROSE** CRYSTAL LAKE, IL

START TO FINISH: 25 MIN. • **MAKES:** 12 SERVINGS (1⅓ CUPS EACH)

- ¼ cup red wine vinegar
- 1 tablespoon reduced-sodium soy sauce
- 2 garlic cloves, minced
- 2 teaspoons sesame oil
- 2 teaspoons honey
- 1 teaspoon minced fresh gingerroot or ½ teaspoon ground ginger
- ⅛ teaspoon Louisiana-style hot sauce
- ½ cup grapeseed or canola oil

SALAD
- 2 heads Boston or Bibb lettuce, torn
- 1 head red leaf lettuce
- 1 medium sweet red pepper, julienned
- 2 celery ribs, sliced
- 1 cup sliced English cucumber
- 1 cup frozen peas, thawed
- 1 cup grape tomatoes, halved
- 1 cup sliced almonds, toasted

1. In a small bowl, whisk the first seven ingredients. Gradually whisk in grapeseed oil until blended.

2. In a large bowl, combine lettuces, red pepper, celery, cucumber, peas and tomatoes. Just before serving, pour dressing over salad and toss to coat. Sprinkle with almonds.

NOTE *To toast nuts, bake in a shallow pan in a 350° oven for 5-10 minutes or cook in a skillet over low heat until lightly browned, stirring occasionally.*

Quick Chicken & Wild Rice Soup

My mother-in-law raves about the chicken and rice soup that we serve at our house. I tweaked the recipe several times to get it just right.

—TERESA JACOBSON ST. JOHNS, FL

START TO FINISH: 30 MIN.
MAKES: 4 SERVINGS

- 1 package (6.2 ounces) fast-cooking long grain and wild rice mix
- 2 tablespoons butter
- 1 small onion, finely chopped
- 1 celery rib, finely chopped
- 1 medium carrot, finely chopped
- 1 garlic clove, minced
- 2 tablespoons all-purpose flour
- 3 cups 2% milk
- 1½ cups chicken broth
- 2 cups cubed cooked chicken

1. Cook the rice mix according to package directions.
2. Meanwhile, in a large saucepan, heat butter over medium-high heat. Add onion, celery and carrot; cook and stir 6-8 minutes or until tender. Add garlic; cook 1 minute longer. Stir in flour until blended; gradually whisk in milk and broth. Bring to a boil, stirring constantly; cook and stir 1-2 minutes or until slightly thickened.
3. Stir in chicken and rice mixture; heat through.

Colorful Corn Bread Salad

When my garden comes in, I harvest the veggies for potluck dishes. I live in the South, and we think bacon and corn bread make everything better, even salad!

—REBECCA CLARK WARRIOR, AL

PREP: 45 MIN. + CHILLING
MAKES: 14 SERVINGS (¾ CUP EACH)

- 1 package (8½ ounces) corn bread/ muffin mix
- 1 cup mayonnaise
- ½ cup sour cream
- 1 envelope ranch salad dressing mix
- 1 to 2 tablespoons adobo sauce from canned chipotle peppers
- 4 to 6 cups torn romaine
- 4 medium tomatoes, chopped
- 1 medium green pepper, chopped
- 1 medium onion, chopped
- 1 pound bacon strips, cooked and crumbled
- 4 cups shredded cheddar cheese
  Additional chopped tomato and crumbled bacon, optional

1. Preheat oven to 400°. Prepare the corn bread batter according to package directions. Pour into a greased 8-in. square baking pan. Bake 15-20 minutes or until a toothpick inserted in center comes out clean. Cool completely in pan on a wire rack.
2. Coarsely crumble corn bread into a large bowl. In a small bowl, mix mayonnaise, sour cream, salad dressing mix and adobo sauce.
3. In a 3-qt. trifle bowl or glass bowl, layer a third of the corn bread and half of each of the following ingredients: romaine, tomatoes, pepper, onion, bacon, cheese and the mayonnaise mixture. Repeat layers. Top with remaining corn bread and, if desired, additional chopped tomato and bacon. Refrigerate salad, covered, 2-4 hours before serving.

Roasted Butternut Squash Panzanella

Squash was a hard sell with our family until I paired it with fall flavors using pumpkin seeds, cranberries and horseradish. Now they love it!

—**DEVON DELANEY** WESTPORT, CT

PREP: 25 MIN. • **BAKE:** 45 MIN.
MAKES: 8 SERVINGS

- 4 cups cubed sourdough bread
- 5 tablespoons olive oil, divided
- 1 medium butternut squash (about 3 pounds), peeled and cut into 1-inch cubes
- ½ teaspoon each salt, ground ginger, ground cumin and pepper
- 1 cup salted shelled pumpkin seeds (pepitas)
- 1 cup dried cranberries
- 4 shallots, finely chopped (about ½ cup)

DRESSING

- ⅓ cup red wine vinegar
- ¼ cup maple syrup
- 2 tablespoons prepared horseradish
- ½ teaspoon salt
- ½ teaspoon pepper
- ¼ teaspoon dried rosemary, crushed
- ¼ cup olive oil

1. Preheat the oven to 425°. Place bread cubes in a 15x10x1-in. baking pan; toss with 2 tablespoons oil. Bake for 10-15 minutes or until toasted, stirring twice.

2. Place squash in a greased 15x10x1-in. baking pan. Mix the seasonings and remaining 3 tablespoons oil; drizzle over squash and toss to coat. Roast 35-45 minutes or until tender and lightly browned, stirring occasionally.

3. In a large bowl, combine bread cubes, squash, pumpkin seeds, cranberries and shallots. In a small saucepan, combine the first six dressing ingredients; heat through, stirring to blend. Remove from heat; gradually whisk in oil until blended.

4. Drizzle ½ cup dressing over salad and toss to combine. (Save remaining dressing for another use.)

Contest Winner

Quick & Easy Turkey Sloppy Joes

When we were first married, I found this simple recipe and adjusted it to our tastes. The fresh bell pepper and red onion give it a wonderful twist.

—**KALLEE TWINER** MARYVILLE, TN

START TO FINISH: 30 MIN.
MAKES: 8 SERVINGS

- 1 pound lean ground turkey
- 1 large red onion, chopped
- 1 large green pepper, chopped
- 1 can (8 ounces) tomato sauce
- ½ cup barbecue sauce
- 1 teaspoon dried oregano
- 1 teaspoon ground cumin
- 1 teaspoon chili powder
- ¼ teaspoon salt
- 8 hamburger buns, split

1. In a large skillet, cook the turkey, onion and pepper over medium heat 6-8 minutes or until turkey is no longer pink and vegetables are tender, breaking up turkey into crumbles.

2. Stir in tomato sauce, barbecue sauce and seasonings. Bring to a boil. Reduce heat; simmer, uncovered, 10 minutes to allow flavors to blend, stirring occasionally. Serve on buns.

Chicken Potpie Soup

My grandmother hand-wrote a cookbook, and this pie crust recipe comes from her. I like to make little pastries out of it to serve with soup.
—**KAREN LEMAY** SEABROOK, TX

PREP: 20 MIN. + CHILLING • **COOK:** 20 MIN. • **MAKES:** 6 SERVINGS

- 2 cups all-purpose flour
- 1¼ teaspoons salt
- ⅔ cup shortening
- 5 to 6 tablespoons 2% milk

SOUP
- 2 tablespoons butter
- 1 cup cubed peeled potatoes
- 1 cup chopped sweet onion
- 2 celery ribs, chopped
- 2 medium carrots, chopped
- ½ cup all-purpose flour
- ½ teaspoon salt
- ¼ teaspoon pepper
- 3 cans (14½ ounces each) chicken broth
- 2 cups shredded cooked chicken
- 1 cup frozen petite peas
- 1 cup frozen corn

1. In a large bowl, mix flour and salt; cut in shortening until crumbly. Gradually add milk, tossing with a fork until dough holds together when pressed. Shape into a disk; wrap in plastic wrap. Refrigerate for 30 minutes or overnight.
2. On a lightly floured surface, roll the dough to ⅛-in. thickness. Using a floured 2½-in. heart-shaped or round cutter, cut 18 shapes. Place 1 in. apart on ungreased baking sheets. Bake at 425° for 8-11 minutes or until golden brown. Cool on a wire rack.
3. For soup, heat butter in a Dutch oven over medium-high heat. Add the potatoes, onion, celery and carrots; cook and stir for 5-7 minutes or until onion is tender.

4. Stir in the flour, salt and pepper until blended; gradually whisk in broth. Bring to a boil over medium-high heat, stirring occasionally. Reduce heat; simmer, uncovered, for 8-10 minutes or until potatoes are tender. Stir in remaining ingredients; heat through. Serve with pastries.

Red, White & Blue Potato Salad

Tossing the cooked potatoes with stock and wine right after you drain them infuses them with flavor. The liquid absorbs like magic.
—**GEORGE LEVINTHAL** GOLETA, CA

PREP: 40 MIN. • **COOK:** 10 MIN. • **MAKES:** 12 SERVINGS (1 CUP EACH)

- 1¼ pounds small purple potatoes (about 11), quartered
- 1 pound small Yukon Gold potatoes (about 9), quartered
- 1 pound small red potatoes (about 9), quartered
- ½ cup chicken stock
- ¼ cup white wine or additional chicken stock
- 2 tablespoons sherry vinegar
- 2 tablespoons white wine vinegar
- 1½ teaspoons Dijon mustard
- 1½ teaspoons stone-ground mustard
- ¾ teaspoon salt
- ½ teaspoon coarsely ground pepper
- 6 tablespoons olive oil
- 3 celery ribs, chopped
- 1 small sweet red pepper, chopped
- 8 green onions, chopped
- ¾ pound bacon strips, cooked and crumbled
- 3 tablespoons each minced fresh basil, dill and parsley
- 2 tablespoons toasted sesame seeds

1. Place all potatoes in a Dutch oven; add water to cover. Bring to a boil. Reduce heat; cook, uncovered, 10-15 minutes or until tender. Drain; transfer to a large bowl. Drizzle the potatoes with stock and wine; toss gently, allowing the liquids to absorb.
2. In a small bowl, whisk vinegars, mustards, salt and pepper. Gradually whisk in oil until blended. Add the vinaigrette, vegetables, bacon and herbs to potato mixture; toss to combine. Sprinkle with sesame seeds. Serve warm.

3. Divide salad greens among four serving plates; top with tomatoes, blueberries, oranges, onions and turkey strips.
4. In a blender, combine the vinegar, blueberries, honey and mustard. While processing, gradually add oil in a steady stream. Serve with salad.

Feta Mushroom Burgers

My son-in-law gave me this recipe and I tweaked it to make it even healthier. The burgers are so quick to whip up on the grill.
—**DOLORES BLOCK** FRANKENMUTH, MI

START TO FINISH: 25 MIN. • **MAKES:** 6 SERVINGS

- 1 **pound lean ground beef (90% lean)**
- 3 **Italian turkey sausage links (4 ounces each), casings removed**
- 2 **teaspoons Worcestershire sauce**
- ½ **teaspoon garlic powder**
- 2 **tablespoons balsamic vinegar**
- 1 **tablespoon olive oil**
- 6 **large portobello mushrooms, stems removed**
- 1 **large onion, cut into ½-inch slices**
- 6 **tablespoons crumbled feta or blue cheese**
- 6 **whole wheat hamburger buns or sourdough rolls, split**
- 10 **fresh basil leaves, thinly sliced**

1. Combine the first four ingredients; mix lightly but thoroughly. Shape into six ½-in.-thick patties. Mix vinegar and oil; brush over mushrooms.
2. Place burgers, mushrooms and onion on an oiled grill rack over medium heat. Grill, covered, over medium heat 4-6 minutes per side or until a thermometer inserted in burger reads 165° and mushrooms and onion are tender.
3. Place cheese in mushroom caps. Grill mushrooms, covered, until cheese is melted, 1-2 minutes. Grill buns, cut side down, until toasted, 30-60 seconds. Serve burgers on buns; top with mushrooms, basil and onion.

Summer Turkey Salads

Tender turkey is treated to a yummy walnut coating in this dressy salad that just begs to be served outside. Add a cold glass filled with Arnold Palmer mix—lemonade and iced tea—and enjoy!
—*TASTE OF HOME* TEST KITCHEN

START TO FINISH: 25 MIN. • **MAKES:** 4 SERVINGS

- ¼ **cup all-purpose flour**
- ½ **teaspoon salt**
- 1 **large egg, beaten**
- ¾ **cup finely chopped walnuts**
- ½ **teaspoon dried rosemary, crushed**
- 8.8 **ounces turkey breast cutlets, cut into strips**
- 1 **tablespoon olive oil**
- 1 **package (5 ounces) spring mix salad greens**
- 2 **plum tomatoes, cut into wedges**
- 1 **cup fresh blueberries**
- ½ **cup mandarin oranges**
- 2 **green onions, thinly sliced**

BLUEBERRY VINAIGRETTE
- ¼ **cup red wine vinegar**
- ½ **cup fresh blueberries**
- 1 **tablespoon honey**
- 2 **teaspoons Dijon mustard**
- ¼ **cup olive oil**

1. Combine flour and salt in a shallow bowl. Place egg in a separate shallow bowl. Combine walnuts and rosemary in another shallow bowl. Coat turkey in flour mixture, then dip in egg and coat with walnut mixture.
2. In a large skillet over medium heat, cook turkey in oil in batches for 2-3 minutes on each side or until meat is no longer pink.

Swiss Chicken Sliders

Some of our friends came over for a spur-of-the-moment bonfire, and I dreamed up these quick chicken sliders so we'd have something to eat. Bake them until the cheese is nice and gooey.

—**SARA MARTIN** WHITEFISH, MT

START TO FINISH: 25 MIN.
MAKES: 6 SERVINGS

- ½ cup mayonnaise
- 3 tablespoons yellow mustard
- 12 mini buns, split
- 12 slices deli ham
- 3 cups shredded rotisserie chicken
- 6 slices Swiss cheese, cut in half

1. Preheat oven to 350°. In a small bowl, mix mayonnaise and mustard. Spread bun bottoms and tops with mayonnaise mixture. Layer bottoms with ham, chicken and cheese; replace tops. Arrange in a single layer in a 15x10x1-in. baking pan.
2. Bake, covered, for 10-15 minutes or until heated through and cheese is melted.

Contest Winner

Deluxe German Potato Salad

I make this salad for all occasions because it goes well with any kind of meat. I often take the warm salad to bring-a-dish events, and there are rarely leftovers!

—**BETTY PERKINS** HOT SPRINGS, AR

START TO FINISH: 30 MIN.
MAKES: 14-16 SERVINGS

- ½ pound sliced bacon, diced
- 1 cup thinly sliced celery
- 1 cup chopped onion
- 1 cup sugar
- 2 tablespoons all-purpose flour
- 1 teaspoon salt
- ¾ teaspoon ground mustard
- 1 cup cider vinegar
- ½ cup water
- 5 pounds unpeeled small red potatoes, cooked and sliced
- 2 medium carrots, shredded
- 2 tablespoons minced fresh parsley
  Additional salt, optional

1. In a large skillet, cook the bacon over medium heat until it is crisp.

Remove bacon to paper towels. Drain the skillet, reserving ¼ cup drippings. Saute celery and onion in drippings until tender.
2. In a large bowl, combine the sugar, flour, salt, mustard, vinegar and water until smooth. Add to the skillet. Bring to a boil. Cook and stir for 1-2 minutes until thickened.
3. In a large serving bowl, combine the potatoes, carrots and parsley. Drizzle with sauce; stir gently to coat. Season with additional salt if desired. Crumble bacon; sprinkle on salad. Serve warm. Refrigerate leftovers.

ZIPPY POTATO SALAD

To kick up my potato salad a notch, I stir in some prepared horseradish, some grated Parmesan cheese and a few drops of hot pepper sauce. It's a welcome twist on this classic recipe.
—**ALLEN R.** DIBOLL, TX

Chipotle-Black Bean Chili

I love soup weather, and this chili will warm you up when there's a chill in the air. The whole can of chipotles in adobo make this pretty spicy, so you can cut back and adjust to your taste.
—**KARLA SHEELEY** WORDEN, IL

PREP: 20 MIN. • **COOK:** 1¼ HOURS
MAKES: 10 SERVINGS (3 QUARTS)

- 1 tablespoon Creole seasoning
- 1 beef top sirloin steak (2 pounds), cut into ½-inch cubes
- 3 tablespoons olive oil
- 1 large sweet onion, chopped
- 3 chipotle peppers in adobo sauce, seeded and finely chopped
- 2 tablespoons minced garlic
- ⅓ cup masa harina
- 2 tablespoons chili powder
- 2 tablespoons Worcestershire sauce
- 1 tablespoon ground cumin
- 1 teaspoon ground cinnamon
- ¼ teaspoon salt
- ¼ teaspoon cayenne pepper
- 4 cups reduced-sodium beef broth
- 1 can (28 ounces) diced tomatoes, undrained
- 3 cans (15 ounces each) black beans, rinsed and drained
  Shredded cheddar cheese and/or finely chopped red onion, optional

1. Place Creole seasoning in a large resealable plastic bag. Add beef, a few pieces at a time, and shake to coat.
2. In a Dutch oven, saute beef in oil in batches. Stir in the onion, chipotle peppers and garlic. Cook 3 minutes longer or until onion is tender. Drain.
3. Stir in the masa harina, chili powder, Worcestershire sauce, cumin, cinnamon, salt and cayenne. Cook and stir for 3-5 minutes. Stir in broth and tomatoes. Bring to a boil. Reduce heat; simmer, uncovered, for 45 minutes or until beef is tender.
4. Stir in beans; heat through. Garnish with cheddar cheese and/or red onion if desired.
NOTE *Wear disposable gloves when cutting hot peppers; the oils can burn skin. Avoid touching your face.*

Contest Winner

South-of-the-Border Caprese Salad

Plump heirloom tomatoes are the stars of this garden-fresh medley, topped with a sweet-tart dressing and crumbled cheese.
—**KATHLEEN MERKLEY** LAYTON, UT

START TO FINISH: 30 MIN.
MAKES: 6 SERVINGS (1 CUP DRESSING)

CILANTRO VINAIGRETTE
- ⅓ cup white wine vinegar
- ½ cup fresh cilantro leaves
- 3 tablespoons sugar
- 1 jalapeno pepper, seeded and chopped
- 1 garlic clove, peeled and quartered
- ¾ teaspoon salt
- ⅔ cup olive oil

SALAD
- 4 cups torn mixed salad greens
- 3 large heirloom or other tomatoes, sliced
- ½ cup crumbled queso fresco or diced part-skim mozzarella cheese
- ¼ teaspoon salt
- ⅛ teaspoon pepper
- 1½ teaspoons fresh cilantro leaves

1. In a blender, combine the first six ingredients. While processing, gradually add oil in a steady stream.
2. Arrange greens on a serving platter; top with tomatoes. Sprinkle with cheese, salt and pepper.
3. Just before serving, drizzle the salad with ½ cup dressing; garnish with cilantro leaves. Refrigerate the leftover dressing.
NOTE *Wear disposable gloves when cutting hot peppers; the oils can burn skin. Avoid touching your face.*

BREADS, ROLLS & MORE

Made-from-scratch rolls, loaves, muffins and biscuits may seem like a lot of work, but these recipes prove you can make something homemade without much fuss at all. Give them a try and see for yourself!

Ginger & Lemon Muffins

A microplane grater (which is also good for citrus zest and hard cheese) works well for grating ginger. Fresh ginger can be frozen up to 6 months; just break off what you need for this recipe.

—LINDA GREEN KILAUEA, HI

START TO FINISH: 30 MIN.
MAKES: 1 DOZEN

- ½ cup butter, softened
- ¾ cup sugar
- 2 large eggs
- ¼ cup minced fresh gingerroot
- 2 tablespoons grated lemon peel
- 2 cups all-purpose flour
- ¾ teaspoon baking soda
- ½ teaspoon salt
- 1 cup buttermilk

TOPPING
- 2 tablespoons coarse sugar
- 2 tablespoons finely chopped crystallized ginger

1. Preheat oven to 375°. In a small bowl, cream butter and sugar until light and fluffy. Add eggs, one at a time, beating well after each addition. Beat in ginger and lemon peel. In another bowl, whisk flour, baking soda and salt; add to creamed mixture alternately with buttermilk, beating well after each addition.

2. Fill greased or paper-lined muffin cups three-fourths full. In a bowl, mix topping ingredients; sprinkle over muffins. Bake 14-16 minutes or until a toothpick inserted in center comes out clean. Cool 5 minutes before removing from pan to a wire rack. Serve warm.

Contest Winner

Surprise Sausage Bundles

Kielbasa and sauerkraut star in a tasty filling for these scrumptious stuffed rolls, which make for a great dinner with soup or salad. My family also loves leftover bundles right out of the refrigerator for a quick lunch.

—BARB RUIS GRANDVILLE, MI

PREP: 45 MIN. + RISING • **BAKE:** 20 MIN.
MAKES: 16 SERVINGS

- 6 bacon strips, diced
- 1 cup chopped onion
- 1 can (16 ounces) sauerkraut, rinsed and well drained
- ½ pound smoked kielbasa or Polish sausage, coarsely chopped
- 2 tablespoons brown sugar
- ½ teaspoon garlic salt
- ¼ teaspoon caraway seeds
- ⅛ teaspoon pepper
- 1 package (16 ounces) hot roll mix
- 2 large eggs, divided use
- 1 cup warm water (120° to 130°)
- 2 tablespoons butter, softened
  Poppy seeds

1. In a large skillet, cook bacon until crisp; remove to paper towels. Reserve 2 tablespoons drippings. Saute onion in drippings until tender. Stir in the sauerkraut, sausage, brown sugar, garlic salt, caraway and pepper. Cook and stir for 5 minutes. Remove from the heat; add bacon. Set aside to cool.

2. In a large bowl, combine contents of the roll mix and its yeast packet. Stir in one egg, water and butter to form a soft dough. Turn onto a floured surface; knead until smooth and elastic, about 5 minutes. Cover dough with a large bowl; let stand for 5 minutes.

3. Divide dough into 16 pieces. On a floured surface, roll out each piece into a 4-in. circle. Top each with ¼ cup filling. Fold dough around filling, forming a ball; pinch edges to seal. Place seam side down on greased baking sheets. Cover loosely with plastic wrap that has been coated with cooking spray. Let rise in a warm place for 15 minutes.

4. Beat remaining egg; brush over bundles. Sprinkle with poppy seeds. Bake at 350° for 16-17 minutes or until golden brown. Serve warm.

FREEZE OPTION *Freeze cooled bundles in a freezer container, separating the layers with waxed paper. To use, reheat bundles on a greased baking sheet in a preheated 325° oven until heated through.*

New England Walnut Bread

Pumpkin bread is for chilly mornings when you long for some home-style New England food. Slice and serve it with a warm and soothing beverage.

—**KIM FORNI** LACONIA, NH

PREP: 25 MIN. • **BAKE:** 1 HOUR + COOLING
MAKES: 2 LOAVES (16 SLICES EACH)

- ½ cup old-fashioned oats
- ⅛ teaspoon ground cinnamon
- ¼ teaspoon sugar

BREAD

- 1 can (15 ounces) solid-pack pumpkin
- 4 large eggs
- ¾ cup canola oil
- ⅔ cup water
- 2 cups sugar
- 1 cup honey
- 1½ teaspoons vanilla extract
- 3½ cups all-purpose flour
- 2 teaspoons baking soda
- 1½ teaspoons salt
- 1½ teaspoons ground cinnamon
- 1 teaspoon ground nutmeg
- ½ teaspoon ground cloves
- ½ teaspoon ground ginger
- 1 cup coarsely chopped walnuts, toasted

1. Preheat oven to 350°. In a small skillet, combine oats, cinnamon and sugar; cook and stir over medium heat 4-6 minutes or until oats are toasted. Remove from heat.
2. For bread, in a large bowl, beat the pumpkin, eggs, oil, water, sugar, honey and vanilla until well blended. In another bowl, whisk the flour, baking soda, salt and spices; gradually beat into the pumpkin mixture. Fold in the walnuts.
3. Transfer to two greased 9x5-in. loaf pans. Sprinkle tops with oat mixture.
4. Bake for 60-70 minutes or until a toothpick inserted in center comes out clean. Cool in the pan 10 minutes before removing to a wire rack to cool.
NOTE *To toast nuts, bake in a shallow pan in a 350° oven for 5-10 minutes or cook in a skillet over low heat until lightly browned, stirring occasionally.*

Pina Colada Biscuits

Pineapple, coconut and macadamia nuts give biscuits a tropical flavor. The biscuits are quick to make and so good. When you want a taste of Hawaii without leaving home, try these!

—**CAROLYN PIETTE** JOHNSTON, RI

START TO FINISH: 30 MIN.
MAKES: 1 DOZEN

- 2½ cups biscuit/baking mix
- 2 tablespoons sugar
- ¼ cup cold butter, cubed
- ¼ cup 2% milk
- 1 large egg
- ½ teaspoon vanilla extract
- ½ cup unsweetened pineapple tidbits, well drained
- ½ cup flaked coconut
- ¼ cup chopped macadamia nuts

1. Preheat oven to 450°. In a large bowl, whisk biscuit mix and sugar. Cut in the butter until mixture resembles coarse crumbs. In another bowl, whisk milk, egg and vanilla; stir into crumb mixture just until moistened. Stir in remaining ingredients.
2. Turn onto a lightly floured surface; knead gently 8-10 times. Pat or roll dough to ½-in. thickness; cut with a floured 2½-in. biscuit cutter. Place 1 in. apart on an ungreased baking sheet. Bake 7-9 minutes or until golden brown. Serve warm.

Louisiana Pecan Bacon Bread

One Christmas, the baby sitter brought gifts for my daughter and a basket of goodies, including pecan bread. When I make this bread, I remember her fondly.

MARINA CASTLE CANYON COUNTRY, CA

PREP: 20 MIN. • **BAKE:** 50 MIN. + COOLING
MAKES: 1 LOAF (16 SLICES)

- 6 bacon strips, chopped
- 6 ounces cream cheese, softened
- ⅓ cup sugar
- 1 large egg
- 2 cups all-purpose flour
- 2½ teaspoons baking powder
- ½ teaspoon salt
- ¾ cup 2% milk
- 1 cup chopped pecans
- ¼ cup finely chopped onion
- ¼ cup chopped green pepper

1. Preheat oven to 350°. In a large skillet, cook bacon over medium-low heat until crisp, stirring occasionally. Remove with a slotted spoon; drain on paper towels. Reserve the drippings (about 2 tablespoons); cool slightly.
2. In a large bowl, beat cream cheese, sugar and reserved drippings until smooth. Beat in egg. In another bowl, whisk flour, baking powder and salt; add to cream cheese mixture alternately with milk, beating well after each addition. Fold in pecans, onion, pepper and bacon. Transfer to a greased 9x5-in. loaf pan.
3. Bake 50-60 minutes or until a toothpick inserted in the center comes out clean. Cool in the pan 10 minutes before removing to a wire rack to cool.
FREEZE OPTION *Securely wrap cooled loaves in plastic wrap and foil, then freeze. To use, thaw in the refrigerator.*

Flaky Cheddar-Chive Biscuits

These buttery biscuits will complement just about any dinner. Speckled with cheese and chives, they look wonderful—and taste even better!

—**BETSY KING** DULUTH, MN

START TO FINISH: 25 MIN. • **MAKES:** 10 BISCUITS

- 2¼ cups all-purpose flour
- 2½ teaspoons baking powder
- 2 teaspoons sugar
- ½ teaspoon baking soda
- ½ teaspoon salt
- ½ cup cold butter, cubed
- 1 cup shredded cheddar cheese
- 3 tablespoons minced fresh chives
- 1 cup buttermilk

1. Preheat oven to 425°. In a large bowl, whisk the first five ingredients. Cut in butter until mixture resembles coarse crumbs; stir in cheese and chives. Add buttermilk; stir just until moistened. Turn onto a lightly floured surface; knead gently 8-10 times.
2. Pat or roll the dough to ¾-in. thickness; cut it with a floured 2½-in. biscuit cutter. Place 2 in. apart on a greased baking sheet. Bake 10-12 minutes or until golden brown. Serve warm.

Contest Winner

Ginger Pear Muffins

I've had this cherished recipe in my files for years. The chunks of fresh pear make each bite of these muffins moist and delicious.
—**LORRAINE CALAND** SHUNIAH, ON

PREP: 25 MIN. • **BAKE:** 20 MIN. • **MAKES:** 1½ DOZEN

- ¾ cup packed brown sugar
- ⅓ cup canola oil
- 1 large egg
- 1 cup buttermilk
- 2½ cups all-purpose flour
- 1 teaspoon baking soda
- 1 teaspoon ground ginger
- ½ teaspoon salt
- ½ teaspoon ground cinnamon
- 2 cups chopped peeled fresh pears

TOPPING
- ⅓ cup packed brown sugar
- ¼ teaspoon ground ginger
- 2 teaspoons butter, melted

1. Preheat oven to 350°. In a small bowl, beat brown sugar, oil and egg until well blended. Beat in buttermilk. In a small bowl, combine flour, baking soda, ginger, salt and cinnamon; gradually beat into buttermilk mixture until blended. Stir in pears. Fill paper-lined muffin cups two-thirds full.

2. For topping, combine brown sugar and ginger. Stir in butter until crumbly. Sprinkle over batter.

3. Bake 18-22 minutes or until a toothpick inserted near the center comes out clean. Cool 5 minutes before removing from pans to wire racks. Serve warm.

Peppered Bacon and Cheese Scones

Mmm! That's what you'll hear as you serve a platter of these buttery, savory scones. The bacon and cheese combination is a welcomed change of pace from the usual sweet varieties served at brunch.
—**JANICE ELDER** CHARLOTTE, NC

PREP: 20 MIN. • **BAKE:** 20 MIN. • **MAKES:** 8 SCONES

- 3 cups all-purpose flour
- 1 tablespoon baking powder
- 2 teaspoons coarsely ground pepper
- ¼ teaspoon salt
- ¼ teaspoon cayenne pepper
- ½ cup cold butter, cubed
- 1½ cups shredded Gouda cheese
- 4 bacon strips, cooked and crumbled
- 1 shallot, finely chopped
- 1 large egg
- 1 cup buttermilk

1. Preheat oven to 400°. In a large bowl, whisk the first five ingredients. Cut in butter until mixture resembles coarse crumbs. Stir in cheese, bacon and shallot.

2. In a small bowl, whisk the egg and buttermilk until they are blended; reserve 1 tablespoon of the mixture for brushing scones. Stir the remaining mixture into the crumb mixture just until it is moistened.

3. Turn onto a lightly floured surface; knead dough gently 10 times. Pat the dough into an 8-in. circle. Cut into eight wedges. Place wedges on a greased baking sheet. Brush with reserved buttermilk mixture.

4. Bake 20-25 minutes or until golden brown. Serve warm.

Rhubread

We moved into a house that had a yard of fresh rhubarb. To use some of those ruby stalks, we made rhubarb bread with cinnamon and pecans.

—ERIKA ELLIOTT PANOLA, IL

PREP: 15 MIN. • **BAKE:** 50 MIN. + COOLING
MAKES: 2 LOAVES (12 SLICES EACH)

- 3 cups coarsely chopped fresh rhubarb (about 12 ounces)
- 2 tablespoons plus 1¾ cups sugar, divided
- 1 cup canola oil
- 2 large eggs
- 1 tablespoon vanilla extract
- 3 cups all-purpose flour
- 1 teaspoon salt
- 1 teaspoon baking soda
- 1 teaspoon ground cinnamon
- ¼ teaspoon baking powder
- ½ cup chopped pecans, optional

1. Preheat oven to 350°. Grease and flour two 8x4-in. loaf pans.
2. Toss rhubarb with 2 tablespoons sugar; let stand while preparing batter.
3. In a large bowl, beat the oil, eggs, vanilla and remaining sugar until well blended. In another bowl, whisk flour, salt, baking soda, cinnamon and baking powder; gradually beat into oil mixture (batter will be thick). Stir in the rhubarb mixture and, if desired, pecans.
4. Transfer to prepared pans. Bake 50-60 minutes or until a toothpick inserted in center comes out clean. Cool in pans 10 minutes before removing to a wire rack to cool.

Contest Winner

Onion-Beef Muffin Cups

A tube of refrigerated biscuits makes these bites so quick to prep. They're one of my tried-and-true recipes that bring in raves. In fact, I usually double the recipe just to be sure I have leftovers.

—BARBARA CARLUCCI ORANGE PARK, FL

PREP: 25 MIN. • **BAKE:** 15 MIN.
MAKES: 4 SERVINGS

- 3 medium onions, thinly sliced
- ¼ cup butter, cubed
- 1 beef top sirloin steak (1 inch thick and 6 ounces), cut into ⅛-inch slices
- 1 teaspoon all-purpose flour
- 1 teaspoon brown sugar
- ¼ teaspoon salt
- ½ cup beef broth
- 1 tube (16.3 ounces) large refrigerated flaky biscuits
- ¾ cup shredded part-skim mozzarella cheese
- ⅓ cup grated Parmesan cheese, divided

1. In a large skillet, cook onions in butter over medium heat for 10-12 minutes or until very tender. Remove and keep warm. In the same skillet, cook steak for 2-3 minutes or until no longer pink.
2. Return onions to pan. Stir in flour, brown sugar and salt until blended; gradually add broth. Bring the mixture to a boil; cook and stir for 4-6 minutes or until thickened.
3. Separate the biscuits; split each horizontally into three portions. Press onto the bottom and up the sides of eight ungreased muffin cups, overlapping the sides and tops. Fill each with about 2 tablespoons beef mixture.
4. Combine mozzarella cheese and ¼ cup Parmesan cheese; sprinkle over filling. Fold the dough over completely to enclose filling. Sprinkle with remaining Parmesan cheese.
5. Bake at 375° for 12-15 minutes or until golden brown. Let stand for 2 minutes before removing from pan. Serve warm.

GRATE IT YOURSELF

If you decide to buy a chunk of Parmesan cheese from the store and grate your own, be sure to use the finest section on your grating tool.

Almond Tea Bread

My aunt brought her tea bread recipe with her from Scotland, and a fresh-baked loaf has become a family tradition during the holidays. Each slice is loaded with red cherries.

—**KATHLEEN SHOWERS** BRIGGSDALE, CO

PREP: 15 MIN.
BAKE: 1¼ HOURS + COOLING
MAKES: 2 LOAVES (16 SLICES EACH)

- 1 can (8 ounces) almond paste
- ¼ cup butter, softened
- 1 cup sugar
- 3 large eggs
- 1½ cups fresh pitted cherries or blueberries
- 3 cups all-purpose flour, divided
- 4 teaspoons baking powder
- ½ teaspoon salt
- ¾ cup milk

1. In a large bowl, combine almond paste and butter; beat them until well blended. Gradually add sugar, beating until light and fluffy. Add eggs, one at a time, beating well after each addition. In a small bowl, gently toss cherries and 1 tablespoon flour. Set aside.

2. Combine the baking powder, salt and remaining flour; add to creamed mixture alternately with milk, beating well after each addition.

3. Spoon a sixth of the batter into each of two greased and floured 8x4-in. loaf pans; sprinkle layers with half of the fruit. Cover with another layer of the batter and sprinkle with remaining fruit. Top with the remaining batter; smooth with spatula.

4. Bake at 350° for 1¼ hours or until a toothpick inserted near the center comes out clean. Cool for 10 minutes before removing from pans to wire racks to cool.

Homemade Corn Muffins with Honey Butter

I turn classic corn bread muffins into something special by serving them with a honey butter. They're gone in a flash!

—**SUZANNE MCKINLEY** LYONS, GA

PREP: 20 MIN. • **BAKE:** 20 MIN.
MAKES: 16 MUFFINS
(⅓ CUP HONEY BUTTER)

- ¼ cup butter, softened
- ¼ cup reduced-fat cream cheese
- ½ cup sugar
- 2 large eggs
- 1½ cups fat-free milk
- 1½ cups all-purpose flour
- 1½ cups yellow cornmeal
- 4 teaspoons baking powder
- ¾ teaspoon salt

HONEY BUTTER

- ¼ cup butter, softened
- 2 tablespoons honey

1. In a large bowl, cream the butter, cream cheese and sugar until light and fluffy. Add eggs, one at a time, beating well after each addition. Stir in milk. Combine the flour, cornmeal, baking powder and salt; add to the creamed mixture just until moistened.

2. Coat the muffin cups with cooking spray; fill them three-fourths full with batter. Bake at 400° for 18-22 minutes or until a toothpick inserted near the center comes out clean. Cool for 5 minutes before removing them from the pans to wire racks. Beat the butter and honey until blended; serve with warm muffins.

Contest Winner

yum!

GIMME FIVE!

When you're short on ingredients, count on these recipes to save the day!
You need only five ingredients—not including water or salt—to pull these off.

Hurry-Up Biscuits

When I was young, my mom would make these biscuits with fresh cream she got from a local farmer. I don't go to those lengths anymore, but this family recipe is still a real treat.

—BEVERLY SPRAGUE BALTIMORE, MD

START TO FINISH: 30 MIN.
MAKES: 1 DOZEN

- 3 cups all-purpose flour
- 4 teaspoons baking powder
- 4 teaspoons sugar
- 1 teaspoon salt
- 2 cups heavy whipping cream

1. Preheat oven to 375°. In a large bowl, whisk flour, baking powder, sugar and salt. Add cream; stir just until moistened.
2. Drop batter by ¼ cupfuls 1 in. apart onto greased baking sheets. Bake 17-20 minutes or until bottoms are golden brown. Serve warm.

S'mores Crescent Rolls

Here's how to score indoor s'mores: Grab crescent dough and Nutella. Invite the kids to help with this rolled-up version of the campfire classic.

—CATHY TROCHELMAN BROOKFIELD, WI

START TO FINISH: 25 MIN.
MAKES: 8 SERVINGS

- 1 tube (8 ounces) refrigerated crescent rolls
- ¼ cup Nutella, divided
- 2 whole graham crackers, broken up
- 2 tablespoons milk chocolate chips
- ⅔ cup miniature marshmallows

1. Preheat oven to 375°. Unroll the crescent dough; separate into eight triangles. Place 1 teaspoon Nutella at the wide end of each triangle; sprinkle with graham crackers, chocolate chips and marshmallows. Roll up and place on ungreased baking sheets, point side down; curve to form crescents. Bake 9-11 minutes or until golden brown.
2. In a microwave, warm remaining Nutella until it reaches a drizzling consistency; spoon over rolls. Serve rolls warm.

Rustic Cranberry & Orange Bread

Studded with cranberries, slices of this pretty bread make the perfect holiday brunch treat.

—**MEGUMI GARCIA** MILWAUKEE, WI

PREP: 25 MIN. + RISING
BAKE: 50 MIN. + COOLING
MAKES: 1 LOAF (16 SLICES)

- 1½ teaspoons active dry yeast
- 1¾ cups water (70° to 75°)
- 3½ cups plus 1 tablespoon all-purpose flour, divided
- 2 teaspoons salt
- 1 tablespoon cornmeal or additional flour
- 1 cup dried cranberries
- 4 teaspoons grated orange peel

1. In a small bowl, dissolve yeast in water. In a large bowl, mix 3½ cups flour and salt. Using a rubber spatula, stir in yeast mixture to form a soft, sticky dough. Do not knead. Cover with plastic; let dough rise at room temperature 1 hour.

2. Punch down dough. Turn onto a lightly floured surface. Pat into a 9-in. square. Fold dough into thirds, forming a 9x3-in. rectangle. Fold rectangle into thirds, forming a 3-in. square. Turn dough over; place in a greased bowl. Cover with plastic; let rise at room temperature until almost doubled, about 1 hour.

3. Punch down dough and repeat folding process. Return dough to bowl; refrigerate, covered, overnight.

4. Dust bottom of a disposable foil roasting pan with cornmeal. Turn dough onto a floured surface; knead in cranberries and orange peel. Shape into a 6-in. round loaf. Place in prepared pan; dust top with remaining 1 tablespoon flour. Cover pan with plastic; let rise at room temperature until dough expands to a 7½-in. loaf, about 1¼ hours.

5. Preheat oven to 500°. Using a sharp knife, make a slash (¼ inch deep) across top of loaf. Cover pan tightly with foil. Bake on lowest oven rack 25 minutes.

6. Reduce oven setting to 450°. Remove foil; bake 25-30 minutes longer or until deep golden brown. Remove loaf to a wire rack to cool.

French Loaves

My children love to help me make this delicious bread recipe. It's quite easy, and they enjoy the fact that they can be eating fresh bread in less than two hours!

—**DENISE BOUTIN** GRAND ISLE, VT

PREP: 30 MIN. + RISING • **BAKE:** 15 MIN.
MAKES: 2 LOAVES (12 SLICES EACH)

- 2 tablespoons active dry yeast
- 2 cups warm water (110° to 115°)
- 2 teaspoons salt
- 1 teaspoon sugar
- 4½ to 5 cups bread flour
- 1 teaspoon cornmeal

1. In a large bowl, dissolve yeast in warm water. Add salt, sugar and 2 cups flour. Beat until smooth. Stir in enough remaining flour to form a soft dough.

2. Turn onto a floured surface; knead dough until smooth and elastic, about 6-8 minutes. Place in a greased bowl, turning once to grease the top. Cover and let rise in a warm place until doubled, about 1 hour.

3. Punch dough down. Turn onto a lightly floured surface; divide in half. Shape into 12-in.-long loaves.

4. Place seam side down on a greased baking sheet. Cover and let rise until doubled, about 30 minutes.

5. Preheat oven to 450°. Sprinkle the dough with cornmeal. With a sharp knife, make four shallow slashes across the top of each loaf. Bake the loaves for 15-20 minutes or until golden brown. Cool on a wire rack.

Sweet & Moist Corn Bread

We prefer good ol' Southern corn bread with our beans, but sometimes we want it sweeter. Here's a tasty version to hold up the butter.

—STACEY FEATHER JAY, OK

PREP: 10 MIN. • **BAKE:** 25 MIN.
MAKES: 15 SERVINGS

- 2½ cups all-purpose flour
- 1½ cups cornmeal
- 1 cup sugar
- 4 teaspoons baking powder
- 1½ teaspoons salt
- ¾ cup shortening
- 2 large eggs
- 2½ cups whole milk

1. Preheat the oven to 400°. In a large bowl, combine the first five ingredients. Cut in shortening until the mixture resembles coarse crumbs. In another bowl, whisk the eggs and milk; stir into the crumb mixture just until moistened.

2. Pour into a greased 13x9-in. baking pan. Bake 25-30 minutes or until a toothpick inserted in center comes out clean. Serve warm.

Braided Multigrain Loaf

Use oats, rye flour, rice and sunflower seeds for a hearty side. It's so robust, you could make a meal out of it. Just add a little butter!

—JANE THOMAS BURNSVILLE, MN

PREP: 40 MIN. + RISING
BAKE: 30 MIN. + COOLING
MAKES: 1 LOAF (24 SLICES)

- 2 cups whole wheat flour
- 1 cup quick-cooking oats
- ½ cup rye flour
- 2 packages (¼ ounce each) active dry yeast
- 2 teaspoons salt
- 3 cups all-purpose flour
- 2 cups milk
- ½ cup honey
- ⅓ cup water
- 2 tablespoons butter
- 1 cup cooked long-grain rice, cooled

TOPPING

- 1 large egg
- 1 tablespoon water
- ⅓ cup sunflower kernels

1. In a large bowl, mix whole wheat flour, oats, rye flour, yeast, salt and 1 cup all-purpose flour. In a small saucepan, heat milk, honey, water and butter to 120°-130°. Add to the dry ingredients; beat on medium speed 2 minutes. Add 1 cup all-purpose flour; beat 2 minutes longer. Stir in rice and enough remaining flour to form a stiff dough.

2. Turn dough onto a floured surface; knead until it is smooth and elastic, about 6-8 minutes. Place in a greased bowl, turning once to grease the top. Cover the dough with plastic wrap and let rise in a warm place until it is doubled, about 1 hour.

3. Punch down dough. Turn onto a lightly floured surface; divide into thirds. Cover and let rest 5 minutes. Roll each portion into an 18-in. rope. Place ropes on a greased baking sheet and braid. Shape into a ring. Pinch ends to seal; tuck under.

4. Cover with a kitchen towel; let rise in a warm place until doubled, about 30 minutes. Preheat oven to 375°.

5. For topping, in a small bowl, whisk the egg and water; brush over dough. Sprinkle with sunflower kernels. Bake 30-40 minutes or until golden brown. Remove to a wire rack to cool.

Classic Long Johns

I found the recipe for these wonderful treats many years ago. I remember Mom making something similar to them. You can frost them with maple or chocolate glaze, then top with chopped nuts, jimmies, toasted coconut or sprinkles.

—ANN SORGENT FOND DU LAC, WI

PREP: 30 MIN. + RISING
COOK: 5 MIN./BATCH + COOLING
MAKES: 2 DOZEN

- 2 packages (¼ ounce each) active dry yeast
- ½ cup warm water (110° to 115°)
- ½ cup half-and-half cream
- ¼ cup sugar
- ¼ cup shortening
- 1 large egg
- 1 teaspoon salt
- ½ teaspoon ground nutmeg
- 3 to 3½ cups all-purpose flour
  Oil for deep-fat frying

MAPLE FROSTING
- ¼ cup packed brown sugar
- 2 tablespoons butter
- 1 tablespoon half-and-half cream
- ⅛ teaspoon maple flavoring
- 1 cup confectioners' sugar

CHOCOLATE FROSTING
- 2 ounces semisweet chocolate, chopped
- 2 tablespoons butter
- 1 cup confectioners' sugar
- 2 tablespoons boiling water
- 1 teaspoon vanilla extract

1. In a large bowl, dissolve yeast in warm water. Add the cream, sugar, shortening, egg, salt, nutmeg and 3 cups flour. Beat until smooth. Stir in enough remaining flour to form a soft dough (dough will be sticky).

2. Turn onto a floured surface; knead dough until smooth and elastic, about 6-8 minutes. Place in a greased bowl, turning once to grease the top. Cover and let rise in a warm place until doubled, about 1 hour.

3. Punch dough down; divide in half. Turn onto a lightly floured surface; roll each half into a 12x6-in. rectangle. Cut into 3x2-in. rectangles. Place on greased baking sheets. Cover and let rise in a warm place until doubled, about 30 minutes.

4. In an electric skillet or deep fryer, heat oil to 375°. Fry long johns, a few at a time, until golden brown on both sides. Drain on paper towels.

5. For maple frosting, combine brown sugar and butter in a small saucepan. Bring to a boil; cook and stir for about 2 minutes or until sugar is dissolved. Remove from heat; stir in cream and maple flavoring. Add confectioners' sugar; beat for 1 minute or until smooth. Frost cooled long johns.

6. For chocolate frosting, melt the chocolate and butter in a microwave; stir until smooth. Stir in remaining ingredients. Spread over cooled long johns; let stand until set.

Onion Crescents

I make these crescents for my family on Easter and Christmas. We like the sweetness of the sugar with the onions, and how our home gets filled with the aroma of fresh-baked bread.

—MARY MAXEINER LAKEWOOD, CO

PREP: 30 MIN. + RISING • **BAKE:** 10 MIN.
MAKES: 2 DOZEN

- 1 package (¼ ounce) active dry yeast
- 1 cup warm milk (110° to 115°)
- ½ cup butter, softened
- ½ cup sugar
- 2 large eggs
- ½ cup dried minced onion
- ½ teaspoon salt
- 3½ to 4½ cups all-purpose flour
- 2 tablespoons butter, melted

1. In a small bowl, dissolve yeast in warm milk. In a large bowl, cream butter and sugar. Beat in eggs. Add onion, salt, yeast mixture and 2 cups flour; beat until blended. Stir in enough remaining flour to form a soft dough.

2. Turn dough onto a floured surface; knead until smooth and elastic, about 6-8 minutes. Place in a greased bowl, turning once to grease the top. Cover the dough with plastic wrap and let rise in a warm place until doubled, about 1 hour.

3. Punch dough down. Turn onto a lightly floured surface; divide in half. Roll each portion into a 12-in. circle; cut each circle into 12 wedges. Roll up wedges from the wide ends. Place 2 in. apart on greased baking sheets, point side down; curve to form crescents.

4. Cover with a kitchen towel; let rise in a warm place until doubled, about 30 minutes. Preheat oven to 400°. Bake 8-12 minutes or until golden brown. Brush with melted butter; remove to wire racks.

Maple Nut Banana Bread

Banana bread rises to a whole new level when you add maple syrup, sour cream, pecans and a cinnamon-spiced streusel. It's a comforting, home-style treat for breakfast or any time of day.

—DAVID DAHLMAN CHATSWORTH, CA

PREP: 40 MIN. • **BAKE:** 55 MIN. + COOLING
MAKES: 1 LOAF (12 SLICES)

- ½ cup butter, softened
- ½ cup packed brown sugar
- 2 large eggs
- 1 cup mashed ripe bananas (about 2 medium)
- ½ cup sour cream
- ⅓ cup maple syrup
- 1 teaspoon vanilla extract
- 2 cups all-purpose flour
- 1 teaspoon baking powder
- 1 teaspoon baking soda
- 1 teaspoon salt
- 1 cup chopped pecans

STREUSEL

- 2 tablespoons all-purpose flour
- 2 tablespoons sugar
- 1 tablespoon packed brown sugar
- 1 tablespoon butter, softened
- ⅛ teaspoon ground cinnamon
- 2 tablespoons finely chopped pecans

1. Preheat oven to 350°. In a large bowl, cream butter and brown sugar until light and fluffy. Add eggs, one at a time, beating well after each addition. In a small bowl, mix the bananas, sour cream, maple syrup and vanilla. In another bowl, whisk flour, baking powder, baking soda and salt; add to creamed mixture alternately with banana mixture, beating well after each addition. Fold in pecans.

2. Transfer to a greased 9x5-in. loaf pan. For streusel, in a small bowl, mix flour, sugars, butter and cinnamon until blended. Stir in pecans; sprinkle over batter.

3. Bake 55-60 minutes or until a toothpick inserted in center comes out clean. Cool in pan 10 minutes before removing to a wire rack to cool.

FOR MINI LOAVES *Transfer batter to four greased 5¾x3x2-in. loaf pans; top with streusel. Bake in preheated 350° oven for 30-35 minutes or until a toothpick comes out clean.*

Jalapeno Buttermilk Corn Bread

If you're from the South, you have to have a good corn bread recipe. Here's a lightened-up version of my mom's traditional corn bread.

—**DEBI MITCHELL** FLOWER MOUND, TX

PREP: 15 MIN. • **BAKE:** 20 MIN. • **MAKES:** 8 SERVINGS

- 1 cup self-rising flour
- 1 cup yellow cornmeal
- 1 cup buttermilk
- ¼ cup egg substitute
- 3 tablespoon canola oil, divided
- 2 tablespoons honey
- 1 tablespoon reduced-fat mayonnaise
- ¼ cup fresh or frozen corn, thawed
- 3 tablespoons shredded reduced-fat cheddar cheese
- 3 tablespoons finely chopped sweet red pepper
- ½ to 1 jalapeno pepper, seeded and finely chopped

1. Preheat oven to 425°. In a large bowl, whisk flour and cornmeal. In another bowl, whisk the buttermilk, egg substitute, 2 tablespoons oil, honey and mayonnaise. Pour remaining oil into an 8-in. ovenproof skillet; place skillet in oven for 4 minutes.

2. Meanwhile, add buttermilk mixture to flour mixture; stir just until moistened. Fold in corn, cheese and peppers.

3. Carefully tilt and rotate skillet to coat bottom with oil; add batter. Bake 20-25 minutes or until a toothpick inserted in center comes out clean. Serve warm.

NOTES *As a substitute for 1 cup of self-rising flour, place 1½ teaspoons baking powder and ½ teaspoon salt in a measuring cup. Add all-purpose flour to measure 1 cup. Wear disposable gloves when cutting hot peppers; the oils can burn skin. Avoid touching your face.*

Favorite Banana Chip Muffins

These muffins are one of the first things my husband, U.S. Army Major John Duda Jr., gets hungry for when he's home from deployment. I make sure to have the overripe bananas ready.

—**KIMBERLY DUDA** SANFORD, NC

PREP: 20 MIN. • **BAKE:** 20 MIN. • **MAKES:** 1 DOZEN

- 1½ cups all-purpose flour
- ⅔ cup sugar
- 1 teaspoon baking soda
- ¼ teaspoon ground cinnamon
- ⅛ teaspoon salt
- 1 large egg
- 1⅓ cups mashed ripe bananas (about 3 medium)
- ⅓ cup butter, melted
- 1 teaspoon vanilla extract
- ½ cup semisweet chocolate chips

1. Preheat oven to 375°. In a large bowl, whisk flour, sugar, baking soda, cinnamon and salt. In another bowl, whisk egg, bananas, melted butter and vanilla until blended. Add to flour mixture; stir just until moistened. Fold in chocolate chips.

2. Fill greased or paper-lined muffin cups three-fourths full. Bake 17-20 minutes or until a toothpick inserted in center comes out clean. Cool 5 minutes before removing from pan to a wire rack. Serve warm.

Blueberry Cornmeal Muffins

When I bring treats to the staff at my school, I try to keep many of them healthy, which this moist muffin is. The cornmeal adds a fun texture.

—ELIZABETH BERGERON DENVER, CO

PREP: 20 MIN. • **BAKE:** 20 MIN.
MAKES: 1 DOZEN

- 1 cup yellow cornmeal
- ½ cup all-purpose flour
- ½ cup whole wheat flour
- ½ cup plus 1½ teaspoons sugar, divided
- 4 teaspoons baking powder
- ½ teaspoon salt
- 2 large eggs
- ¾ cup fat-free milk
- ¼ cup canola oil
- 1 teaspoon vanilla extract
- 2 cups fresh or frozen blueberries

1. In a small bowl, combine cornmeal, flours, ½ cup sugar, baking powder and salt. In another bowl, combine eggs, milk, oil and vanilla. Stir into dry ingredients just until moistened. Fold in blueberries.

2. Fill greased muffin cups three-fourths full; sprinkle with remaining sugar. Bake at 350° for 18-22 minutes or until a toothpick inserted in muffin comes out clean. Cool for 5 minutes before removing from pan to a wire rack. Serve warm.

NOTE *If using frozen blueberries, use without thawing to avoid discoloring the batter.*

Roasted Butternut Squash Bread

Butternut squash is so versatile, I use it to make a sweet and savory bread that's perfect for breakfast, snacking or even dessert.

—SARAH MEUSER NEW MILFORD, CT

PREP: 40 MIN. • **BAKE:** 55 MIN. + COOLING
MAKES: 1 LOAF (16 SLICES)

- 3½ cups cubed peeled butternut squash (1-inch pieces)
- 2 tablespoons olive oil
- ½ cup butter, softened
- ½ cup sugar
- ½ cup packed brown sugar
- 2 large eggs
- 1 teaspoon vanilla extract
- 1½ cups whole wheat pastry flour
- 1 teaspoon baking soda
- 1 teaspoon ground cinnamon
- ¾ teaspoon salt
- ½ cup fat-free plain Greek yogurt
- ¼ teaspoon fine sea salt

1. Preheat oven to 375°. Place squash in a greased 15x10x1-in. baking pan. Drizzle with oil; toss to coat. Roast 25-30 minutes or until tender. Reduce oven setting to 325°.

2. Transfer the squash to a bowl; mash coarsely. In a large bowl, beat the butter and sugars until blended. Add eggs, one at a time, beating well after each addition. Beat in mashed squash and vanilla. In another bowl, whisk flour, baking soda, cinnamon and salt; add to the butter mixture alternately with yogurt, beating well after each addition.

3. Transfer to a greased 9x5-in. loaf pan; sprinkle with the sea salt. Bake 55-65 minutes or until a toothpick inserted in center comes out clean. Cool in the pan 10 minutes before removing to a wire rack to cool.

Can't-Eat-Just-One Cinnamon Rolls

Once I dropped off a dozen of these incredible rolls for my brothers, and they emptied the pan in 10 minutes.

—REGINA FARMWALD

WEST FARMINGTON, OH

PREP: 1 HOUR + RISING • **BAKE:** 20 MIN.
MAKES: 2 DOZEN

- 1 package (¼ ounce) active dry yeast
- 1 tablespoon sugar
- ¼ cup warm water (110° to 115°)
- 1 cup 2% milk
- ⅓ cup instant vanilla pudding mix (half of a 3.4-ounce package)
- 1 large egg
- ¼ cup butter, melted
- 1 teaspoon salt
- 3 to 3½ cups all-purpose flour

FILLING
- ¾ cup sugar
- 1 tablespoon ground cinnamon
- ¼ cup butter, melted

FROSTING
- ½ cup butter, softened
- 2 teaspoons vanilla extract
- 1 teaspoon water
- 1½ to 1¾ cups confectioners' sugar

1. In a small bowl, dissolve yeast and 1 tablespoon sugar in warm water. In a large bowl, beat milk and pudding mix on low speed 1 minute. Let stand 1 minute or until soft-set. Add egg, melted butter, salt, yeast mixture and 2 cups flour; beat on medium until smooth. Stir in enough remaining flour to form a soft dough (dough will be sticky).

2. Turn the dough onto a floured surface; knead until smooth and elastic, about 6-8 minutes. Place in a greased bowl, turning once to grease the top. Cover with plastic wrap and let rise in a warm place until doubled, about 1 hour.

3. For filling, in a small bowl, mix sugar and cinnamon. Punch down dough; divide in half. Turn one portion of dough onto a lightly floured surface; roll into an 18x10-in. rectangle. Brush with half of melted butter to within ¼ in. of the edges; sprinkle with half of the sugar mixture. Roll up jelly-roll style, starting with a long side; pinch the seam to seal. Cut into 12 slices. Repeat with the remaining dough and filling ingredients.

4. Place all slices in a greased 13x9-in. baking pan, cut side down. Cover with a kitchen towel; let rise in a warm place until almost doubled, about 45 minutes. Preheat oven to 350°.

5. Bake 20-25 minutes or until golden brown. Cool in pan on a wire rack.

6. For frosting, in a small bowl, beat butter until creamy. Beat in vanilla, water and enough confectioners' sugar to reach desired consistency. Spread over warm rolls. Serve warm.

Flaky Whole Wheat Biscuits

Whole wheat flour gives these biscuits a nutty flavor. Ever since I started making these, white flour biscuits just don't taste as good! Pair them with soup or slather them with whipped cream and sweetened berries for a dessert treat.

—TRISHA KRUSE EAGLE, ID

START TO FINISH: 25 MIN.
MAKES: 10 BISCUITS

- 1 cup all-purpose flour
- 1 cup whole wheat flour
- 3 teaspoons baking powder
- 1 tablespoon brown sugar
- 1 teaspoon baking soda
- ½ teaspoon salt
- ¼ cup cold butter
- 1 cup 2% milk

1. In a large bowl, combine the first six ingredients. Cut in butter until mixture resembles coarse crumbs. Stir in milk just until moistened. Turn onto a lightly floured surface; knead 8-10 times.

2. Pat or roll out to ½-in. thickness; cut with a floured 2½-in. biscuit cutter. Place biscuits 2 in. apart on an ungreased baking sheet. Bake at 425° for 8-10 minutes or until biscuits are golden brown.

Contest Winner

MAIN DISHES

There's no denying it—a stunning entree can turn an ordinary weeknight dinner into a special event. Home cooks just like you shared these main courses, which means they're already well-loved!

Parmesan Chicken with Mushroom Wild Rice

We call this dish "OMG Chicken." Frozen veggies and rice make the meal a cinch.

—**WENDY GORTON** OAK HARBOR, OH

PREP: 15 MIN. • **BAKE:** 45 MIN.
MAKES: 6 SERVINGS

- ½ **pound sliced fresh mushrooms**
- 1 **tablespoon canola oil**
- ½ **cup grated Parmesan cheese**
- ½ **cup mayonnaise**
- ½ **teaspoon Italian seasoning**
- 2 **packages (10 ounces each) frozen brown and wild rice with broccoli and carrots**
- ¼ **teaspoon salt**
- ⅛ **teaspoon pepper**
- 6 **boneless skinless chicken thighs**

1. Saute the mushrooms in oil in a large skillet until tender. Meanwhile, combine the cheese, mayonnaise and Italian seasoning in small bowl; set aside.
2. Place the frozen rice mixture in a greased 13x9-in. baking dish; sprinkle with salt and pepper. Top with the mushrooms and chicken. Spread cheese mixture over chicken.
3. Bake dish, uncovered, at 325° for 45-50 minutes or until a thermometer reads 170°.

Contest Winner

Individual Pork & Cranberry Potpies

My neighbor gave me this recipe some years ago, and I love how these pies are different from the usual chicken potpie. Being able to freeze these allows my family to enjoy them any time of year. They are especially good for an easy dinner during the cold winter months.

—**MARY SHENK** DEKALB, IL

PREP: 45 MIN. • **BAKE:** 15 MIN.
MAKES: 8 SERVINGS

- 2 **cups fresh or frozen cranberries, thawed**
- 4 **celery ribs, sliced**
- 1 **medium onion, chopped**
- 2½ **cups apple cider or juice**
- 3 **tablespoons brown sugar**
- 4 **garlic cloves, minced**
- 4 **teaspoons grated orange peel**
- 1 **tablespoon beef or chicken bouillon granules**
- 1 **teaspoon dried rosemary, crushed, or dried thyme**
- 6 **tablespoons all-purpose flour**
- ¾ **cup water**
- 5 **cups chopped cooked pork**
- 1 **package (14.1 ounces) refrigerated pie pastry**

1. Preheat oven to 450°. In a large saucepan, combine the first nine ingredients; bring to a boil. Reduce heat; simmer, uncovered, until berries pop, about 10 minutes.
2. In a small bowl, mix flour and water until smooth; stir into the cranberry mixture. Return to a boil, stirring constantly; cook and stir 1-2 minutes or until thickened. Stir in pork; remove from heat.
3. On a work surface, unroll pastry sheets. Roll each to a 12-in. circle. Using a 5-in. disposable foil potpie pan as a guide (top side down), cut out eight 5½-in. pastry circles, rerolling scraps as needed.
4. Divide pork mixture among eight 5-in. disposable foil pans. Place pastry circles over tops; flute edges. Cut slits in pastry.
5. Place potpies on baking sheets. Bake 15-20 minutes or until crust is golden brown and filling is bubbly.
FREEZE OPTION *Cover and freeze unbaked potpies. To use, bake frozen pies on baking sheets in a preheated 400° oven 40-50 minutes or until golden brown and a thermometer inserted in the center reads 165°.*

Turkey-Thyme Stuffed Peppers

My 3-year-old, Chloe, is a big fan of these healthy peppers, which have a great thyme flavor. She likes to help mix the ingredients and make meals with me.

—**JENNIFER KENT** PHILADELPHIA, PA

PREP: 30 MIN. • **COOK:** 10 MIN.
MAKES: 4 SERVINGS

- 1 **pound lean ground turkey**
- 1 **medium onion, finely chopped**
- 3 **garlic cloves, minced**
- ½ **teaspoon dried thyme**
- ¼ **teaspoon salt**
- ¼ **teaspoon dried rosemary, crushed**
- ⅛ **teaspoon pepper**
- 1 **can (14½ ounces) diced tomatoes, undrained**
- 1 **package (8.8 ounces) ready-to-serve brown rice**
- ½ **cup seasoned bread crumbs**
- 4 **medium sweet yellow or orange peppers**
- ¼ **cup shredded part-skim mozzarella cheese**

1. In a large skillet, cook turkey and onion over medium heat 8-10 minutes or until the turkey is no longer pink and onion is tender, breaking up turkey into crumbles. Add garlic and seasonings; cook 1 minute longer. Stir in tomatoes, rice and bread crumbs.
2. Cut sweet peppers lengthwise in half; remove seeds. Arrange pepper halves in a 13x9-in. microwave-safe dish; fill with turkey mixture. Sprinkle with cheese. Microwave, covered, on high for 7-9 minutes or until peppers are crisp-tender.
NOTE *This recipe was tested in a full-size 1,100-watt microwave. If your microwave does not accommodate a 13x9-in. dish, microwave stuffed peppers, half at a time, in an 8-in. square dish for 6-8 minutes or until peppers are crisp-tender.*

Chili-Beer Glazed Steaks

Bold ingredients give these grilled steaks a smoky-sweet taste you won't soon forget.

—**GEORDYTH SULLIVAN** CUTLER BAY, FL

PREP: 25 MIN. • **GRILL:** 10 MIN.
MAKES: 4 SERVINGS

- ⅔ **cup chili sauce**
- ⅔ **cup spicy steak sauce**
- ½ **cup chopped shallots**
- ½ **cup beer or nonalcoholic beer**
- 4 **boneless beef top loin steaks (8 ounces each)**
- ½ **teaspoon salt**
- ½ **teaspoon pepper**

1. In a small saucepan, combine chili sauce, steak sauce, shallots and beer. Bring to a boil. Reduce heat; simmer, uncovered, for 12-15 minutes or until slightly thickened. Set aside ½ cup for serving and keep warm. Sprinkle steaks with salt and pepper.
2. Moisten a paper towel with cooking oil; using long-handled tongs, lightly coat the grill rack. Grill the steaks, covered, over medium heat or broil 4 in. from the heat for 4-6 minutes on each side or until the meat reaches desired doneness (for medium-rare, a thermometer should read 145°; medium, 160°; well-done, 170°), basting occasionally with sauce mixture. Serve with reserved sauce.
NOTE *Top loin steak may be labeled as strip steak, Kansas City steak, NY strip steak, ambassador steak or boneless club steak in your region.*

Contest Winner

Wintertime Braised Beef Stew

This wonderful beef stew makes an easy Sunday meal. It's even better a day or two later, so we make a double batch for leftovers.
—**MICHAELA ROSENTHAL** WOODLAND HILLS, CA

PREP: 40 MIN. • **BAKE:** 2 HOURS • **MAKES:** 8 SERVINGS (2 QUARTS)

- 2 pounds boneless beef sirloin steak or chuck roast, cut into 1-inch pieces
- 2 tablespoons all-purpose flour
- 2 teaspoons Montreal steak seasoning
- 2 tablespoons olive oil, divided
- 1 large onion, chopped
- 2 celery ribs, chopped
- 2 medium parsnips, peeled and cut into 1½-inch pieces
- 2 medium carrots, peeled and cut into 1½-inch pieces
- 2 garlic cloves, minced
- 1 can (14½ ounces) diced tomatoes, undrained
- 1 cup dry red wine or reduced-sodium beef broth
- 2 tablespoons red currant jelly
- 2 bay leaves
- 2 fresh oregano sprigs
- 1 can (15 ounces) white kidney or cannellini beans, rinsed and drained
  Minced fresh parsley, optional

1. Preheat oven to 350°. Toss beef with flour and steak seasoning.

2. In an ovenproof Dutch oven, heat 1 tablespoon oil over medium heat. Brown the beef in batches; remove with a slotted spoon.

3. In same pan, heat remaining oil over medium heat. Add onion, celery, parsnips and carrots; cook and stir until onion is tender. Add garlic; cook 1 minute longer. Stir in tomatoes, wine, jelly, bay leaves, oregano and beef; bring to a boil.

4. Bake, covered, 1½ hours. Stir in beans; bake, covered, 30-40 minutes longer or until beef and vegetables are tender. Remove bay leaves and oregano sprigs. If desired, sprinkle with parsley.
FREEZE OPTION *Freeze cooled stew in freezer containers. To use, partially thaw in refrigerator overnight. Heat through in a saucepan, stirring occasionally and adding a little broth or water if necessary.*

Chicken & Egg Noodle Casserole

After a fire at my friend Michelle's home, my heart broke for her and her family. Bringing over this casserole was the one thing I could think of to help her out in a tiny way and let her know I was thinking of them.
—**LIN KRANKEL** OXFORD, MI

PREP: 20 MIN. • **BAKE:** 30 MIN. • **MAKES:** 8 SERVINGS

- 6 cups uncooked egg noodles (about 12 ounces)
- 2 cans (10¾ ounces each) condensed cream of chicken soup, undiluted
- 1 cup (8 ounces) sour cream
- ¾ cup 2% milk
- ¼ teaspoon salt
- ¼ teaspoon pepper
- 3 cups cubed cooked chicken breasts
- 1 cup crushed Ritz crackers (about 20 crackers)
- ¼ cup butter, melted

1. Preheat oven to 350°. Cook noodles according to package directions for al dente; drain.

2. In a large bowl, whisk soup, sour cream, milk, salt and pepper until blended. Stir in chicken and noodles. Transfer to a greased 13x9-in. baking dish. In a small bowl, mix crushed crackers and butter; sprinkle over top. Bake for 30-35 minutes or until bubbly.

Buffalo Chicken Lasagna

This recipe was inspired by my daughter's favorite food—Buffalo wings! It tastes just like it came from a restaurant, and it's perfect for game day potlucks.

—MELISSA MILLWOOD LYMAN, SC

PREP: 1 HOUR 40 MIN. • **BAKE:** 40 MIN. + STANDING
MAKES: 12 SERVINGS

- 1 tablespoon canola oil
- 1½ pounds ground chicken
- 1 small onion, chopped
- 1 celery rib, finely chopped
- 1 large carrot, grated
- 2 garlic cloves, minced
- 1 can (14½ ounces) diced tomatoes, drained
- 1 bottle (12 ounces) Buffalo wing sauce
- ½ cup water
- 1½ teaspoons Italian seasoning
- ½ teaspoon salt
- ¼ teaspoon pepper
- 9 lasagna noodles
- 1 carton (15 ounces) ricotta cheese
- 1¾ cups (7 ounces) crumbled blue cheese, divided
- ½ cup minced Italian flat leaf parsley
- 1 large egg, lightly beaten
- 3 cups part-skim mozzarella cheese
- 2 cups white cheddar cheese

1. In a Dutch oven, heat oil over medium heat. Add the chicken, onion, celery and carrot; cook and stir until meat is no longer pink and vegetables are tender. Add garlic; cook 2 minutes longer. Stir in tomatoes, wing sauce, water, Italian seasoning, salt and pepper; bring to a boil. Reduce heat; cover and simmer 1 hour.

2. Meanwhile, cook noodles according to the package directions; drain. In a small bowl, mix the ricotta cheese, ¾ cup blue cheese, parsley and egg. Preheat oven to 350°.

3. Spread 1½ cups sauce into a greased 13x9-in. baking dish. Layer with three noodles, 1½ cups sauce, ⅔ cup ricotta mixture, 1 cup mozzarella cheese, ⅔ cup cheddar cheese and ⅓ cup blue cheese. Repeat layers twice.

4. Bake, covered, 20 minutes. Uncover; bake 20-25 minutes longer or until bubbly and the cheese is melted. Let stand 10 minutes before serving.

Cod with Bacon & Balsamic Tomatoes

Let's face it, everything really is better with bacon. I fry it up, add cod fillets to the pan, and finish with a big, tomato-y pop.

—MAUREEN MCCLANAHAN ST. LOUIS, MO

START TO FINISH: 30 MIN. • **MAKES:** 4 SERVINGS

- 4 center-cut bacon strips, chopped
- 4 cod fillets (5 ounces each)
- ½ teaspoon salt
- ¼ teaspoon pepper
- 2 cups grape tomatoes, halved
- 2 tablespoons balsamic vinegar

1. In a large skillet, cook bacon over medium heat until crisp, stirring occasionally. Remove with a slotted spoon; drain on paper towels.

2. Sprinkle fillets with salt and pepper. Add fillets to bacon drippings; cook over medium-high heat 4-6 minutes on each side or until fish just begins to flake easily with a fork. Remove and keep warm.

3. Add tomatoes to skillet; cook and stir 2-4 minutes or until tomatoes are softened. Stir in vinegar; reduce heat to medium-low. Cook 1-2 minutes longer or until sauce is thickened. Serve cod with tomato mixture and bacon.

Oven-Fried Chicken Drumsticks

This fabulous chicken uses Greek yogurt to create an amazing marinade that makes the chicken incredibly moist. No one will guess that it's been lightened up and not even deep-fried!

—KIMBERLY WALLACE DENNISON, OH

PREP: 20 MIN. + MARINATING
BAKE: 40 MIN. • **MAKES:** 4 SERVINGS

- 1 cup fat-free plain Greek yogurt
- 1 tablespoon Dijon mustard
- 2 garlic cloves, minced
- 8 chicken drumsticks (4 ounces each), skin removed
- ½ cup whole wheat flour
- 1½ teaspoons paprika
- 1 teaspoon baking powder
- 1 teaspoon salt
- 1 teaspoon pepper
  Olive oil-flavored cooking spray

1. In a large resealable plastic bag, combine yogurt, mustard and garlic. Add chicken; seal bag and turn to coat. Refrigerate 8 hours or overnight.
2. Preheat oven to 425°. In another plastic bag, mix flour, paprika, baking powder, salt and pepper. Remove chicken from marinade and add, one piece at a time, to flour mixture; close bag and shake to coat. Place on a wire rack over a baking sheet; spritz with cooking spray. Bake 40-45 minutes or until a thermometer reads 180°.

Ultimate Grilled Pork Chops

A little brining and a special dry rub go a long way to making the perfect pork chop.
—MATTHEW HASS FRANKLIN, WI

PREP: 20 MIN. + BRINING • **GRILL:** 10 MIN.
MAKES: 4 SERVINGS

- ¼ cup kosher salt
- ¼ cup sugar
- 2 cups water
- 2 cups ice water
- 4 bone-in pork center-cut rib chops (1 inch thick and 8 ounces each)
- 2 tablespoons canola oil

BASIC RUB
- 3 tablespoons paprika
- 1 teaspoon each garlic powder, onion powder, ground cumin and ground mustard
- 1 teaspoon coarsely ground pepper
- ½ teaspoon ground chipotle pepper

1. In a large saucepan, combine salt, sugar and 2 cups water; cook and stir over medium heat until salt and sugar are dissolved. Remove from heat. Add 2 cups of ice water to cool the brine to room temperature.

2. Place the pork chops in a large resealable plastic bag; add cooled brine. Seal bag, pressing out as much air as possible; turn to coat chops. Place in a 13x9-in. baking dish. Refrigerate 8-12 hours.
3. Remove chops from brine; rinse and pat dry. Discard brine. Brush both sides of chops with oil. In a small bowl, mix rub ingredients; rub over pork chops. Let stand at room temperature 30 minutes. Grill chops on an oiled rack, covered, over medium heat 4-6 minutes on each side or until a thermometer reads 145°. Let stand 5 minutes before serving.

FOR SMOKY PORK RUB *Prepare rub as directed, using smoked paprika in place of regular paprika.*
FOR SPICY PORK RUB *Add ½ teaspoon of cayenne pepper to the rub mixture.*
FOR SWEET PORK RUB *Add 3 tablespoons of brown sugar to the rub mixture.*

Turkey & Vegetable Pasta

This recipe freezes beautifully and is a wonderful way to use up leftover turkey and vegetables. It's also a great way to get the kids to eat their veggies!

—VERONICA MCCANN COLUMBUS, OH

PREP: 25 MIN. • **COOK:** 35 MIN.
MAKES: 6 SERVINGS

- 1¾ cups uncooked penne or gemelli pasta (about 6 ounces)
- 1 tablespoon olive oil
- 3 celery ribs, chopped
- 1 cup chopped sweet onion
- 1 cup chopped red onion
- 1 cup chopped fresh broccoli
- 1 cup chopped carrots
- 3 garlic cloves, minced
- 1 tablespoon minced fresh parsley
- 1 tablespoon minced fresh tarragon or 1 teaspoon dried tarragon
- 1 teaspoon poultry seasoning
- 1 teaspoon lemon-pepper seasoning
- ¼ teaspoon white pepper
- 1½ cups sliced baby portobello mushrooms
- 1 cup frozen peas
- 2 cups cubed cooked turkey
- 1½ cups vegetable broth
- 1 can (10¾ ounces) condensed cream of mushroom soup, undiluted
- ⅔ cup plain Greek yogurt
- 1 tablespoon Worcestershire sauce
- 2 tablespoons reduced-fat cream cheese

1. Cook pasta according to package directions; drain. Meanwhile, in a Dutch oven, heat oil over medium-high heat. Add the celery, onions, broccoli and carrots; cook and stir 10-12 minutes or until onions are tender. Add garlic, parsley, tarragon and seasonings; cook 1 minute longer.

2. Add mushrooms and peas; cook and stir 3-5 minutes or until mushrooms are tender. Stir in turkey, broth, soup, yogurt, Worcestershire sauce and cream cheese. Bring to a boil. Reduce heat; simmer, uncovered, for 10-15 minutes or until slightly thickened, stirring occasionally. Add pasta; toss to combine and heat through.

FREEZE OPTION *Freeze cooled pasta mixture in freezer containers. To use, partially thaw it in the refrigerator overnight. Heat through in a saucepan, stirring occasionally and adding a little broth or milk if necessary.*

Bacon Cheeseburger Tater Tot Bake

Chores are completed quickly when my kids know this yummy casserole is on the menu.

—DEANNA ZEWEN UNION GROVE, WI

PREP: 15 MIN. • **BAKE:** 35 MIN.
MAKES: 12 SERVINGS

- 2 pounds ground beef
- 1 large onion, chopped and divided
- 1 can (15 ounces) tomato sauce
- 1 package (8 ounces) process cheese (Velveeta)
- 1 tablespoon ground mustard
- 1 tablespoon Worcestershire sauce
- 2 cups shredded cheddar cheese
- 12 bacon strips, cooked and crumbled
- 1 package (32 ounces) frozen Tater Tots
- 1 cup grape tomatoes, chopped
- ⅓ cup sliced dill pickles

1. Preheat oven to 400°. In a large skillet over medium heat, cook beef and 1 cup onion, crumbling the meat, until the beef is no longer pink and onion is tender, 6-8 minutes. Drain. Stir in tomato sauce, process cheese, mustard and Worcestershire sauce until cheese is melted, 4-6 minutes.

2. Transfer to a greased 13x9-in. or 3½-qt. baking dish. Sprinkle with cheddar cheese and bacon. Top with Tater Tots. Bake, uncovered, 35-40 minutes or until bubbly. Top with tomato, pickles and remaining onion.

Quick & Easy Deep-Dish Pizza

I was trying to impress my boyfriend with my cooking, so I made this meaty pizza. I think it worked! Here we are 17 years later, and I still make it for our family at least once a month, if not more.

—STACEY WHITE FUQUAY-VARINA, NC

PREP: 30 MIN. • **BAKE:** 30 MIN. • **MAKES:** 8 SERVINGS

- 1 pound ground beef
- 1 medium green pepper, chopped
- 1 small onion, chopped
- 1 jar (14 ounces) pizza sauce
- 10 slices Canadian bacon (about 6 ounces), coarsely chopped
- 2 packages (6½ ounces each) pizza crust mix
- 2 cups shredded part-skim mozzarella cheese
- 4 ounces sliced pepperoni

1. Preheat oven to 425°. In a large skillet, cook beef, pepper and onion over medium heat 8-10 minutes or until beef is no longer pink, breaking up beef into crumbles; drain. Stir in pizza sauce and Canadian bacon; remove from heat.

2. Prepare dough for pizza crust according to package directions. Press dough to fit bottom and 1 in. up sides of a greased 13x9-in. baking pan.

3. Spoon meat sauce into crust. Sprinkle with cheese; top with pepperoni. Bake, covered, 25 minutes. Uncover; bake 5-10 minutes longer or until the crust and cheese are golden brown.

FREEZE OPTION *Cool meat sauce before assembling pizza. Securely cover and freeze unbaked pizza. To use, bake frozen pizza, covered with foil, in a preheated 425° oven 25 minutes. Uncover; bake 15-20 minutes longer or until golden brown and heated through.*

Winter Squash, Sausage & Feta Bake

During the fall, I can't resist butternut squash because of its bright color and autumnal flavor. I make this casserole for potlucks—it's a guaranteed hit.

—CRAIG SIMPSON SAVANNAH, GA

PREP: 30 MIN. • **BAKE:** 45 MIN. • **MAKES:** 20 SERVINGS (¾ CUP EACH)

- 1 pound bulk Italian sausage
- 2 large onions, chopped
- ½ teaspoon crushed red pepper flakes, divided
- ¼ cup olive oil
- 2 teaspoons minced fresh rosemary
- 1 teaspoon Worcestershire sauce
- 1½ teaspoons salt
- 1 teaspoon pepper
- 1 medium butternut squash (about 4 pounds), peeled and cut into 1-inch cubes
- 1 medium acorn squash, peeled and cut into 1-inch cubes
- 2 cups (8 ounces) crumbled feta cheese
- 2 small sweet red peppers, chopped

1. Preheat oven to 375°. In a large skillet, cook the sausage, onions and ¼ teaspoon pepper flakes over medium heat 8-10 minutes or until sausage is no longer pink and onions are tender, breaking up sausage into crumbles; drain.

2. In a large bowl, combine oil, rosemary, Worcestershire sauce, salt, pepper and remaining pepper flakes. Add butternut and acorn squash, cheese, red peppers and sausage mixture; toss to coat.

3. Transfer to an ungreased shallow roasting pan. Cover and bake 35 minutes. Uncover; bake 10-15 minutes longer or until squash is tender.

Contest Winner

Meatball Pie

I grew up on a farm, so I took part in 4-H Club cooking activities. I still love to prepare and serve classic, wholesome recipes such as this meat and veggie pie.

—SUSAN KEITH FORT PLAIN, NY

PREP: 50 MIN. • **BAKE:** 45 MIN. + STANDING • **MAKES:** 6 SERVINGS

- 1 **pound ground beef**
- ¾ **cup soft bread crumbs**
- ¼ **cup chopped onion**
- 2 **tablespoons minced fresh parsley**
- 1 **teaspoon salt**
- ½ **teaspoon dried marjoram**
- ⅛ **teaspoon pepper**
- ¼ **cup milk**
- 1 **large egg, lightly beaten**
- 1 **can (14½ ounces) stewed tomatoes**
- 1 **tablespoon cornstarch**
- 2 **teaspoons beef bouillon granules**
- 1 **cup frozen peas**
- 1 **cup sliced carrots, cooked**

CRUST

- 2⅔ **cups all-purpose flour**
- ½ **teaspoon salt**
- 1 **cup shortening**
- 7 **to 8 tablespoons ice water**
  Half-and-half cream

1. In a large bowl, combine the first nine ingredients (mixture will be soft). Divide into fourths; shape each portion into 12 small meatballs. Brown meatballs in batches in a large skillet; drain and set aside.

2. Drain tomatoes, reserving liquid. Combine liquid with cornstarch; pour into skillet. Add tomatoes and bouillon; bring to a boil over medium heat, stirring constantly. Stir in peas and carrots. Remove from heat and set aside.

3. Preheat oven to 400°. For crust, in a large bowl, combine flour and salt. Cut in shortening until mixture resembles coarse crumbs. Add water, 1 tablespoon at a time, tossing lightly with a fork. Transfer to a lightly floured surface. Knead gently to form a dough. (The mixture will be very crumbly at first, but will come together and form a dough as it's kneaded.) Divide dough in half.

4. Roll each half of dough between two pieces of lightly floured waxed paper to a ⅛-in.-thick circle. Remove top piece of waxed paper from one pastry circle; invert onto a 9-in. deep-dish pie plate. Remove remaining waxed paper. Trim pastry even with rim. Add meatballs; spoon tomato mixture over top.

5. Remove top piece of waxed paper from remaining pastry circle; invert onto pie. Remove remaining waxed paper. Trim, seal and flute edge. Cut slits in top; brush with cream.

MEATLESS MEALS

No meat? No problem! With dishes this filling, comforting and just plain delicious, you not only won't miss the meat, you'll be adding these to your regular dinner rotation.

Vegetable Jambalaya

Trust me, this entree won't leave you hungry since it uses convenient canned beans in place of the meat.
—**CRYSTAL JO BRUNS** ILIFF, CO

PREP: 10 MIN. • **COOK:** 30 MIN.
MAKES: 6 SERVINGS

- 1 **tablespoon canola oil**
- 1 **medium green pepper, chopped**
- 1 **medium onion, chopped**
- 1 **celery rib, chopped**
- 3 **garlic cloves, minced**
- 2 **cups water**
- 1 **can (14½ ounces) diced tomatoes, undrained**
- 1 **can (8 ounces) tomato sauce**
- ½ **teaspoon Italian seasoning**
- ¼ **teaspoon salt**
- ¼ **teaspoon crushed red pepper flakes**
- ⅛ **teaspoon fennel seed, crushed**
- 1 **cup uncooked long grain rice**
- 1 **can (16 ounces) butter beans, rinsed and drained**
- 1 **can (16 ounces) red beans, rinsed and drained**

1. In a Dutch oven, heat the oil over medium-high heat. Add green pepper, onion and celery; cook and stir until tender. Add garlic; cook 1 minute longer.
2. Add the water, tomatoes, tomato sauce and seasonings. Bring to a boil; stir in rice. Reduce heat; cover and simmer for 15-18 minutes or until liquid is absorbed and rice is tender. Stir in beans; heat through.

Five-Cheese Jumbo Shells

Using five cheeses in one dish doesn't usually translate to something that's considered light, but this meatless meal is proof that it can be done with great success (and great taste!). The shells freeze beautifully, so leftovers are a cinch to save for another quick dinner.
—**LISA RENSHAW** KANSAS CITY, MO

PREP: 45 MIN. • **BAKE:** 50 MIN. + STANDING
MAKES: 8 SERVINGS

- 24 **uncooked jumbo pasta shells**
- 1 **tablespoon olive oil**
- 1 **medium zucchini, shredded and squeezed dry**
- ½ **pound baby portobello mushrooms, chopped**
- 1 **medium onion, finely chopped**
- 2 **cups reduced-fat ricotta cheese**
- ½ **cup shredded part-skim mozzarella cheese**
- ½ **cup shredded provolone cheese**
- ½ **cup grated Romano cheese**
- 1 **large egg, lightly beaten**
- 1 **teaspoon Italian seasoning**
- ½ **teaspoon crushed red pepper flakes**
- 1 **jar (24 ounces) meatless spaghetti sauce**
- ¼ **cup grated Parmesan cheese**

1. Preheat oven to 350°. Cook shells according to package directions for al dente; drain and rinse in cold water.
2. In a large skillet, heat the oil over medium-high heat. Add vegetables; cook and stir until tender. Remove from heat. In a bowl, combine ricotta, mozzarella, provolone and Romano cheeses; stir in the egg, seasonings and vegetables.
3. Spread 1 cup sauce into a 13x9-in. baking dish coated with cooking spray. Fill the pasta shells with the cheese mixture; place in baking dish. Top with remaining sauce. Sprinkle with Parmesan cheese.
4. Bake, covered, 40 minutes. Bake, uncovered, 10 minutes longer or until cheese is melted. Let stand 10 minutes before serving.
FREEZE OPTION *Cool unbaked casserole; cover and freeze. To use, partially thaw in the refrigerator overnight. Remove from refrigerator 30 minutes before baking. Preheat oven to 350°. Cover the casserole with foil; bake 50 minutes. Uncover; bake 15-20 minutes longer or until heated through and a thermometer inserted in center reads 165°.*

Contest-Winning Pesto Veggie Pizza

When I was thinking about what my family likes to eat and what I like to cook, the answer was simple—pizza!

—**DANA DIRKS** SAN DIEGO, CA

PREP: 30 MIN. + STANDING • **BAKE:** 10 MIN.
MAKES: 6 SERVINGS

- 1 package (¼ ounce) active dry yeast
- 1 cup warm water (110° to 115°)
- ⅓ cup grated Parmesan cheese
- 2 tablespoons canola oil
- 1 tablespoon sugar
- 1 tablespoon dried basil
- ½ teaspoon salt
- ¾ cup all-purpose flour
- 1 to 1½ cups whole wheat flour
- 3½ cups fresh baby spinach
- ¼ cup prepared pesto
- 1¾ cups coarsely chopped fresh broccoli
- ¾ cup chopped green pepper
- 2 green onions, chopped
- 4 garlic cloves, minced
- 2 cups shredded part-skim mozzarella cheese

1. In a small bowl, dissolve yeast in warm water. Add Parmesan cheese, oil, sugar, basil, salt, all-purpose flour and ¾ cup whole wheat flour. Beat until smooth. Stir in enough of the remaining whole wheat flour to form a soft dough (dough will be sticky).

2. Turn onto a lightly floured surface; knead until smooth and elastic, about 6-8 minutes. Cover and let rest for 10 minutes.

3. Roll the dough into a 16x12-in. rectangle. Transfer to a baking sheet coated with cooking spray; build up edges slightly. Prick dough with a fork. Bake at 375° for 8-10 minutes or until lightly browned.

4. Meanwhile, in a large saucepan, bring ½ in. of water to a boil. Add spinach; cover and boil for 3-5 minutes or until wilted. Drain and place in a food processor. Add pesto; cover and process until blended.

5. Spread over the pizza crust. Top with broccoli, green pepper, green onions, garlic and mozzarella cheese. Bake 10-12 minutes or until the cheese is melted.

Lemon-Garlic Cream Fettuccine

I've been making this for my family for years. It's both simple and indulgent enough to make it a go-to recipe.

—**ANNE MILLER** GLENFIELD, NY

PREP: 25 MIN. • **COOK:** 15 MIN.
MAKES: 4 SERVINGS

- 3 teaspoons grated lemon peel
- 2 teaspoons minced fresh parsley
- 2 garlic cloves, minced
- 8 ounces uncooked fettuccine

SAUCE
- ¼ cup butter
- 1 small onion, chopped
- 2 garlic cloves, minced
- 1 teaspoon grated lemon peel
- ½ cup heavy whipping cream
- ¼ teaspoon salt
- ⅛ teaspoon pepper
- 4 ounces cream cheese, cubed
- 2 tablespoons lemon juice
- 2 plum tomatoes, chopped
- 2 teaspoons minced fresh parsley
  Grated Parmesan cheese, optional

1. In a small bowl, mix lemon peel, parsley and garlic. Cook fettuccine according to package directions; drain.

2. For sauce, in a large skillet, heat butter over medium-high heat. Add onion; cook and stir 2-3 minutes or until tender. Add garlic and lemon peel; cook 1 minute longer. Stir in cream, salt and pepper. Whisk in cream cheese until melted. Remove from heat; cool slightly. Stir in lemon juice.

3. Add pasta, tomatoes and parsley to the skillet; toss to combine. Serve immediately with lemon peel mixture and, if desired, Parmesan cheese.

Contest Winner

Grilled Sausages with Summer Vegetables

After 30 years of camping, we've come up with a collection of go-to recipes. These grilled sausages with veggies will shine at your next potluck or summer get-together.
—**NANCY DAUGHERTY** CORTLAND, OH

PREP: 35 MIN. • **GRILL:** 25 MIN. • **MAKES:** 12 SERVINGS

- ¾ **cup peach preserves**
- ½ **cup reduced-sodium soy sauce**
- 3 **tablespoons minced fresh gingerroot**
- 3 **tablespoons water**
- 3 **garlic cloves, minced**
  Dash hot pepper sauce, optional
- 4 **medium sweet red peppers**
- 1 **medium eggplant**
- 3 **small zucchini**
- 2 **small yellow summer squash**
- 12 **hot Italian pork or turkey sausage links (4 ounces each)**

1. Place the first five ingredients in a blender; if desired, add pepper sauce. Cover and process until blended.
2. Cut the peppers lengthwise in half; remove seeds. Cut eggplant lengthwise into ½-in.-thick slices. Cut zucchini and yellow squash lengthwise into quarters. Place all vegetables in a large bowl; drizzle with ½ cup of the sauce and toss to coat.
3. Place vegetables on a greased grill rack. Grill, covered, over medium heat 8-10 minutes or until tender and lightly charred, turning once. Cool slightly. Reduce the grill temperature to medium-low heat.
4. Cut vegetables into bite-size pieces. Toss with additional ¼ cup sauce; keep warm.
5. Grill the sausages, covered, over medium-low heat 15-20 minutes or until a thermometer reads 160° for pork sausages (165° for turkey sausages), turning occasionally. Remove sausages from grill; toss with remaining sauce. Serve with vegetables.

Fiesta Beef & Cheese Skillet Cobbler

I tweaked my beefy skillet cobbler until it achieved the wow factor. I must have gotten it right, as it's now a family tradition. Top it off with lettuce, avocado, cherry tomatoes and a dollop of sour cream.
—**GLORIA BRADLEY** NAPERVILLE, IL

PREP: 40 MIN. • **BAKE:** 15 MIN. + STANDING • **MAKES:** 8 SERVINGS

- 1 **pound ground beef**
- 1 **can (15 ounces) black beans, rinsed and drained**
- 1 **can (14½ ounces) diced tomatoes with mild green chilies**
- 1 **can (10 ounces) enchilada sauce**
- 1 **teaspoon ground cumin**
- 4 **tablespoons chopped fresh cilantro or parsley, divided**
- 1½ **cups biscuit/baking mix**
- 1½ **cups shredded Colby-Monterey Jack cheese, divided**
- 4 **bacon strips, cooked and crumbled**
- ⅔ **cup 2% milk**
- 1 **large egg, lightly beaten**
  Sour cream, optional

1. Preheat oven to 400°. In a 10-in. ovenproof skillet, cook beef over medium heat 5-7 minutes or until no longer pink, breaking into crumbles; drain. Stir in beans, tomatoes, enchilada sauce and cumin; bring to a boil. Reduce heat; simmer, uncovered, 20 minutes to allow flavors to blend, stirring occasionally. Stir in 2 tablespoons cilantro.
2. In a bowl, combine baking mix, ½ cup cheese, bacon and remaining cilantro. Add milk and beaten egg; stir just until a soft dough is formed. Spoon over beef mixture.
3. Bake, uncovered, 13-15 minutes or until golden brown. Sprinkle with remaining cheese; bake 2-3 minutes longer or until cheese is melted. Let stand 10 minutes before serving. If desired, serve with sour cream.

Contest Winner

Cheesy Chicken and Leek Phyllo Pie

In our house, chicken potpie is a year-round staple. For a springtime feel, we use leeks, mushrooms and a lighter phyllo dough crust. If you don't have Gruyere, try Parmesan.
—**ANDREA STEWART** TORONTO, ON

PREP: 35 MIN. • **BAKE:** 30 MIN. • **MAKES:** 6 SERVINGS

- 6 tablespoons olive oil, divided
- 2 medium leeks (white portion only), thinly sliced
- 1 cup sliced fresh mushrooms
- 1 tablespoon all-purpose flour
- 1 cup chicken stock
- 1 can (5 ounces) evaporated milk
- 3 cups cubed cooked chicken
- ¾ cup plus 2 tablespoons shredded Gruyere cheese, divided
- 1½ teaspoons minced fresh thyme or ½ teaspoon dried thyme
- ½ teaspoon salt
- ½ teaspoon pepper
- 10 sheets phyllo dough (14x9-inch size)

1. Preheat the oven to 350°. In a large skillet, heat the 2 tablespoons oil over medium-high heat. Add leeks and mushrooms; cook and stir 3-4 minutes or until vegetables are tender. Stir in flour until blended; gradually stir in stock and milk. Bring to a boil, stirring constantly; cook and stir 3-4 minutes or until thickened. Stir in the chicken, ¾ cup cheese, thyme, salt and pepper.

2. Brush a 9-in. pie plate with some of the remaining oil. Place one sheet of phyllo dough into prepared pie plate, allowing ends to extend over edges of dish; brush with oil. (Keep remaining phyllo covered with plastic wrap and a damp towel to prevent it from drying out.) Layer with seven additional phyllo sheets, brushing each layer with oil and rotating sheets to cover the pie plate. Transfer chicken mixture to crust.

3. Gently fold in ends of phyllo over filling, leaving an opening in the center. Crumble the remaining phyllo sheets over filling; sprinkle with remaining cheese. Brush edges with remaining oil. Bake 30-35 minutes or until golden brown.

4. Bake until the crust is golden brown, 45-50 minutes. Cover edges loosely with foil during the last 10 minutes if needed to prevent overbrowning. Let stand 10 minutes before cutting.

Rigatoni with Sausage & Peas

With a hearty tomato sauce and tangy goat cheese, this weeknight wonder is my version of comfort food. You just want to have bowl after bowl.
—**LIZZIE MUNRO** BROOKLYN, NY

START TO FINISH: 30 MIN. • **MAKES:** 6 SERVINGS

- 12 ounces uncooked rigatoni or large tube pasta
- 1 pound bulk Italian sausage
- 4 garlic cloves, minced
- ¼ cup tomato paste
- 1 can (28 ounces) crushed tomatoes
- ½ teaspoon dried basil
- ¼ to ½ teaspoon crushed red pepper flakes
- 1½ cups frozen peas
- ½ cup heavy whipping cream
- ½ cup crumbled goat or feta cheese
  Thinly sliced fresh basil, optional

1. Cook the rigatoni according to package directions.

2. Meanwhile, in a Dutch oven, cook sausage over medium heat 6-8 minutes or until no longer pink, breaking into crumbles. Add garlic; cook 1 minute longer. Drain. Add tomato paste; cook and stir 2-3 minutes or until meat is coated. Stir in tomatoes, dried basil and pepper flakes; bring to a boil. Reduce heat; simmer, uncovered, 10-15 minutes or until thickened, stirring occasionally.

3. Drain rigatoni; stir into the sausage mixture. Add peas and cream; heat through. Top with cheese and, if desired, fresh basil.

Chili-Stuffed Poblano Peppers

I tasted chiles relleno and wanted to make them at home. My husband and I teamed up to create this new recipe.

—LORRIE GRABCZYNSKI
COMMERCE TOWNSHIP, MI

START TO FINISH: 30 MIN.
MAKES: 4 SERVINGS

- 1 pound lean ground turkey
- 1 can (15 ounces) chili without beans
- ¼ teaspoon salt
- 1½ cups shredded Mexican cheese blend, divided
- 1 medium tomato, finely chopped
- 4 green onions, chopped
- 4 large poblano peppers
- 1 tablespoon olive oil

1. Preheat broiler. In a skillet, cook turkey over medium heat 5-7 minutes or until no longer pink, breaking into crumbles; drain. Add chili and salt; heat through. Stir in ½ cup cheese, tomato and green onions.
2. Meanwhile, cut peppers lengthwise in half; remove the seeds. Place them on a foil-lined 15x10x1-in. baking pan, cut side down; brush with oil. Broil 4 in. from the heat until skins blister, about 5 minutes.
3. With tongs, turn peppers. Fill with the turkey mixture; sprinkle with the remaining cheese. Broil 1-2 minutes longer or until cheese is melted.
NOTE *Wear disposable gloves when cutting hot peppers; the oils can burn skin. Avoid touching your face.*

Contest Winner

Five-Cheese Macaroni with Prosciutto Bits

Macaroni is baked with smoked Gouda, Swiss, white cheddar, goat cheese and Parmesan and topped with crispy prosciutto—so worth it!

—MYA ZERONIS PITTSBURGH, PA

PREP: 25 MIN. • **BAKE:** 20 MIN.
MAKES: 12 SERVINGS (1¼ CUPS EACH)

- 1 package (16 ounces) elbow macaroni
- ⅓ cup unsalted butter, cubed
- 1 medium onion, halved and thinly sliced
- 1 garlic clove, minced
- ⅓ cup all-purpose flour
- ½ cup white wine or reduced-sodium chicken broth
- 4 cups heavy whipping cream
- 1 teaspoon white pepper
- ¼ teaspoon salt
- 5 ounces fresh goat cheese, crumbled
- 5 ounces white cheddar cheese, shredded
- 5 ounces Swiss cheese, shredded
- 3 ounces smoked Gouda cheese, shredded
- ¾ cup grated Parmesan cheese
- ½ cup panko (Japanese) bread crumbs
- 4 ounces thinly sliced prosciutto, chopped

1. Cook macaroni according to package directions until al dente.
2. Meanwhile, in a Dutch oven, heat butter over medium-high heat. Add onion; cook and stir for 4-6 minutes or until golden brown. Add garlic; cook 1 minute longer. Stir in flour until blended; gradually stir in wine. Add cream, pepper and salt; bring to a boil, stirring constantly. Cook and stir for 2 minutes or until thickened.
3. Reduce heat to medium-low. Add goat cheese; stir gently until melted. Gradually stir in remaining cheeses; cook until melted. Remove from heat.
4. Drain macaroni; stir into the sauce. Transfer to a greased 13x9-in. baking dish. Sprinkle with bread crumbs. Bake, uncovered, at 375° for 15-20 minutes or until lightly browned.
5. Meanwhile, in a small nonstick skillet, cook prosciutto over medium heat for 5-7 minutes or until crisp, stirring frequently. Sprinkle over macaroni just before serving.

Mushroom Beef

Top this hearty stew with crumbled blue cheese just before serving to add a burst of flavor. Serve some now and store the rest in the freezer for another meal.

—NANCY LATULIPPE SIMCOE, ON

PREP: 35 MIN. • **COOK:** 2 HOURS
MAKES: 9 SERVINGS

- 1 carton (32 ounces) beef broth
- 1 ounce dried mixed mushrooms
- ¼ cup all-purpose flour
- 1 teaspoon salt
- 1 teaspoon pepper
- 1 boneless beef chuck roast (2 pounds), cubed
- 3 tablespoons canola oil
- 1 pound sliced baby portobello mushrooms
- 5 medium carrots, chopped
- 1 large onion, chopped
- 3 garlic cloves, minced
- 3 teaspoons minced fresh rosemary or 1 teaspoon dried rosemary, crushed
- 2 tablespoons cornstarch
- 2 tablespoons cold water
  Hot cooked egg noodles, optional
- ¼ cup crumbled blue cheese

1. Bring broth and dried mushrooms to a boil in a large saucepan. Remove from heat; let stand 15-20 minutes or until mushrooms are softened. Drain mushrooms, reserving liquid; finely chop mushrooms. Set aside.

2. Combine flour, salt and pepper in a large resealable plastic bag; set aside 1 tablespoon for sauce. Add beef, a few pieces at a time, to the remaining flour mixture and shake to coat.

3. Brown the beef in oil in batches in a Dutch oven. Add the portobello mushrooms, carrots and onion; saute until the onion is tender. Add the garlic, rosemary and rehydrated mushrooms; cook 1 minute. Stir in reserved flour mixture until blended; gradually add mushroom broth.

4. Bring to a boil. Reduce heat; cover and simmer 1½-2 hours or until beef is tender. Combine cornstarch and water until smooth; gradually stir into pan. Bring to a boil; cook and stir 2 minutes or until thickened. Serve with egg noodles if desired; top with blue cheese.

FREEZE OPTION *Freeze cooled stew in freezer containers up to 6 months. To use, thaw stew in the refrigerator overnight. Place it in a Dutch oven; reheat. Serve dish with egg noodles if desired; top with blue cheese.*

Contest Winner

Glazed BBQ Ribs

After trying a fruit salad at a backyard barbecue, I wanted to make a rib sauce that tasted as sweet. Everyone loves the raspberry-red wine combo in this sauce.

—STEVE MARINO NUTLEY, NJ

PREP: 2 HOURS • **BROIL:** 10 MIN.
MAKES: 4 SERVINGS

- 4 pounds pork baby back ribs
- ½ cup olive oil
- 2 teaspoons salt
- 2 teaspoons pepper
- 1 bottle (18 ounces) barbecue sauce
- 1 cup seedless raspberry preserves
- ¼ cup dry red wine
- ½ teaspoon onion powder
- ½ teaspoon cayenne pepper

1. Preheat oven to 325°. Place the ribs in a shallow roasting pan, bone side down. In a small bowl, mix oil, salt and pepper; rub over ribs. Bake, covered, 1½ to 2 hours or until tender; drain.

2. In another bowl, mix remaining ingredients; reserve ¾ cup for serving with ribs. Brush some of remaining sauce over ribs. Bake, uncovered, 25-30 minutes or until the ribs are glazed, basting occasionally with additional sauce.

3. Preheat broiler. Transfer the ribs to a broiler pan, bone side down. Broil 4-5 in. from heat 8-10 minutes or until browned. Serve with reserved sauce.

Dr Spicy BBQ Pork

I served this at my son's graduation party and kept it warm in a slow cooker after roasting it in the oven. The pork is great by itself or piled high on rolls.

—**MICHELLE GAUER** SPICER, MN

PREP: 25 MIN. • **BAKE:** 4 HOURS • **MAKES:** 12 SERVINGS (⅔ CUP EACH)

- 1 boneless pork shoulder roast (5 to 7 pounds)
- 1 teaspoon garlic powder
- ½ teaspoon salt
- ½ teaspoon freshly ground pepper
- 6 chipotle peppers in adobo sauce, finely chopped (about ⅓ cup)
- 1 large sweet onion, halved and sliced
- 2 tablespoons brown sugar
- 2 cans (12 ounces each) Dr Pepper
- 1 cup barbecue sauce
   French-fried onions, optional

1. Preheat oven to 325°. Sprinkle roast with garlic powder, salt and pepper; rub with chipotle peppers. Place in a Dutch oven. Top with sweet onion; sprinkle with brown sugar. Pour Dr Pepper around roast. Bake, covered, 4 to 4½ hours or until meat is tender.
2. Remove the roast; cool slightly. Strain cooking juices, reserving onion; skim fat from juices.
3. Shred pork with two forks. Return juices, onion and pork to Dutch oven. Stir in barbecue sauce; heat through over medium heat, stirring occasionally. If desired, sprinkle with French-fried onions.

Garlic Spaghetti Squash with Meat Sauce

I was looking for filling, comforting meals without pasta or potatoes. When I was tinkering with this recipe, I discovered that spaghetti squash is a great pasta replacement.

—**BECKY RUFF** MCGREGOR, IA

PREP: 15 MIN. • **BAKE:** 45 MIN. • **MAKES:** 4 SERVINGS

- 1 medium spaghetti squash (about 4 pounds)
- 1 pound lean ground beef (90% lean)
- 2 cups sliced fresh mushrooms
- 4 garlic cloves, minced, divided
- 4 plum tomatoes, chopped
- 2 cups pasta sauce
- ½ teaspoon pepper, divided
- 1 tablespoon olive oil
- ¼ teaspoon salt
   Grated Parmesan cheese, optional

1. Preheat oven to 375°. Cut the squash lengthwise in half; remove and discard seeds. Place squash in a 13x9-in. baking pan, cut side down; add ½ in. of hot water. Bake, uncovered, 40 minutes. Drain water from pan; turn squash cut side up. Bake 5-10 minutes longer or until squash is tender.
2. Meanwhile, in a large skillet, cook beef and mushrooms over medium heat 6-8 minutes or until beef is no longer pink and mushrooms are tender, breaking up beef into crumbles; drain. Add half of the garlic; cook 1 minute longer. Stir in tomatoes, pasta sauce and ¼ teaspoon pepper; bring to a boil. Reduce heat; simmer, uncovered, 15-20 minutes.
3. When squash is cool enough to handle, use a fork to separate strands. In a large skillet, heat oil over medium heat. Add remaining garlic; cook and stir 1 minute. Stir in squash, salt and remaining pepper; heat through. Serve with meat sauce and, if desired, cheese.

Pan-Roasted Chicken and Vegetables

This one-dish meal tastes like it needs hours of hands-on time to put together, but it's just minutes to prep the simple ingredients. So easy!

—**SHERRI MELOTIK** OAK CREEK, WI

PREP: 15 MIN. • **BAKE:** 45 MIN. • **MAKES:** 6 SERVINGS

- 2 pounds red potatoes (about 6 medium), cut into ¾-inch pieces
- 1 large onion, coarsely chopped
- 2 tablespoons olive oil
- 3 garlic cloves, minced
- 1¼ teaspoons salt, divided
- 1 teaspoon dried rosemary, crushed, divided
- ¾ teaspoon pepper, divided
- ½ teaspoon paprika
- 6 bone-in chicken thighs (about 2¼ pounds), skin removed
- 6 cups fresh baby spinach (about 6 ounces)

1. Preheat oven to 425°. In a large bowl, combine potatoes, onion, oil, garlic, ¾ teaspoon salt, ½ teaspoon rosemary and ½ teaspoon pepper; toss to coat. Transfer the mixture to a 15x10x1-in. baking pan coated with cooking spray.
2. In a bowl, mix paprika and the remaining salt, rosemary and pepper. Sprinkle chicken with paprika mixture; arrange over vegetables. Roast until a thermometer inserted in chicken reads 170°-175° and vegetables are just tender, 35-40 minutes.
3. Remove chicken to a serving platter; keep warm. Top vegetables with spinach. Roast until vegetables are tender and spinach is wilted, 8-10 minutes longer. Stir vegetables to combine; serve with chicken.

Hearty Shrimp Risotto

Given the white wine, goat cheese and fresh spinach, guests will think you picked up this dish from an Italian restaurant!

—**LYDIA JENSEN** KANSAS CITY, MO

PREP: 15 MIN. • **COOK:** 35 MIN. • **MAKES:** 4 SERVINGS

- 4 cups reduced-sodium chicken broth
- 1 small onion, finely chopped
- 1 tablespoon olive oil
- 1 cup uncooked arborio rice
- 1 fresh thyme sprig
- 1 bay leaf
- ¼ teaspoon pepper
- ¾ cup white wine or additional reduced-sodium chicken broth
- 1 pound uncooked medium shrimp, peeled and deveined
- 2 cups chopped fresh spinach
- 4 ounces fresh goat cheese, crumbled

1. In a small saucepan, heat broth and keep warm. In a large nonstick skillet coated with cooking spray, saute onion in oil until tender. Add the rice, thyme, bay leaf and pepper; cook and stir for 2-3 minutes. Reduce heat; stir in wine. Cook and stir until all of the liquid is absorbed.
2. Add heated broth, ½ cup at a time, stirring constantly. Allow the liquid to absorb between additions. Cook just until risotto is creamy and rice is almost tender. (Cooking time is about 20 minutes.) Add the shrimp and spinach; cook until shrimp turn pink and spinach is wilted.
3. Stir in the cheese. Discard the thyme and the bay leaf. Serve immediately.

Contest Winner

Sweet & Tangy Salmon with Green Beans

I'm always up for new ways to cook salmon. In this dish, a sweet sauce gives the fish and green beans some down-home barbecue zip. Even our kids love it.
—**ALIESHA CALDWELL** ROBERSONVILLE, NC

PREP: 20 MIN. • **BAKE:** 15 MIN.
MAKES: 4 SERVINGS

- 4 **salmon fillets (6 ounces each)**
- 1 **tablespoon butter**
- 2 **tablespoons brown sugar**
- 2 **tablespoons reduced-sodium soy sauce**
- 2 **tablespoons Dijon mustard**
- 1 **tablespoon olive oil**
- ½ **teaspoon pepper**
- ⅛ **teaspoon salt**
- 1 **pound fresh green beans, trimmed**

1. Preheat oven to 425°. Place fillets on a 15x10x1-in. baking pan coated with cooking spray. In a small skillet, melt butter; stir in brown sugar, soy sauce, mustard, oil, pepper and salt. Brush half of the mixture over salmon.
2. Place green beans in a large bowl; drizzle with remaining brown sugar mixture and toss to coat. Arrange green beans around fillets. Roast 14-16 minutes or until fish just begins to flake easily with a fork and green beans are crisp-tender.

Chicken Tacos with Avocado Salsa

My family has special dietary needs, and these zesty tacos suit everyone. For extra toppings, add cilantro, red onion, black olives, jalapeno and lettuce.
—**CHRISTINE SCHENHER** EXETER, CA

START TO FINISH: 30 MIN.
MAKES: 4 SERVINGS

- 1 **pound boneless skinless chicken breasts, cut into ½-inch strips**
- ⅓ **cup water**
- 1 **teaspoon sugar**
- 1 **tablespoon chili powder**
- 1 **teaspoon onion powder**
- 1 **teaspoon dried oregano**
- 1 **teaspoon ground cumin**
- 1 **teaspoon paprika**
- ½ **teaspoon salt**
- ½ **teaspoon garlic powder**
- 1 **medium ripe avocado, peeled and cubed**
- 1 **cup fresh or frozen corn, thawed**
- 1 **cup cherry tomatoes, quartered**
- 2 **teaspoons lime juice**
- 8 **taco shells, warmed**

1. Place a large nonstick skillet coated with cooking spray over medium-high heat. Brown chicken. Add water, sugar and seasonings. Cook 4-5 minutes or until the chicken is no longer pink, stirring occasionally.
2. Meanwhile, in a small bowl, gently mix avocado, corn, tomatoes and lime juice. Spoon chicken mixture into taco shells; top with avocado salsa.
FREEZE OPTION *Freeze cooled meat mixture in freezer containers. To use, partially thaw in refrigerator overnight. Heat mixture through in a saucepan, stirring occasionally and adding a little water if necessary.*

Farmhouse Pork and Apple Pie

I've always loved pork and apples together, and this recipe combines them nicely to create a comforting main dish. It calls for a bit of preparation, but my family and I agree that the taste makes it well worth the extra effort.

—SUZANNE STROCSHER BOTHELL, WA

PREP: 70 MIN. • **BAKE:** 2 HOURS
MAKES: 10 SERVINGS

- 1 pound sliced bacon, cut into 2-inch pieces
- 3 medium onions, chopped
- 3 pounds boneless pork, cut into 1-inch cubes
- ¾ cup all-purpose flour
  Canola oil, optional
- 3 medium tart apples, peeled and chopped
- 1 teaspoon rubbed sage
- ½ teaspoon ground nutmeg
- 1 teaspoon salt
- ¼ teaspoon pepper
- 1 cup apple cider
- ½ cup water
- 4 medium potatoes, peeled and cubed
- ½ cup milk
- 5 tablespoons butter, divided
  Additional salt and pepper
  Minced fresh parsley, optional

1. Cook the bacon in an ovenproof 12-in. skillet until crisp. Remove with a slotted spoon to paper towels to drain. In the drippings, saute onions until tender; remove with slotted spoon and set aside. Dust pork lightly with flour. Brown a third at a time in drippings, adding oil if needed. Remove from the heat and drain.

2. To the pork, add the bacon, onions, apples, sage, nutmeg, salt and pepper. Stir in the cider and water. Cover and bake at 325° for 2 hours or until pork is tender.

3. Place potatoes in a large saucepan and cover with water. Bring to a boil. Reduce the heat; cover and cook for 10-15 minutes or until tender.

4. Drain and mash with milk and 3 tablespoons butter. Add salt and pepper to taste. Remove skillet from the oven and spread potatoes over pork mixture.

5. Melt the remaining butter; brush over potatoes. Broil 6 in. from heat for 5 minutes or until topping is browned. Sprinkle with parsley if desired.

Pretzel-Coated Chicken Nuggets

Chicken nuggets with a crushed pretzel crust have a guaranteed wow factor. Enjoy them as a quick weeknight supper or serve 'em as a party app.

—CARRIE FARIAS OAK RIDGE, NJ

START TO FINISH: 30 MIN.
MAKES: 6 SERVINGS (½ CUP SAUCE)

- 2 large eggs
- ¼ cup 2% milk
- 3 cups buttermilk ranch or cheddar cheese pretzel pieces, finely crushed
- 1 cup all-purpose flour
- 1½ pounds boneless skinless chicken breasts, cut into 1-inch pieces
  Cooking spray

SAUCE
- ¼ cup Dijon mustard
- ¼ cup honey

1. Preheat oven to 425°. In a shallow bowl, whisk eggs and milk. Place the pretzels and flour in separate shallow bowls. Dip chicken in flour to coat all sides; shake off excess. Dip in egg mixture, then in pretzels, patting to help coating adhere.

2. Place the chicken on foil-lined baking sheets; spritz with cooking spray. Bake 12-15 minutes or until chicken is no longer pink. In a small bowl, mix mustard and honey. Serve with chicken.

Contest Winner

Spinach-Stuffed Chicken Parmesan

Every time I buy a loaf of bread, I use the heels to make bread crumbs. Just pop them in the toaster and then crush them in a resealable plastic bag. That way I always have them on hand for quick recipes like this.
—**KELLIE FOGLIO** SALEM, WI

PREP: 25 MIN. • **BAKE:** 30 MIN. • **MAKES:** 4 SERVINGS

- 4 cups fresh spinach
- 2 garlic cloves, minced
- 2 teaspoons olive oil
- 2 tablespoons grated Parmesan cheese, divided
- ¼ teaspoon salt
- ¼ teaspoon pepper
- 4 boneless skinless chicken breast halves (4 ounces each)
- ½ cup dry whole wheat bread crumbs
- 1 large egg, lightly beaten
- 2 cans (8 ounces each) no-salt-added tomato sauce
- 1 teaspoon dried basil
- 1 teaspoon dried oregano
- ¾ cup shredded part-skim mozzarella cheese

1. Preheat oven to 375°. In a large skillet, cook and stir spinach and garlic in oil just until wilted. Drain. Stir in 1 tablespoon Parmesan cheese, salt and pepper.

2. Pound chicken breasts with a meat mallet to ¼-in. thickness. Spread each with 1 tablespoon spinach mixture. Fold the chicken in half, enclosing the filling; secure the meat with toothpicks.

3. Place bread crumbs and egg in separate shallow bowls. Dip chicken in egg, then roll in crumbs to coat. Place seam side down in an 8-in. square baking dish coated with cooking spray. Bake, uncovered, 20 minutes.

4. Meanwhile, in a large bowl, combine tomato sauce, basil and oregano. Pour over chicken. Sprinkle with mozzarella cheese and remaining Parmesan cheese. Bake, uncovered, 10-15 minutes longer or until a thermometer reads 165°. Discard toothpicks before serving.

Salisbury Steak Supreme

When I was running late one night, a go-to recipe of my mom's popped into my head. Now it's one of my husband's favorites. It's also a fast answer to unexpected company.
—**PATRICIA SWART** GALLOWAY, NJ

PREP: 20 MIN. • **COOK:** 15 MIN. • **MAKES:** 4 SERVINGS

- 2 medium red onions, divided
- ½ cup soft bread crumbs
- ¾ teaspoon salt-free seasoning blend
- ½ teaspoon pepper
    Dash ground nutmeg
- 1 pound lean ground beef (90% lean)
- 1 teaspoon cornstarch
- 1 teaspoon reduced-sodium beef bouillon granules
- ½ cup cold water
- 2 teaspoons butter
- 1½ cups sliced fresh mushrooms

1. Thinly slice 1½ onions; finely chop remaining onion half. In a large bowl, toss bread crumbs with chopped onion and seasonings. Add beef; mix lightly but thoroughly. Shape into four ½-in.-thick oval patties.

2. Place a large nonstick skillet coated with cooking spray over medium heat. Add patties; cook 5-6 minutes on each side or until a thermometer reads 160°. Remove from pan. Discard drippings from pan.

3. In a small bowl, mix cornstarch, bouillon and water until smooth. In the same skillet, heat the butter over medium-high heat. Add mushrooms and sliced onions; cook and stir 5-7 minutes or until onions are tender.

4. Stir in cornstarch mixture. Bring to a boil; cook and stir 1-2 minutes or until thickened. Return Salisbury steaks to pan, turning to coat with sauce; heat through.

NOTE *To make soft bread crumbs, tear bread into pieces and place in a food processor or blender. Cover and pulse until crumbs form. One slice of bread yields ½ to ¾ cup crumbs.*

Contest Winner

My Mom's Best Meat Loaf

The Rice Krispies used here are my mother's secret ingredient. While they may seem odd, they help hold the meat loaf together. And once they are cooked, no one realizes they were even there.
—**KELLY SIMMONS** HOPKINSVILLE, KY

PREP: 10 MIN. • **BAKE:** 1 HOUR + STANDING • **MAKES:** 8 SERVINGS

- ½ **cup chili sauce**
- ¼ **cup ketchup**
- 2 **cups Rice Krispies**
- 1 **medium onion, finely chopped**
- 1 **small green or sweet red pepper, finely chopped**
- ¾ **cup shredded part-skim mozzarella cheese**
- 1 **large egg, lightly beaten**
- ½ **teaspoon salt**
- ¼ **teaspoon pepper**
- 2 **pounds ground beef**

1. Preheat oven to 350°. In a small bowl, mix chili sauce and ketchup. In a large bowl, combine Rice Krispies, onion, green pepper, cheese, egg, salt and pepper; stir in half of the chili sauce mixture. Add beef; mix lightly but thoroughly.
2. Transfer beef mixture to an ungreased 9x5-in. loaf pan. Make a shallow indentation down the center of the loaf. Spread the remaining chili sauce mixture over the loaf, being sure to fill the indentation.
3. Bake 60-70 minutes or until a thermometer reads 160°; use a turkey baster to remove drippings every 20 minutes. Let stand 10 minutes before slicing.
NOTE *This recipe was tested with Heinz chili sauce.*

Jalapeno-Bacon Mac & Cheese

All my dishes use ingredients that are usually available in the pantry of our fire department. I simply adjust the amounts depending on how many people we have on duty that day. Mac and cheese with jalapenos and bacon is always popular.
—**NICK KACZOR** NEW HUDSON, MI

PREP: 25 MIN. • **BAKE:** 10 MIN. • **MAKES:** 8 SERVINGS

- 1 **package (16 ounces) elbow macaroni**
- 3 **tablespoons butter**
- 3 **tablespoons all-purpose flour**
- 2 **cans (12 ounces each) evaporated milk**
- 3 **tablespoons yellow mustard**
- 3 **to 4 tablespoons chopped pickled jalapenos**
- 4 **cups shredded cheddar cheese, divided**
- ½ **pound thick-sliced bacon strips (about 7 strips), cooked and crumbled**

1. Preheat oven to 350°. In a 6-qt. stockpot, cook macaroni according to package directions.
2. Meanwhile, in a large saucepan, melt the butter over medium heat. Stir in flour until smooth; gradually whisk in milk and mustard. Bring to a boil, stirring constantly; cook and stir 1-2 minutes or until thickened. Stir in jalapenos and 3 cups cheese until the cheese is melted. Reserve ¼ cup crumbled bacon; stir remaining bacon into sauce.
3. Drain macaroni and return to pot; stir in cheese sauce. Transfer to a greased 13x9-in. baking dish; sprinkle with remaining cheese and reserved bacon. Bake, uncovered, 8-10 minutes or until cheese is melted.

Maple-Dijon Sprouts & Sausage

You can substitute any vegetables that you have on hand or that you prefer in this recipe. Just make sure to test them to make sure they are cooked through.
—*TASTE OF HOME* TEST KITCHEN

START TO FINISH: 30 MIN.
MAKES: 4 SERVINGS

- 4 Italian sausage links, casings removed
- 1 package (16 ounces) frozen Brussels sprouts
- ½ pound sliced fresh mushrooms
- 1 cup fresh baby carrots, halved
- 1 medium onion, chopped
- 2 tablespoons maple syrup
- 2 tablespoons Dijon mustard
- ½ teaspoon dried sage leaves
- ½ teaspoon pepper
- 1 package (5.8 ounces) roasted garlic and olive oil couscous
- ¼ cup grated Parmesan cheese

1. Cook the sausage in a large skillet until no longer pink; drain. Add the Brussels sprouts, mushrooms, carrots and onion; cook until the vegetables are crisp-tender. Add syrup, mustard, sage and pepper; cover and cook for 4-6 minutes longer or until Brussels sprouts are tender.

2. Meanwhile, prepare the couscous according to package directions. Serve with sausage mixture and sprinkle with cheese.

Contest Winner

Chicken Chile Relleno Casserole

My husband enjoys Mexican food and casseroles, so I combined them. This dish with chicken, poblanos and chilies tastes like dinner out at a Mexican restaurant.
—ERICA INGRAM LAKEWOOD, OH

PREP: 20 MIN. • **BAKE:** 35 MIN. + STANDING
MAKES: 8 SERVINGS

- 2 tablespoons butter
- 2 poblano peppers, seeded and coarsely chopped
- 1 small onion, finely chopped
- 2 tablespoons all-purpose flour
- 1 teaspoon ground cumin
- 1 teaspoon smoked paprika
- ¼ teaspoon salt
- ⅔ cup 2% milk
- 1 package (8 ounces) cream cheese, cubed
- 2 cups shredded pepper jack cheese
- 2 cups coarsely shredded rotisserie chicken
- 1 can (4 ounces) chopped green chilies
- 2 packages (8½ ounces each) corn bread/muffin mix

1. Preheat oven to 350°. In a large skillet, heat butter over medium-high heat. Add peppers and onion; cook and stir 4-6 minutes or until peppers are tender.

2. Stir in flour and seasonings until blended; gradually stir in milk. Bring to a boil, stirring constantly; cook and stir until thickened, about 1 minute. Stir in cream cheese until blended. Add pepper jack cheese, chicken and green chilies; heat through, stirring to combine. Transfer to a greased 11x7-in. baking dish.

3. Prepare the corn muffin batter according to package directions. Spread over chicken mixture. Bake, uncovered, 35-40 minutes or until golden brown and a toothpick inserted in topping comes out clean. Let stand 10 minutes before serving.

Ultimate Pot Roast

When juicy pot roast simmers in garlic, onions and veggies, everyone comes running to ask, "When can we eat?" The answer? Just wait—it will be worth it.

—NICK IVERSON MILWAUKEE, WI

PREP: 55 MIN. • **BAKE:** 2 HOURS
MAKES: 8 SERVINGS

- 1 boneless beef chuck-eye or other chuck roast (3 to 4 pounds)
- 2 teaspoons pepper
- 2 teaspoons salt, divided
- 2 tablespoons canola oil
- 2 medium onions, cut into 1-inch pieces
- 2 celery ribs, chopped
- 3 garlic cloves, minced
- 1 tablespoon tomato paste
- 1 tablespoon minced fresh thyme or 1 teaspoon dried thyme
- 2 bay leaves
- 1 cup dry red wine or reduced-sodium beef broth
- 2 cups reduced-sodium beef broth
- 1 pound small red potatoes, quartered
- 4 medium parsnips, peeled and cut into 2-inch pieces
- 6 medium carrots, cut into 2-inch pieces
- 1 tablespoon red wine vinegar
- 2 tablespoons minced fresh parsley
  Salt and pepper to taste

1. Preheat oven to 325°. Pat roast dry with a paper towel; tie at 2-in. intervals with kitchen string. Sprinkle roast with pepper and 1½ teaspoons salt. In a Dutch oven, heat oil over medium-high heat. Brown roast on all sides. Remove from pan.
2. Add onions, celery and ½ teaspoon salt to the same pan; cook and stir over medium heat 8-10 minutes or until onions are browned. Add garlic, tomato paste, thyme and bay leaves; cook and stir 1 minute longer.
3. Add the wine, stirring to loosen browned bits from pan; stir in broth. Return roast to pan. Arrange potatoes, parsnips and carrots around roast; bring to a boil. Bake, covered, until meat is fork-tender, 2 to 2½ hours.
4. Remove roast and vegetables from pan; keep warm. Discard bay leaves; skim fat from cooking juices. On the stovetop, bring juices to a boil; cook until liquid is reduced by half (about 1½ cups), 10-12 minutes. Stir in the vinegar and parsley; season with salt and pepper to taste.
5. Remove string from roast. Serve with vegetables and sauce.

Contest Winner

Haddock with Lime-Cilantro Butter

In Louisiana, the good times roll when we broil fish and serve it with lots of lime juice, cilantro and butter.

—DARLENE MORRIS FRANKLINTON, LA

START TO FINISH: 15 MIN.
MAKES: 4 SERVINGS

- 4 haddock fillets (6 ounces each)
- ½ teaspoon salt
- ¼ teaspoon pepper
- 3 tablespoons butter, melted
- 2 tablespoons minced fresh cilantro
- 1 tablespoon lime juice
- 1 teaspoon grated lime peel

1. Preheat broiler. Sprinkle the fillets with salt and pepper. Place them on a greased broiler pan. Broil 4-5 in. from heat 5-6 minutes or until fish flakes easily with a fork.
2. In a small bowl, mix remaining ingredients. Serve over fish.

KEEP IT FRESH
Fresh cilantro should be used as soon as possible. For short-term storage, immerse the freshly cut stems in water about 2 inches deep. Cover leaves loosely with a plastic bag and refrigerate for several days. Wash just before using.

MEALS IN MINUTES

When you've got a half hour and dinnertime is fast approaching, turn to this quick-hits chapter for a tasty success. Time will be on your side when you choose one of these savory dishes.

Rosemary Pork Medallions with Peas

It's nice to have a quick meal to fix after coming home from work. This one is simple to prepare and doesn't use a lot of ingredients, so it's great for beginner cooks, too.

—LAURA MCALLISTER MORGANTON, NC

START TO FINISH: 25 MIN.
MAKES: 4 SERVINGS

- 1 pork tenderloin (1 pound), cut into ½-inch slices
- ½ teaspoon salt
- ¼ teaspoon pepper
- ¼ cup all-purpose flour
- 1 tablespoon olive oil
- 2 teaspoons butter
- 1 cup reduced-sodium chicken broth
- 1 garlic clove, minced
- 1 teaspoon dried rosemary, crushed
- 2 cups frozen peas

1. Sprinkle pork with salt and pepper. Toss with flour to coat lightly; shake off excess.

2. In a large skillet, heat oil and butter over medium heat. Add pork; cook 1-2 minutes on each side or until tender. Remove from pan; keep warm.

3. In the same pan, add broth, garlic and rosemary; bring to a boil, stirring to loosen browned bits from the pan. Cook 2-3 minutes or until liquid is reduced by a third. Stir in peas; cook 2-3 minutes longer or until heated through. Serve with pork.

Grilled Garden Pizza

Dazzle your family and friends with pizzas that are fresh off the grill. We top them with Asiago, Parmesan, veggies and fresh basil. Pile on the toppings you love.

—TERI RASEY CADILLAC, MI

START TO FINISH: 30 MIN.
MAKES: 6 SERVINGS

- 2 plum tomatoes, thinly sliced
- ½ teaspoon sea salt or kosher salt
- 1 loaf (1 pound) frozen pizza dough, thawed
- 2 tablespoons olive oil, divided
- ½ cup shredded Parmesan or Asiago cheese
- ½ cup fresh or frozen corn, thawed
- ¼ cup thinly sliced red onion
- 8 ounces fresh mozzarella cheese, sliced
- ½ cup thinly sliced fresh spinach
- 3 tablespoons chopped fresh basil

1. Sprinkle tomatoes with salt; set aside. On a lightly floured surface, divide dough in half. Roll or press each to ¼-in. thickness; place each on a greased sheet of foil (about 10 in. square). Brush tops with 1 tablespoon oil.

2. Carefully invert crusts onto grill rack, removing foil. Brush tops with remaining oil. Grill, covered, over medium heat 2-3 minutes or until bottom is golden brown. Remove from grill; reduce grill temperature to low.

3. Top grilled sides of crusts with Parmesan or Asiago cheese, tomatoes, corn, onion and mozzarella cheese. Grill, covered, on low heat 4-6 minutes or until cheese is melted. Sprinkle with spinach and basil.

Broccoli Shrimp Alfredo

After tasting fettuccine Alfredo at a restaurant, I tried to duplicate the recipe at home. You can't imagine how pleased I was when I came up with this version. Not only does my family love the creamy dish, but my husband prefers it to the one at the restaurant!

—**RAE NATOLI** KINGSTON, NY

START TO FINISH: 30 MIN.
MAKES: 4 SERVINGS

- 8 **ounces uncooked fettuccine**
- 1 **pound uncooked medium shrimp, peeled and deveined**
- 3 **garlic cloves, minced**
- ½ **cup butter, cubed**
- 1 **package (8 ounces) cream cheese, cubed**
- 1 **cup milk**
- ½ **cup shredded Parmesan cheese**
- 4 **cups frozen broccoli florets**
- ½ **teaspoon salt**
  Dash pepper

1. Cook the fettuccine according to package directions. Meanwhile, in a large skillet, saute shrimp and garlic in butter until shrimp turn pink. Remove and set aside.

2. In the same skillet, combine the cream cheese, milk and Parmesan cheese; cook and stir until cheeses are melted and mixture is smooth.

3. Place 1 in. of water in a saucepan; add the broccoli. Bring to a boil. Reduce heat; cover and simmer for 6-8 minutes or until tender. Drain. Stir the broccoli, shrimp, salt and pepper into cheese sauce; heat through. Drain fettuccine; top with shrimp mixture.

Contest Winner

Skillet BBQ Beef Potpie

Beef potpie is a classic comfort food, but who's got time to see it through? My crowd-pleaser is not only speedy; it uses up leftover stuffing.

—**PRISCILLA YEE** CONCORD, CA

START TO FINISH: 25 MIN.
MAKES: 4 SERVINGS

- 1 **pound lean ground beef (90% lean)**
- ⅓ **cup thinly sliced green onions, divided**
- 2 **cups frozen mixed vegetables, thawed**
- ½ **cup salsa**
- ½ **cup barbecue sauce**
- 3 **cups cooked corn bread stuffing**
- ½ **cup shredded cheddar cheese**
- ¼ **cup chopped sweet red pepper**

1. In a large skillet, cook beef and ¼ cup green onions over medium heat 6-8 minutes or until beef is no longer pink, breaking into crumbles; drain. Stir in mixed vegetables, salsa and barbecue sauce; cook, covered, over medium-low heat 4-5 minutes or until heated through.

2. Layer stuffing over beef; sprinkle with the cheese, red pepper and remaining green onion. Cook, covered, 3-5 minutes longer or until heated through and cheese is melted.

Peppered Portobello Penne

Hearty mushrooms and a kickin' hot cheese sauce take this simple pasta toss from drab to fab! My family loves the fact that it tastes like a restaurant dish but is made at home.
—**VERONICA CALLAGHAN** GLASTONBURY, CT

START TO FINISH: 30 MIN. • **MAKES:** 4 SERVINGS

- 2 **cups uncooked penne pasta**
- 4 **large portobello mushrooms, stems removed, halved and thinly sliced**
- 2 **tablespoons olive oil**
- ½ **cup heavy whipping cream**
- ¾ **teaspoon salt**
- ¼ **teaspoon pepper**
- 1 **cup shredded pepper jack cheese**

1. Cook pasta according to package directions.
2. Meanwhile, in a large skillet, saute mushrooms in oil until tender. Stir in cream, salt and pepper; heat through. Stir in cheese until melted. Drain pasta. Add to skillet and toss to coat.

Sausage & Feta Stuffed Tomatoes

As a professional weight loss coach, I'm all about eating healthy. My clients and blog followers love these tomatoes so much that I included them in my cookbook. They leave you feeling satisfied—not deprived.
—**SHANA CONRADT** GREENVILLE, WI

START TO FINISH: 25 MIN. • **MAKES:** 4 SERVINGS

- 3 **Italian turkey sausage links (4 ounces each), casings removed**
- 1 **cup (4 ounces) crumbled feta cheese, divided**
- 8 **plum tomatoes**
- ¼ **teaspoon salt**
- ¼ **teaspoon pepper**

- 3 **tablespoons balsamic vinegar**
  Minced fresh parsley

1. Preheat oven to 350°. In a large skillet, cook sausage over medium heat 4-6 minutes or until no longer pink, breaking into crumbles. Transfer to a small bowl; stir in ½ cup cheese.
2. Cut tomatoes in half lengthwise. Scoop out pulp, leaving a ½-in. shell; discard pulp. Sprinkle the tomatoes with salt and pepper; transfer to an ungreased 13x9-in. baking dish. Spoon sausage mixture into tomato shells; drizzle with vinegar. Sprinkle with remaining cheese.
3. Bake, uncovered, 10-12 minutes or until heated through. Sprinkle with parsley.

Waffle Iron Pizzas

These little pizza pockets are a fun mashup using the waffle iron. Try your different toppings or even breakfast fillings like ham and eggs.
—**AMY LENTS** GRAND FORKS, ND

START TO FINISH: 30 MIN. • **MAKES:** 4 SERVINGS

- 1 **package (16.3 ounces) large refrigerated buttermilk biscuits**
- 1 **cup shredded part-skim mozzarella cheese**
- 24 **slices turkey pepperoni (about 1½ ounces), quartered**
- 2 **ready-to-serve fully cooked bacon strips, chopped**
  Pizza sauce, warmed

1. Roll or press the biscuits into 6-in. circles. On one biscuit, place ¼ cup cheese, 6 slices pepperoni and a scant tablespoon chopped bacon to within ½ in. of edges. Top with a second biscuit, folding bottom edge over top edge and pressing to seal completely.
2. Bake in a preheated waffle iron according to the manufacturer's directions until golden brown, about 4-5 minutes. Meanwhile, repeat with remaining ingredients. Serve with pizza sauce.

Ham & Veggie Casserole

I've paired ham with broccoli and cauliflower for years. To complete this casserole dinner, I pass around the dinner rolls.
—**SHERRI MELOTIK** OAK CREEK, WI

START TO FINISH: 30 MIN. • **MAKES:** 4 SERVINGS

- 1 package (16 ounces) frozen broccoli florets
- 1 package (16 ounces) frozen cauliflower
- 2 teaspoons plus 2 tablespoons butter, divided
- ¼ cup seasoned bread crumbs
- 2 tablespoons all-purpose flour
- 1½ cups 2% milk
- ¾ cup shredded sharp cheddar cheese
- ½ cup grated Parmesan cheese
- 1½ cups cubed fully cooked ham (about 8 ounces)
- ¼ teaspoon pepper

1. Preheat oven to 425°. Cook broccoli and cauliflower according to package directions; drain.
2. Meanwhile, in a small skillet, melt 2 teaspoons butter. Add the bread crumbs; cook and stir over medium heat 2-3 minutes or until lightly toasted. Remove from heat.
3. In a large saucepan, melt remaining butter over medium heat. Stir in flour until smooth; gradually whisk in milk. Bring to a boil, stirring constantly; cook and stir 1-2 minutes or until thickened. Remove from heat; stir in cheeses until blended. Stir in ham, pepper and vegetables.
4. Transfer to a greased 8-in. square baking dish. Sprinkle with toasted crumbs. Bake, uncovered, 10-15 minutes or until heated through.

One-Pot Chilighetti

Grab your stockpot for my meal-in-one chili and spaghetti. I've got a large family, and this hearty pasta takes care of everybody.
—**JENNIFER TRENHAILE** EMERSON, NE

START TO FINISH: 30 MIN. • **MAKES:** 8 SERVINGS

- 1½ pounds ground beef
- 1 large onion, chopped
- 1 can (46 ounces) tomato juice
- 1 cup water
- 2 tablespoons Worcestershire sauce
- 4 teaspoons chili powder
- ½ teaspoon salt
- ½ teaspoon ground cumin
- ½ teaspoon pepper
- 1 package (16 ounces) spaghetti, broken into 2-inch pieces
- 2 cans (16 ounces each) kidney beans, rinsed and drained
  Sour cream and shredded cheddar cheese

1. In a 6-qt. stockpot, cook beef and onion over medium-high heat 8-10 minutes or until beef is no longer pink and onion is tender, breaking up beef into crumbles; drain.
2. Stir in tomato juice, water, Worcestershire sauce and seasonings; bring to a boil. Add spaghetti. Reduce heat; simmer, covered, 9-11 minutes or until the pasta is tender. Stir in beans; heat through. Top servings with sour cream and cheese.
FREEZE OPTION *Freeze cooled pasta mixture in freezer containers. To use, partially thaw in refrigerator overnight. Heat through in a saucepan, stirring occasionally and adding a little water if necessary.*

Ham and Pea Pasta Alfredo

When I want a filling meal that even the kids enjoy, I toss ham and sugar snap peas with Romano cream sauce and pasta.

—C.R. MONACHINO KENMORE, NY

START TO FINISH: 25 MIN.
MAKES: 8 SERVINGS

- 1 package (16 ounces) fettuccine
- 2 tablespoons butter
- 1½ pounds sliced fully cooked ham, cut into strips (about 5 cups)
- 2 cups fresh sugar snap peas
- 2 cups heavy whipping cream
- ½ cup grated Romano cheese
- ¼ teaspoon pepper

1. Cook the fettuccine according to package directions. Meanwhile, in a large skillet, heat butter over medium heat. Add ham and peas; cook and stir 5 minutes. Stir in cream, cheese and pepper; bring to a boil. Reduce heat; simmer, uncovered, 1-2 minutes or until sauce is slightly thickened and peas are crisp-tender.
2. Drain fettuccine; add to skillet and toss to coat. Serve immediately.

Sweet Potatoes with Cilantro Black Beans

As a vegan, I'm always looking for impressive dishes to share. Sweet potatoes loaded with beans and a touch of peanut butter is one of my standout recipes.

—KAYLA CAPPER OJAI, CA

START TO FINISH: 20 MIN.
MAKES: 4 SERVINGS

- 4 medium sweet potatoes (about 8 ounces each)
- 1 tablespoon olive oil
- 1 small sweet red pepper, chopped
- 2 green onions, chopped
- 1 can (15 ounces) black beans, rinsed and drained
- ½ cup salsa
- ¼ cup frozen corn
- 2 tablespoons lime juice
- 1 tablespoon creamy peanut butter
- 1 teaspoon ground cumin
- ¼ teaspoon garlic salt
- ¼ cup minced fresh cilantro
  Additional minced fresh cilantro, optional

1. Scrub sweet potatoes; pierce several times with a fork. Place on a microwave-safe plate. Microwave, uncovered, on high 6-8 minutes or until tender, turning once.
2. Meanwhile, in a large skillet, heat oil over medium-high heat. Add pepper and green onions; cook and stir 3-4 minutes or until tender. Stir in beans, salsa, corn, lime juice, peanut butter, cumin and garlic salt; heat through. Stir in cilantro.
3. With a sharp knife, cut an "X" in each sweet potato. Fluff pulp with a fork. Spoon bean mixture over potatoes. If desired, sprinkle with additional cilantro.

Chicken & Wild Rice Strudels

I wanted the buttery crunch of layered pastry without the sweet filling of strudel. Using rotisserie chicken from the store, I found my savory answer.
—JOHNNA JOHNSON SCOTTSDALE, AZ

START TO FINISH: 30 MIN.
MAKES: 6 SERVINGS

- 1 package (8.8 ounces) ready-to-serve long grain and wild rice
- 1½ cups coarsely chopped rotisserie chicken
- ½ cup shredded Swiss cheese
- ½ teaspoon Italian seasoning
- ¼ teaspoon salt
- ¼ teaspoon pepper
- 12 sheets phyllo dough (14x9-inch size)
- 6 tablespoons butter, melted

1. Preheat oven to 400°. Place the first six ingredients in a large bowl; toss to combine.
2. Place one sheet of phyllo dough on a work surface; brush lightly with the melted butter. Layer with five additional sheets, brushing each layer. (Keep remaining phyllo covered with plastic wrap and a damp towel to prevent it from drying out.)
3. Spoon half of the rice mixture down the center of the phyllo dough to within 1 in. of ends. Fold up short sides to enclose filling. Roll up tightly, starting with a long side.
4. Transfer, seam side down, to a 15x10x1-in. baking pan lined with parchment paper. Brush with the additional butter. Repeat with the remaining ingredients. Bake 20-25 minutes or until golden brown and heated through.

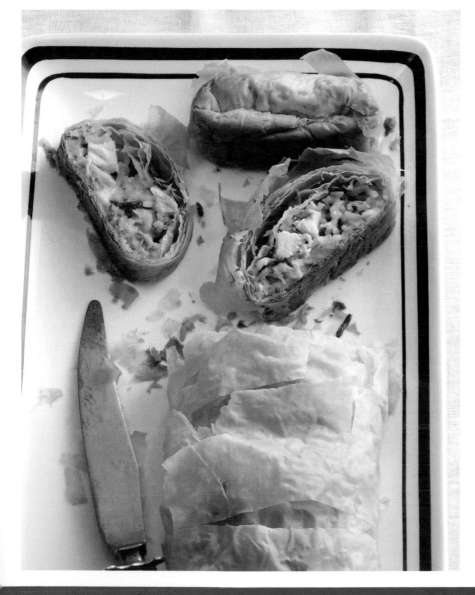

Bruschetta-Topped Chicken & Spaghetti

I like making healthy recipes for my family. If you find yourself craving Italian food, this 30-minute meal hits the spot.
—SUSAN WHOLLEY FAIRFIELD, CT

START TO FINISH: 30 MIN.
MAKES: 4 SERVINGS

- 8 ounces uncooked whole wheat spaghetti
- 4 boneless skinless chicken breast halves (5 ounces each)
- ½ teaspoon pepper
- 1 cup prepared bruschetta topping
- ⅓ cup shredded Italian cheese blend
- 2 tablespoons grated Parmesan cheese

1. Preheat broiler. Cook spaghetti according to package directions; drain. Pound chicken breasts with a meat mallet to ½-in. thickness. Sprinkle with pepper. In a large nonstick skillet coated with cooking spray, cook chicken over medium heat 5-6 minutes on each side or until no longer pink.
2. Transfer to an 8-in. square baking pan. Spoon the bruschetta topping over chicken; sprinkle with cheeses. Broil 3-4 in. from heat 5-6 minutes or until cheese is golden brown. Serve with spaghetti.

BRUNCH IN A FLASH

When it comes to the most important meal of the day, skip the cereal and go for homemade goodness. These breakfast options come together so fast, you'll have time to enjoy your coffee, too!

Zucchini-Parmesan Bake

When my garden is overflowing with zucchini, I turn to this recipe as a tasty way to use it up.

—**SHANNON DAVIS** MASON, MI

START TO FINISH: 30 MIN.
MAKES: 6 SERVINGS

- 3 **large eggs**
- ½ **cup canola oil**
- 3 **cups shredded zucchini (about 1 pound)**
- 1 **cup reduced-fat biscuit/baking mix**
- ½ **cup shredded Parmesan cheese**

1. Preheat oven to 375°. In a large bowl, whisk eggs and oil until blended. Stir in remaining ingredients.
2. Transfer mixture to a greased 10-in. ovenproof skillet. Bake 25-30 minutes or until golden brown.

Egg Biscuit Bake

Convenient refrigerated biscuits create a golden border around this all-in-one brunch dish. It's a variation of a simple egg-cheese combination my mother used to make. It's become our favorite comfort food.

—**ALICE LE DUC** CEDARBURG, WI

START TO FINISH: 30 MIN.
MAKES: 4-6 SERVINGS

- 1 **can (5 ounces) evaporated milk**
- 8 **ounces process cheese (Velveeta), cubed**
- 1 **teaspoon prepared mustard**
- ¾ **cup cubed fully cooked ham**
- ½ **cup frozen peas**
- 2 **tablespoons butter**
- 10 **large eggs, lightly beaten**
- 1 **tube (12 ounces) refrigerated buttermilk biscuits**

1. Preheat oven to 375°. In a large saucepan, combine milk, cheese and mustard; cook over low heat until smooth, stirring constantly. Stir in ham and peas.
2. Melt butter in a large skillet, heat butter until hot. Add eggs; cook and stir over medium heat until eggs are completely set. Add cheese sauce and stir gently.
3. Spoon into an ungreased shallow 2-qt. baking dish. Separate biscuits and cut in half. Place with cut side down around outer edge of dish.
4. Bake, uncovered, 15-20 minutes or until a knife inserted near the center comes out clean and biscuits are golden brown.

Egg-Topped Biscuit Waffles

Breakfast for dinner is always a hit at our house. As a mom, I like transforming an ordinary breakfast sandwich into something magical and kid-friendly. These biscuit waffles definitely earn an enthusiastic thumbs-up.

—AMY LENTS GRAND FORKS, ND

START TO FINISH: 25 MIN.
MAKES: 4 SERVINGS

- 1½ cups biscuit/baking mix
- ¾ cup shredded Swiss cheese
- ⅛ teaspoon pepper
- ½ cup 2% milk
- 4 large eggs
- 4 bacon strips, cooked and crumbled
  Cubed avocado and pico de gallo, optional

1. Preheat a four-square waffle iron. Place the baking mix, cheese and pepper in a bowl. Add milk; stir just until moistened. Transfer to a lightly floured surface; knead dough gently 4-6 times. Pat or roll into an 8-in. square; cut into four 4-in. squares.

2. Generously grease top and bottom grids of the waffle maker. Place one portion of dough on each section of waffle maker, pressing an indentation in each for eggs.

3. Break an egg over each biscuit; sprinkle with bacon. Close the lid carefully over eggs; cook until biscuits are golden brown. If desired, top with avocado and pico de gallo.

NOTE *Recipe may also be baked in a round waffle maker. Divide biscuit dough into four portions; pat each into a 4½-in. circle. Assemble and cook one serving at a time.*

Contest Winner

BBQ Chicken, Polenta & Eggs

When I was in college, I'd make this in the morning before heading out to class and it kept me full until I got home later that evening. I cook it now when I have friends or family over for brunch on Sundays.

—EVAN JANNEY LOS ANGELES, CA

START TO FINISH: 25 MIN.
MAKES: 4 SERVINGS

- 2 cups shredded cooked chicken breasts
- ¾ cup barbecue sauce
- 1 tablespoon minced fresh cilantro
- 2 tablespoons olive oil, divided
- 1 tube (1 pound) polenta, cut into 8 slices
- 1 small garlic clove, minced
- 4 large eggs

1. In a small saucepan, combine the chicken, barbecue sauce and cilantro; heat through over medium heat, stirring occasionally.

2. In a large skillet, heat 1 tablespoon oil over medium-high heat. Add the polenta; cook 2-3 minutes on each side or until lightly browned. Transfer to a serving plate; keep warm.

3. In the same pan, heat remaining oil over medium-high heat. Add garlic; cook and stir 1 minute. Break eggs, one at a time, into pan. Reduce heat to low. Cook until desired doneness, turning after whites are set, if desired. Serve over polenta with chicken mixture.

Ravioli with Apple Chicken Sausage

I love butternut squash ravioli but was never quite sure what flavors would best go with it. Turns out that creamy spinach, chicken sausage and a hint of sweet spice are the perfect go-alongs.

—MARY BRODEUR MILLBURY, MA

START TO FINISH: 30 MIN.
MAKES: 4 SERVINGS

- 1 package (18 ounces) frozen butternut squash ravioli
- 2 packages (10 ounces each) frozen creamed spinach
- 1 tablespoon olive oil
- 1 package (12 ounces) fully cooked apple chicken sausage links or flavor of your choice, cut into ½-inch slices
- 1 teaspoon maple syrup
- ¼ teaspoon pumpkin pie spice

1. Cook ravioli according to package directions. Prepare spinach according to package directions. Meanwhile, in a large skillet, heat oil over medium heat. Add the sausage; cook and stir 2-4 minutes or until browned.
2. Drain ravioli. Add ravioli, spinach, maple syrup and pie spice to sausage; heat through.

Cajun Boil on the Grill

I came up with these everything-in-one seafood packets for a family reunion, since the recipe can be increased to feed a bunch. The foil steams up inside, so open carefully.

—ALLISON BROOKS FORT COLLINS, CO

START TO FINISH: 30 MIN.
MAKES: 4 SERVINGS

- 1 package (20 ounces) refrigerated red potato wedges
- 2 salmon fillets (6 ounces each), halved
- ¾ pound uncooked shrimp (31–40 per pound), peeled and deveined
- ½ pound summer sausage, cubed
- 2 medium ears sweet corn, halved
- 2 tablespoons olive oil
- 1 teaspoon seafood seasoning
- ½ teaspoon salt
- ¼ teaspoon pepper
- 1 medium lemon, cut into 4 wedges

1. Divide potatoes, salmon, shrimp, sausage and corn among four pieces of heavy-duty foil (about 18x12-in. rectangles). Drizzle with oil; sprinkle with seasonings. Squeeze lemon juice over top; place squeezed wedges in packets. Fold foil around mixture, sealing tightly.
2. Grill, covered, over medium heat 12-15 minutes or until fish just begins to flake easily with a fork, shrimp turn pink and potatoes are tender. Open foil carefully to allow steam to escape.

Parmesan Bow Tie with Chicken

On lazy summer weekends, we like chicken and yellow squash tossed with bow tie pasta. Fresh grated Parmesan adds a special touch.

—**SARAH SMILEY** BANGOR, ME

START TO FINISH: 30 MIN.
MAKES: 6 SERVINGS

- 1 package (16 ounces) bow tie pasta
- 5 tablespoons butter, divided
- 1 pound boneless skinless chicken breasts, cut into 1-inch pieces
- 1 teaspoon salt, divided
- 1 teaspoon pepper, divided
- 2 medium yellow summer squash or zucchini, cut into 1-inch pieces
- 3 tablespoons all-purpose flour
- 2 garlic cloves, minced
- 1½ cups fat-free milk
- ¾ cup grated Parmesan cheese

1. In a 6-qt. stockpot, cook pasta according to package directions.
2. In a large skillet, heat 1 tablespoon butter over medium heat. Add chicken; cook and stir 7-9 minutes or until no longer pink. Add ¼ teaspoon each salt and pepper; remove from pan. In same pan, heat 1 tablespoon butter over medium heat. Add squash; cook and stir 3-5 minutes or until tender. Remove from heat.
3. In a saucepan, melt remaining 3 tablespoons butter over medium heat. Stir in flour and garlic until blended; gradually whisk in milk. Bring to a boil, stirring constantly; cook and stir 1-2 minutes or until thickened. Remove from heat; stir in cheese and remaining salt and pepper.
4. Drain pasta; return to pot. Add chicken, squash and sauce; heat through, stirring to combine.

Scallops with Wilted Spinach

Two of my favorite foods are bacon and seafood. In this dish, I get them together with white wine, shallots and baby spinach. Serve with bread to soak up the tasty broth.

—**DEBORAH WILLIAMS** PEORIA, AZ

START TO FINISH: 25 MIN.
MAKES: 4 SERVINGS

- 4 bacon strips, chopped
- 12 sea scallops (about 1½ pounds), side muscles removed
- 2 shallots, finely chopped
- ½ cup white wine or chicken broth
- 8 cups fresh baby spinach (about 8 ounces)

1. In a large nonstick skillet, cook the bacon over medium heat until crisp, stirring occasionally. Remove it with a slotted spoon and drain on paper towels. Discard drippings, reserving 2 tablespoons. Wipe skillet clean if necessary.
2. Pat scallops dry with paper towels. In the same skillet, heat 1 tablespoon drippings over medium-high heat. Add scallops; cook 2-3 minutes on each side or until golden brown and firm. Remove from pan; keep warm.
3. Heat remaining drippings in same pan over medium-high heat. Add the shallots; cook and stir 2-3 minutes or until tender. Add wine; bring to a boil, stirring to loosen the browned bits from pan. Add spinach; cook and stir 1-2 minutes or until wilted. Stir in bacon. Serve with scallops.

Broccoli, Rice and Sausage Dinner

The first recipe my kids requested when they left home was broccoli with sausage and rice. If fresh zucchini or summer squash is available, add it to the mix, too.

—JOANN PARMENTIER BRANCH, MI

START TO FINISH: 25 MIN. • **MAKES:** 6 SERVINGS

- 1 tablespoon canola oil
- 1 package (13 ounces) smoked turkey sausage, sliced
- 4 cups small fresh broccoli florets
- 2 cups water
- 1 can (14½ ounces) diced tomatoes, drained
- ¼ teaspoon seasoned salt
- ¼ teaspoon garlic powder
- ¼ teaspoon dried oregano
- 2 cups uncooked instant brown rice
- ½ cup shredded sharp cheddar cheese
    Reduced-fat sour cream and Louisiana-style hot sauce, optional

1. In a large skillet, heat oil over medium-high heat. Add sausage; cook and stir 2-3 minutes or until browned. Stir in broccoli; cook and stir 2 minutes longer.

2. Add water, tomatoes and seasonings; bring to a boil. Stir in rice. Reduce heat; simmer, covered, 5 minutes.

3. Remove from heat; stir rice mixture and sprinkle with cheese. Let stand, covered, 5 minutes or until liquid is almost absorbed and cheese is melted. If desired, serve with sour cream and hot sauce.

> ### SKILLET RICE CAKES
> When I have extra rice, I use it to make breakfast the next day. I mix the rice with a beaten egg or two, then drop spoonfuls into hot butter in a skillet. I cook both sides until they are lightly browned and serve them with maple syrup.
> **—LAURA G.** POWHATAN, VA

Chicken with Pear & Sweet Potato

When my husband was deployed to Iraq, one of my girlfriends shared this yummy chicken. I served it when he returned home, and now it's a tradition at our house.
—**CATHRYN ECKLEY** FORT MEADE, MD

START TO FINISH: 30 MIN. • **MAKES:** 4 SERVINGS

- 4 boneless skinless chicken breast halves (5 ounces each)
- ¼ teaspoon pepper
- ¾ teaspoon salt, divided
- 1 tablespoon canola oil
- 1 medium sweet potato (about ¾ pound), peeled and cut into ½-inch pieces
- ½ cup plus 3 tablespoons water, divided
- 1 medium ripe pear, cut into ½-inch pieces
- 1 tablespoon red wine vinegar
- 1 tablespoon Dijon mustard
- 1 teaspoon minced fresh tarragon or ¼ teaspoon dried tarragon

1. Pound chicken breasts with a meat mallet to ½-in. thickness; sprinkle with pepper and ½ teaspoon salt.
2. In a large nonstick skillet, heat oil over medium heat. Add chicken; cook 3-4 minutes on each side or until no longer pink. Remove from pan; keep warm.
3. In the same pan, combine sweet potato and ½ cup water; bring to a boil. Reduce heat; simmer, covered, 5 minutes. Stir in pear; cook, covered, 4-5 minutes longer or until potato is tender. Add vinegar, mustard and tarragon; stir in remaining water and heat through. Serve with chicken.

Fresh Corn & Tomato Fettuccine

This recipe combines whole wheat pasta with the best of fresh garden produce. It's tossed with heart-healthy olive oil, and a little feta cheese gives it bite.
—**ANGELA SPENGLER** TAMPA, FL

START TO FINISH: 30 MIN. • **MAKES:** 4 SERVINGS

- 8 ounces uncooked whole wheat fettuccine
- 2 medium ears sweet corn, husks removed
- 2 teaspoons plus 2 tablespoons olive oil, divided
- ½ cup chopped sweet red pepper
- 4 green onions, chopped
- 2 medium tomatoes, chopped
- ½ teaspoon salt
- ½ teaspoon pepper
- 1 cup crumbled feta cheese
- 2 tablespoons minced fresh parsley

1. In a Dutch oven, cook fettuccine according to package directions, adding corn during the last 8 minutes of cooking.
2. Meanwhile, in a small skillet, heat 2 teaspoons oil over medium-high heat. Add red pepper and green onions; cook and stir until tender.
3. Drain pasta and corn; transfer pasta to a large bowl. Cool corn slightly; cut corn from cob and add to pasta. Add tomatoes, salt, pepper, remaining oil and the pepper mixture; toss to combine. Sprinkle with cheese and parsley.

Cheesy Chicken & Broccoli Orzo

Broccoli and rice casserole tops my family's comfort food list, but when we need something fast, this is the stuff. Chicken and veggie orzo cooked on the stovetop speeds up everything.
—MARY SHIVERS ADA, OK

START TO FINISH: 30 MIN.
MAKES: 6 SERVINGS

- 1¼ cups uncooked orzo pasta
- 2 packages (10 ounces each) frozen broccoli with cheese sauce
- 2 tablespoons butter
- 1½ pounds boneless skinless chicken breasts, cut into ½-inch cubes
- 1 medium onion, chopped
- ¾ teaspoon salt
- ½ teaspoon pepper

1. Cook orzo according to package directions. Meanwhile, heat broccoli with cheese sauce according to the package directions.
2. In a large skillet, heat butter over medium heat. Add chicken, onion, salt and pepper; cook and stir 6-8 minutes or until chicken is no longer pink and onion is tender. Drain orzo. Stir orzo and broccoli with cheese sauce into skillet; heat through.

Shrimp Lettuce Wraps

Lettuce forms a crispy shell that's full of possibilities, depending on what's in your fridge. Swap shrimp for cooked chicken, pork or tofu. Mix in any veggies you want: Carrots, broccoli, snow peas and chopped zucchini are all fantastic add-ins.
—*TASTE OF HOME* TEST KITCHEN

START TO FINISH: 30 MIN.
MAKES: 4 SERVINGS

- ¼ cup reduced-sodium soy sauce
- 3 tablespoons lime juice
- 2 tablespoons plus 1 teaspoon apricot preserves
- 2 tablespoons water
- 2 garlic cloves, minced
- ¼ teaspoon ground ginger
- 1 large sweet red pepper, chopped
- 2 medium carrots
- 6 green onions
- 3 teaspoons olive oil, divided
- 1 pound uncooked medium shrimp, peeled and deveined
- 2 cups hot cooked rice
- 8 large lettuce leaves

1. In a small bowl, mix the first six ingredients. Using a vegetable peeler, shave carrots lengthwise into very thin strips. Slice the white parts of the green onions; cut each green top in half lengthwise.
2. In a large skillet, heat 2 teaspoons oil over medium-high heat. Add shrimp; stir-fry until shrimp turn pink. Remove from pan.
3. Stir-fry the red pepper and carrots in remaining oil for 4 minutes. Add the white parts of the onions; stir-fry 1-2 minutes longer or until the vegetables are crisp-tender.
4. Add ⅓ cup soy sauce mixture to pan. Bring to a boil. Add shrimp; heat through. Place ¼ cup rice on each lettuce leaf; top with ½ cup shrimp mixture. Drizzle with remaining soy sauce mixture and roll up. Tie each with a green onion strip.

Spicy Tilapia Rice Bowl

I love eating well, and tilapia is a staple in my kitchen. Fresh vegetables are always good but take more prep time, so I like the frozen veggie blend here.

—ROSALIN JOHNSON TUPELO, MS

START TO FINISH: 30 MIN.
MAKES: 4 SERVINGS

- 4 tilapia fillets (4 ounces each)
- 1¼ teaspoons Cajun seasoning
- 3 tablespoons olive oil, divided
- 1 medium yellow summer squash, halved lengthwise and sliced
- 1 package (16 ounces) frozen pepper and onion stir-fry blend
- 1 can (14½ ounces) diced tomatoes, drained
- 1 envelope fajita seasoning mix
- 1 can (15 ounces) black beans, rinsed and drained
- ⅛ teaspoon salt
- ⅛ teaspoon pepper
- 3 cups hot cooked brown rice
    Optional toppings: cubed avocado, sour cream and salsa

1. Sprinkle the fillets with Cajun seasoning. In a large skillet, heat 2 tablespoons oil over medium heat. Add fillets; cook 4-6 minutes on each side or until fish just begins to flake easily with a fork. Remove and keep warm. Wipe pan clean.

2. In same skillet, heat remaining oil. Add squash; cook and stir 3 minutes. Add stir-fry blend and tomatoes; cook 6-8 minutes longer or until vegetables are tender. Stir in fajita seasoning mix; cook and stir 1-2 minutes longer or until slightly thickened.

3. In a small bowl, mix the beans, salt and pepper. Divide the rice among four serving bowls; layer with beans, vegetables and fillets. Serve with toppings as desired.

Contest Winner

Dressed-Up Meatballs

For a last-minute meal, I put together meatballs, veggies, and sweet and sour sauce. Popped in the microwave, they're a lifesaver and wonderful.

—IVY ERESMAS DADE CITY, FL

START TO FINISH: 20 MIN.
MAKES: 8 SERVINGS

- 2 pounds frozen fully cooked homestyle meatballs, thawed
- 2 medium carrots, julienned
- 1 small onion, halved and sliced
- 1 small green pepper, julienned
- 1 garlic clove, minced
- 1 jar (10 ounces) sweet-and-sour sauce
- 4½ teaspoons soy sauce
    Hot cooked rice

1. Place the meatballs in a 3-qt. microwave-safe dish; top with carrots, onion, pepper and garlic. In a small bowl, mix sweet-and-sour sauce and soy sauce; pour over meatballs.

2. Microwave, covered, on high for 6-8 minutes or until the vegetables are tender and the meatballs are heated through, stirring twice. Serve with the rice.

NOTE *This recipe was tested in a 1,100-watt microwave.*

Chicken Sausage & Gnocchi Skillet

I had a bunch of fresh veggies and combined them with sausage, gnocchi and goat cheese when I needed a quick dinner. Mix and match the ingredients you have on hand to give it your own spin.
—**DAHLIA ABRAMS** DETROIT, MI

START TO FINISH: 30 MIN. • **MAKES:** 4 SERVINGS

- 1 package (16 ounces) potato gnocchi
- 1 tablespoon butter
- 1 tablespoon olive oil
- 2 fully cooked Italian chicken sausage links (3 ounces each), sliced
- ½ pound sliced baby portobello mushrooms
- 1 medium onion, finely chopped
- 1 pound fresh asparagus, trimmed and cut into ½-inch pieces
- 2 garlic cloves, minced
- 2 tablespoons white wine or chicken broth
- 2 ounces herbed fresh goat cheese
- 2 tablespoons minced fresh basil or 2 teaspoons dried basil
- 1 tablespoon lemon juice
- ¼ teaspoon salt
- ⅛ teaspoon pepper
  Grated Parmesan cheese

1. Cook gnocchi according to package directions; drain. Meanwhile, in a large skillet, heat the butter and oil over medium-high heat. Add sausage, mushrooms and onion; cook and stir until sausage is browned and vegetables are tender. Add the asparagus and garlic; cook and stir for 2-3 minutes longer.

2. Stir in wine. Bring to a boil; cook until liquid is almost evaporated. Add goat cheese, basil, lemon juice, salt and pepper. Stir in gnocchi; heat through. Sprinkle with Parmesan cheese.

Angel Hair with Chicken & Cherries

Nutmeg is the secret something that really makes this dish. My vegetarian friend likes it just as much without the chicken.
—**MARY ANN SANDER** CENTRALIA, MO

START TO FINISH: 30 MIN. • **MAKES:** 4 SERVINGS

- 8 ounces uncooked multigrain angel hair pasta
- ¾ pound boneless skinless chicken breasts, cut into ½-inch cubes
- 1 tablespoon cornstarch
- ½ teaspoon salt
- ⅛ teaspoon pepper
- 1 tablespoon olive oil
- 1 package (6 ounces) fresh baby spinach
- ½ cup dried cherries
- ¼ teaspoon ground nutmeg
- ½ cup shredded Parmesan cheese
- ⅓ cup chopped pecans, toasted
- ¼ cup pine nuts, toasted

1. Cook the pasta according to package directions.

2. Meanwhile, in a small bowl, toss chicken with cornstarch, salt and pepper. In a large nonstick skillet, heat the oil over medium-high heat. Add chicken mixture; cook and stir until chicken is no longer pink. Stir in spinach and cherries; cook 3-4 minutes longer or until spinach is wilted.

3. Drain the pasta, reserving ¾ cup pasta water. Place pasta in a large bowl; sprinkle with nutmeg and toss to combine, adding enough reserved pasta water to moisten pasta. Serve with chicken mixture. Sprinkle with cheese and nuts.

NOTE *To toast nuts, bake in a shallow pan in a 350° oven for 5-10 minutes or cook in a skillet over low heat until lightly browned, stirring occasionally.*

Weeknight Cabbage Kielbasa Skillet

I like the challenge of cooking lighter meals that pack big flavor. This one, which came from a dear friend, does the trick. My son rated it a 10 out of 10!

—**BEVERLY BATTY** FOREST LAKE, MN

START TO FINISH: 30 MIN. • **MAKES:** 4 SERVINGS

- 1½ teaspoons cornstarch
- ¼ cup cider vinegar
- 1 tablespoon honey
- 1 teaspoon Dijon mustard
- ¼ teaspoon salt
- ¼ teaspoon pepper
- 1 tablespoon canola oil
- 1 package (14 ounces) smoked turkey kielbasa, cut into ¼-inch slices
- 2 medium red potatoes (about 8 ounces), cut into ½-inch cubes
- ½ cup sliced sweet onion
- ½ cup chopped sweet red pepper
- 4 bacon strips, cooked and crumbled
- ½ cup water
- 1 teaspoon beef bouillon granules
- 1 package (14 ounces) coleslaw mix

1. In a small bowl, whisk the first six ingredients until smooth. In a large skillet, heat oil over medium-high heat. Add kielbasa, potatoes, onion, red pepper and bacon; cook and stir 3-5 minutes or until kielbasa is lightly browned.
2. Add water and bouillon; bring to a boil. Reduce heat; simmer, covered, 6-8 minutes or until potatoes are almost tender. Add coleslaw; cook, covered, 4-6 minutes longer or until tender, stirring occasionally.
3. Stir cornstarch mixture and add to pan. Bring to a boil; cook and stir 1-2 minutes or until sauce is thickened.

Almond Chicken Salad

My mother used to prepare this salad for an evening meal during the hot summer months. It also serves well as a quick luncheon or potluck dish. You can't beat the tasty combination of chicken, grapes and almonds.

—**KATHY KITTELL** LENEXA, KS

START TO FINISH: 15 MIN. • **MAKES:** 6-8 SERVINGS

- 4 cups cubed cooked chicken
- 1½ cups seedless green grapes, halved
- 1 cup chopped celery
- ¾ cup sliced green onions
- 3 hard-cooked large eggs, chopped
- ½ cup Miracle Whip
- ¼ cup sour cream
- 1 tablespoon prepared mustard
- 1 teaspoon salt
- ½ teaspoon pepper
- ¼ teaspoon onion powder
- ¼ teaspoon celery salt
- ⅛ teaspoon ground mustard
- ⅛ teaspoon paprika
- ½ cup slivered almonds, toasted
- 1 kiwifruit, peeled and sliced, optional

1. In a large bowl, combine the chicken, grapes, celery, onions and eggs. In another bowl, combine the next nine ingredients; stir until smooth.
2. Pour over the chicken mixture and toss gently. Stir in almonds and serve immediately, or refrigerate and add the almonds just before serving. Garnish with kiwi if desired.

Contest Winner

COOKING FOR TWO

When you want a recipe that starts small and doesn't leave you with leftovers for days, turn here. These scaled-down dishes perfectly serve a duo without much fuss!

Lemon & Garlic New Potatoes for Two

This is a simplified version of a dish my Costa Rican host sister used to make when I was in the Peace Corps. It has become a favorite side dish at my house ever since.
—**KATIE BARTLE** PARKVILLE, MO

START TO FINISH: 25 MIN.
MAKES: 2 SERVINGS

- ½ **pound baby red potatoes (1¾-inch wide, about 6), halved**
- 1 **tablespoon olive oil**
- 1 **garlic clove, minced**
- 2 **tablespoons shredded Parmesan cheese**
- 1 **tablespoon lemon juice**
- ⅛ **teaspoon salt**
- ⅛ **teaspoon pepper**

1. Place potatoes in a saucepan; add water to cover. Bring to a boil. Reduce the heat; cook, uncovered, 10-15 minutes or until tender. Drain; remove from pan.

2. In the same pan, heat the oil over medium-high heat. Return potatoes to pan; cook and stir 4-5 minutes or until lightly browned. Add the garlic; cook 1 minute longer. Remove from heat. Add the remaining ingredients; toss to combine.

Bacon & Mushroom Omelets

I had grown tired of the same breakfast meals, so I wanted to make something more interesting. This fresh omelet comes with a versatile sauce that can also be used as a nacho dip or topping, over mashed potatoes or inside burritos.
—**SUSAN KIEBOAM** STREETSBORO, OH

START TO FINISH: 25 MIN.
MAKES: 2 SERVINGS

- 3 **bacon strips, chopped**
- 4 **medium fresh mushrooms, sliced**
- 4 **large eggs**
- ¼ **teaspoon salt**
- 2 **teaspoons butter, divided**

SAUCE

- 1 **tablespoon butter**
- 1 **tablespoon all-purpose flour**
- ½ **cup 2% milk**
- 3 **tablespoons shredded cheddar cheese**
- 1 **teaspoon shredded Parmesan cheese**
- 1 **teaspoon taco seasoning**
  Optional toppings: shredded lettuce, chopped tomatoes and thinly sliced green onions

1. In a small nonstick skillet, cook bacon and mushrooms over medium heat until mushrooms are tender and bacon is crisp, stirring occasionally. Remove with a slotted spoon; drain on paper towels. Discard drippings.

2. In a small bowl, whisk the eggs and salt. In a small nonstick skillet, heat 1 teaspoon butter over medium-high heat. Pour in half of the egg mixture. The mixture should set immediately at the edges.

3. As eggs set, push cooked portions toward the center, letting uncooked eggs flow underneath. When eggs are thickened and no liquid egg remains, spoon half of the mushroom mixture on one side. Fold the omelet in half; slide it onto a plate. Repeat for the remaining omelet.

4. Meanwhile, for sauce, in a small saucepan, melt 1 tablespoon butter over medium heat. Stir in flour until smooth; gradually whisk in milk. Bring to a boil, stirring constantly; cook and stir 2-3 minutes or until thickened.

5. Stir in cheeses and taco seasoning until cheese is melted. Serve with omelets and toppings as desired.

Parmesan Herb Loaf

I turn to this savory quick bread recipe often. I like to serve warm slices of bread accompanied by individual ramekins filled with extra virgin olive oil infused with herbs for dipping.

—DIANNE CULLEY NESBIT, MS

PREP: 15 MIN. • **BAKE:** 30 MIN.
MAKES: 1 LOAF (8 SERVINGS)

- 1¼ cups all-purpose flour
- 3 tablespoons plus 1 teaspoon grated Parmesan cheese, divided
- 1½ teaspoons sugar
- 1½ teaspoons dried minced onion
- 1¼ teaspoons Italian seasoning, divided
- ½ teaspoon baking powder
- ¼ teaspoon baking soda
- ¼ teaspoon salt
- ½ cup sour cream
- 2 tablespoons plus 2 teaspoons 2% milk
- 4½ teaspoons butter, melted
- 1 large egg white, lightly beaten

1. In a small bowl, combine the flour, 3 tablespoons Parmesan cheese, sugar, onion, 1 teaspoon Italian seasoning, baking powder, baking soda and salt. In another bowl, whisk sour cream, milk and butter. Stir into the dry ingredients just until moistened.

2. Turn onto a floured surface; knead for 1 minute. Shape into a round loaf; place on a baking sheet coated with cooking spray. With kitchen scissors, cut a ¼-in.-deep cross in the top of the loaf. Brush it with the egg white. Sprinkle with the remaining cheese and Italian seasoning.

3. Bake at 350° for 30-35 minutes or until golden brown. Serve warm.

Parmesan Crisp Baked Apples

A friend and I wanted to make an easy apple crisp. We made a Parmesan filling, stuffed the apples and baked them whole. It's pure genius, we think!

—SUSAN STETZEL GAINESVILLE, NY

START TO FINISH: 25 MIN.
MAKES: 2 SERVINGS

- 2 small Braeburn or Gala apples
- ¼ cup grated Parmesan cheese
- 3 tablespoons quick-cooking oats
- 2 tablespoons all-purpose flour
- 2 tablespoons brown sugar
  Dash ground nutmeg
- 1 tablespoon butter, melted
  Honey, optional

1. Preheat oven to 350°. Cut a ¼-in. slice off top of each apple. Core apples, leaving the bottoms intact; place in a microwave-safe 8-in. square baking dish. Microwave, covered, 3-4 minutes or until tender.

2. In a small bowl, mix cheese, oats, flour, brown sugar and nutmeg; stir in melted butter until crumbly. Carefully fill apples with oat mixture. Bake, uncovered, 12-15 minutes or until topping is golden brown. If desired, drizzle with honey.

Contest Winner

Couscous Tabbouleh with Fresh Mint & Feta

Using couscous instead of bulgur for tabbouleh really speeds up the process of making this colorful salad. Other quick-cooking grains such as barley or quinoa work well, too.

—**ELODIE ROSINOVSKY** BRIGHTON, MA

START TO FINISH: 20 MIN. • **MAKES:** 2 SERVINGS

- ¾ cup water
- ½ cup uncooked couscous
- 1 can (15 ounces) chickpeas, rinsed and drained
- 1 large tomato, chopped
- ½ English cucumber, halved and thinly sliced
- 3 tablespoons lemon juice
- 2 teaspoons grated lemon peel
- 2 teaspoons olive oil
- 2 teaspoons minced fresh mint
- 2 teaspoons minced fresh parsley
- ¼ teaspoon salt
- ⅛ teaspoon pepper
- ¾ cup crumbled feta cheese

1. In a small saucepan, bring water to a boil. Stir in the couscous. Remove from the heat; cover and let stand for 5-8 minutes or until water is absorbed. Fluff with a fork.
2. In a large bowl, combine beans, tomato and cucumber. In a small bowl, whisk the lemon juice, lemon peel, oil and seasonings. Drizzle over the bean mixture. Add couscous; toss to combine. Serve immediately or refrigerate until chilled. Sprinkle with cheese before serving.

Marinated Asparagus with Blue Cheese

Asparagus marinated in vinaigrette and dotted with cheese makes an awesome side. We're blue cheese fans, but you might like Parmesan or feta.

—**SUSAN VAITH** JACKSONVILLE, FL

PREP: 20 MIN. + MARINATING • **MAKES:** 4 SERVINGS

- 1 pound fresh asparagus, trimmed
- 4 green onions, thinly sliced
- ¼ cup olive oil
- 2 tablespoons white wine vinegar
- 1 garlic clove, minced
- ½ teaspoon salt
- ¼ teaspoon pepper
- ½ cup crumbled blue cheese

1. In a large saucepan, bring 6 cups water to a boil. Add asparagus; cook, uncovered, 2-3 minutes or just until crisp-tender. Remove the asparagus and immediately drop into ice water. Drain and pat dry.
2. In a large resealable plastic bag, combine green onions, oil, vinegar, garlic, salt and pepper. Add asparagus; seal bag and turn to coat. Refrigerate at least 1 hour.
3. Drain asparagus, discarding marinade. Place asparagus on a serving plate; sprinkle with cheese.

> ### USE ALL OF THE ASPARAGUS
> Don't throw away those tough ends when trimming fresh asparagus. Cook and drain the ends, then puree them with a bit of water or chicken broth in a blender until the mixture is smooth. Freeze for future use in a variety of soups and casseroles.
> —**PAULINE S.** MOUNT MORRIS, MI

1. In a small saucepan, heat cream until bubbles form around sides of pan. In a small bowl, whisk the egg yolks, brown sugar and cinnamon. Remove cream from the heat; stir a small amount of hot cream into egg mixture. Return all to the pan, stirring constantly. Stir in maple flavoring.
2. Transfer to three 6-oz. ramekins or custard cups. Place in a 6-qt. slow cooker; add 1 in. of boiling water to the slow cooker. Cover and cook on high for 2 to 2½ hours or until centers are just set (mixture will jiggle). Carefully remove the ramekins from slow cooker; cool for 10 minutes. Cover and refrigerate for at least 4 hours.
3. For topping, combine the sugar and brown sugar. If using a creme brulee torch, sprinkle the custards with the sugar mixture. Heat the sugar with the torch until caramelized. Serve immediately.
4. If broiling the custards, place ramekins on a baking sheet; let them stand at room temperature for 15 minutes. Sprinkle with sugar mixture. Broil 8 in. from the heat for 3-5 minutes or until the sugar is caramelized. Refrigerate for 1-2 hours or until firm.

Hearty Asian Lettuce Salad

It may sound surprising, but this meatless version of your favorite restaurant salad packs in 13 grams of protein and is bursting with juicy flavor.
—*TASTE OF HOME* TEST KITCHEN

START TO FINISH: 20 MIN. • **MAKES:** 2 SERVINGS

- 1 cup ready-to-serve brown rice
- 1 cup frozen shelled edamame
- 3 cups spring mix salad greens
- ¼ cup reduced-fat sesame ginger salad dressing
- 1 medium navel orange, peeled and sectioned
- 4 radishes, sliced
- 2 tablespoons sliced almonds, toasted

1. Prepare the rice and edamame according to the package directions.
2. In a large bowl, combine the salad greens, rice and edamame. Drizzle with salad dressing and toss to coat. Divide salad mixture between two plates; top with orange segments, radishes and almonds.

Maple Creme Brulee

The slow cooker is the perfect way to cook a classic dessert creme brulee. The crunchy brown sugar topping is wonderful, and the custard is smooth and creamy.
—*TASTE OF HOME* TEST KITCHEN

PREP: 20 MIN. • **COOK:** 2 HOURS + CHILLING
MAKES: 3 SERVINGS

- 1⅓ cups heavy whipping cream
- 3 large egg yolks
- ½ cup packed brown sugar
- ¼ teaspoon ground cinnamon
- ½ teaspoon maple flavoring
TOPPING
- 1½ teaspoons sugar
- 1½ teaspoons brown sugar

Easy Baked Potato Casserole

This potato salad looks like you've fussed for hours, but only you have to know how quickly it was put together.
—**DEBBIE JOHNSON** CENTERTOWN, MO

START TO FINISH: 30 MIN. • **MAKES:** 2 SERVINGS

- 1½ cups frozen O'Brien potatoes, thawed
- 2 teaspoons canola oil
- ½ cup shredded cheddar-Monterey Jack cheese, divided
- 2 bacon strips, cooked and crumbled
- 2 tablespoons mayonnaise
- ½ teaspoon prepared mustard

1. In a small skillet, saute potatoes in oil until lightly browned. Remove from the heat; stir in ⅓ cup cheese, bacon, mayonnaise and mustard.
2. Transfer to an ungreased 3-cup baking dish. Bake, uncovered, at 375° for 15-20 minutes or until cheese is melted. Sprinkle with remaining cheese.

Spinach & Feta Saute

With just the right level of garlic and a pleasant mix of cheese and almonds, this side will brighten any plate. You could also try it stuffed in a filet—the possibilities are endless.

—SHARON DELANEY-CHRONIS
SOUTH MILWAUKEE, WI

START TO FINISH: 10 MIN.
MAKES: 2 SERVINGS

- 2 garlic cloves, minced
- 2 tablespoons olive oil
- 1 package (6 ounces) fresh baby spinach
- ¼ cup slivered almonds
- ½ cup crumbled feta cheese

In a large skillet, saute garlic in oil for 1 minute. Add the spinach and almonds; saute 2 minutes longer or just until spinach is wilted. Sprinkle with feta cheese.

Roasted Red Pepper Pasta Topper

Give ordinary plain pasta and sauce a big boost in just 5 minutes with this zippy topping.

—KAREN BERNER NEW CANAAN, CT

START TO FINISH: 5 MIN.
MAKES: 1 SERVING

- 3 tablespoons chopped roasted sweet red peppers
- 1 tablespoon chopped fresh parsley
  Dash crushed red pepper flakes
  Hot cooked pasta
  Pasta sauce, optional

Toss peppers with parsley and pepper flakes. Sprinkle over pasta and, if desired, sauce.

FREEZE PARSLEY

To prevent fresh parsley from spoiling before I get a chance to use it all, I place washed sprigs in an ice cube tray, then fill the tray with water. After the cubes are frozen, I store them in a freezer bag. Then I can take out a few cubes whenever needed and drop them in soups and stews.

—SHERRI K.
GRAND JUNCTION, CO

Smoked Salmon Quesadillas with Creamy Chipotle Sauce

These quesadillas taste extra-special, but they take just minutes to make. A fresh burst of chopped fresh cilantro is the perfect finishing touch.

—DANIEL SHEMTOB IRVINE, CA

START TO FINISH: 25 MIN.
MAKES: 3 SERVINGS (⅔ CUP SAUCE)

- ½ cup creme fraiche or sour cream
- 2 tablespoons minced chipotle peppers in adobo sauce
- 2 tablespoons lime juice
- ⅛ teaspoon salt
- ⅛ teaspoon pepper

QUESADILLAS

- ¼ cup cream cheese, softened
- 2 ounces fresh goat cheese
- 3 flour tortillas (8 inches)
- 3 ounces smoked salmon or lox, chopped
- ¼ cup finely chopped shallots
- ¼ cup finely chopped roasted sweet red pepper
  Coarsely chopped fresh cilantro

1. In a small bowl, mix the first five ingredients. In another bowl, mix cream cheese and goat cheese until blended; spread over tortillas. Top half side of each with the salmon, shallots and red pepper; fold over.
2. Place the quesadillas on a greased griddle. Cook them over medium heat for 1-2 minutes on each side or until they are lightly browned and the cheeses are melted. Serve with sauce; top with cilantro.

Couscous & Sausage-Stuffed Acorn Squash

If you have a tiny apartment, zero counter space and only two people to feed, cumbersome meals are out. This acorn squash with couscous is just the right size.
—JESSICA LEVINSON NYACK, NY

START TO FINISH: 25 MIN.
MAKES: 2 SERVINGS

- 1 medium acorn squash (about 1½ pounds)
- ¼ teaspoon salt
- ¼ teaspoon pepper
- 1 tablespoon olive oil
- 1 medium onion, chopped
- 2 fully cooked spinach and feta chicken sausage links (3 ounces each), sliced
- ½ cup chicken stock
- ½ cup uncooked couscous
   Crumbled feta cheese, optional

1. Cut squash lengthwise in half; remove and discard seeds. Sprinkle the squash with salt and pepper; place in a microwave-safe dish, cut side down. Microwave, covered, on high for 10-12 minutes or until tender.

2. Meanwhile, in a large skillet, heat oil over medium heat. Add onion; cook and stir 5-7 minutes or until tender and lightly browned. Add sausage; cook and stir 2-3 minutes or until lightly browned.

3. Add stock; bring to a boil. Stir in couscous. Remove from heat; let stand, covered, 5 minutes or until stock is absorbed. Spoon over squash. If desired, top with feta cheese.

Southwest Tortilla Scramble

Here's my version of a deconstructed breakfast burrito that is actually good for you. Go for hefty corn tortillas in this recipe because the flour ones can get lost in the scramble.
—CHRISTINE SCHENHER EXETER, CA

START TO FINISH: 15 MIN.
MAKES: 2 SERVINGS

- 4 large egg whites
- 2 large eggs
- ¼ teaspoon pepper
- 2 corn tortillas (6 inches), halved and cut into strips
- ¼ cup chopped fresh spinach
- 2 tablespoons shredded reduced-fat cheddar cheese
- ¼ cup salsa

1. In a large bowl, whisk egg whites, eggs and pepper. Stir in tortillas, spinach and cheese.

2. Heat a large skillet that is coated with cooking spray over medium heat. Pour in the egg mixture; cook and stir until eggs are thickened and no liquid egg remains. Top with salsa.

SIT BACK AND SIP

Tired of the same ol' drink choices? Quench your thirst in the most delicious way possible—these tasty beverages provide a boost morning, noon or night!

A.M. Rush Espresso Smoothie

Want an early morning pick-me-up that's good for you, too? Fruit and flaxseed give this sweet espresso a nutritious twist while filling you up, too.
—**AIMEE WILSON** CLOVIS, CA

START TO FINISH: 10 MIN. • **MAKES:** 1 SERVING

- ½ cup cold fat-free milk
- 1 tablespoon vanilla flavoring syrup
- 1 cup ice cubes
- ½ medium banana, cut up
- 1 to 2 teaspoons instant espresso powder
- 1 teaspoon ground flaxseed
- 1 teaspoon baking cocoa

In a blender, combine all the ingredients; cover and process for 1-2 minutes or until blended. Pour into a chilled glass; serve immediately.
NOTE *This recipe was tested with Torani brand flavoring syrup. Look for it in the coffee section.*

Black-Eyed Susan

The Kentucky Derby has the mint julep; the Preakness has the Black-Eyed Susan. The drink is a sunny mix of vodka, rum, pineapple and orange juices to toast your special events.
—*TASTE OF HOME* **TEST KITCHEN**

START TO FINISH: 5 MIN. • **MAKES:** 1 SERVING

- ½ to ¾ cup crushed ice
- 1 ounce vodka
- 1 ounce light rum
- ½ ounce Triple Sec
- 2 ounces unsweetened pineapple juice
- 2 ounces orange juice
  Lime slice and pitted sweet dark cherry

Place desired amount of ice in a rocks glass. Pour vodka, rum, Triple Sec and juices into glass. Stir; serve with a lime slice and cherry.

Layered Italian Soda

Italian sodas are fun, and your gang will love them. Try making the sodas with differently flavored syrups, or even topping off each glass with a shot of whipped cream and a cherry.

—*TASTE OF HOME* TEST KITCHEN

START TO FINISH: 5 MIN. • **MAKES:** 2 SERVINGS

- ¼ cup black currant or blackberry flavoring syrup
- ½ cup orange juice
- 1⅓ cups carbonated water, chilled

Place 2 tablespoons syrup in each of two tall glasses. Layer each glass with ¼ cup orange juice and ⅔ cup carbonated water, slowly pouring down inside of tilted glass to keep layers separated. Serve immediately.

NOTE *This recipe was tested with Torani brand flavoring syrup. Look for it in the coffee section.*

Thin Mint Milk Shake

Save a sleeve of those yummy chocolate-mint Girl Scout cookies to use for creamy milk shakes. They go over big with kids and adults alike.

—**SHAUNA SEVER** SAN FRANCISCO, CA

START TO FINISH: 5 MIN. • **MAKES:** 2 SERVINGS

- 3 tablespoons creme de menthe or 3 tablespoons 2% milk plus a dash of peppermint extract
- 1¼ to 1½ cups vanilla ice cream
- 7 Girl Scout Thin Mint cookies
  Green food coloring, optional

Place all ingredients in a blender in order listed; cover and process until blended. Serve immediately.

Ginger-Kale Smoothies

Since I started drinking these spiced-up smoothies for breakfast every day, I honestly feel better! Substitute any fruit and juice you like to make this recipe your own blend.

—**LINDA GREEN** KILAUEA, HI

START TO FINISH: 15 MIN. • **MAKES:** 2 SERVINGS

- 1¼ cups orange juice
- 1 teaspoon lemon juice
- 2 cups torn fresh kale
- 1 medium apple, peeled and coarsely chopped
- 1 tablespoon minced fresh gingerroot
- 4 ice cubes
- ⅛ teaspoon ground cinnamon
- ⅛ teaspoon ground turmeric or ¼-inch piece fresh turmeric, peeled and finely chopped
  Dash cayenne pepper

Place all ingredients in a blender; cover and process until blended. Serve immediately.

Grilled Salmon Packets for Two

Cleanup's a snap with this convenient dish that is prepared and cooked in a foil wrapper. It's a welcome quick fix during a hectic week.

—**TIM WEBER** BETTENDORF, IA

START TO FINISH: 25 MIN.
MAKES: 2 SERVINGS

- 2 **salmon steaks (6 ounces each)**
- ½ **teaspoon lemon-pepper seasoning**
- ½ **cup shredded carrots**
- ¼ **cup julienned sweet yellow pepper**
- ¼ **cup julienned green pepper**
- 2 **teaspoons lemon juice**
- ½ **teaspoon dried parsley flakes**
- ¼ **teaspoon salt**
- ⅛ **teaspoon pepper**

1. Sprinkle the salmon with lemon-pepper. Place each salmon steak on a double thickness of heavy-duty foil (about 12 in. square). Top the steaks with carrots and peppers. Sprinkle with remaining ingredients.
2. Fold foil around fish and seal tightly. Grill, covered, over medium heat for 15-20 minutes or until fish flakes easily with a fork.

Quick Crab Melts

Two types of cheese melted over a savory crab mixture make these sandwiches amazing. I usually serve them for dinner, but they make terrific appetizers when you cut them in half.

—**DONNA BENNETT** BRAMALEA, ON

START TO FINISH: 15 MIN.
MAKES: 2 SERVINGS

- 1 **can (6 ounces) crabmeat, drained, flaked and cartilage removed**
- 3 **tablespoons mayonnaise**
- 5 **teaspoons finely chopped celery**
- 1 **tablespoon minced green onion**
- 2 **English muffins, split**
- 4 **slices tomato**
- 4 **thin slices cheddar cheese**
- 4 **thin slices Monterey Jack cheese**
  Paprika

1. Preheat broiler. In a small bowl, mix crab, mayonnaise, celery and green onion until blended. Place muffin halves on an ungreased baking sheet.
2. Broil 4-6 in. from heat until toasted. Spread with crab mixture. Top with tomato and cheeses; sprinkle with paprika. Broil until bubbly.

Michigan Fruit Baked Oatmeal

Whole-grain oatmeal is a delicious way to start each day. For a change, try swapping chunks of Granny Smith apples for the dried fruit. The leftovers warm up well in the microwave.

—**JEANETTE KASS** RAVENNA, MI

PREP: 15 MIN. • **BAKE:** 45 MIN.
MAKES: 3 SERVINGS

- 1 **cup old-fashioned oats**
- ¼ **cup dried cranberries or cherries**
- 1 **tablespoon brown sugar**
- 2 **cups fat-free milk**
- ½ **cup chunky applesauce**
- ¼ **teaspoon almond extract**
- 2 **tablespoons sliced almonds**
  Optional toppings: vanilla yogurt and additional dried cranberries and sliced almonds

1. In a large bowl, combine the first six ingredients. Transfer to a 3-cup baking dish coated with cooking spray; sprinkle with almonds.
2. Bake, uncovered, at 350° for 45-50 minutes or until set. Serve with toppings if desired.

Apple-Bacon Egg Bake

I wanted a healthy egg dish for Sunday brunch, so I came up with this recipe. It's hearty and savory, and the apples give it a slight sweetness.
—**NANCY MILLER** BETTENDORF, IA

PREP: 15 MIN. • **BAKE:** 30 MIN.
MAKES: 2 SERVINGS

- 3 **large eggs**
- 1 **small apple, diced**
- ¾ **cup frozen O'Brien potatoes, thawed**
- ⅓ **cup 2% milk**
- ⅓ **cup sour cream**
- ⅓ **cup shredded cheddar cheese, divided**
- 3 **bacon strips, cooked and crumbled, divided**
  Dash salt and pepper

1. In a small bowl, beat eggs. Stir in apple, hash browns, milk, sour cream, 3 tablespoons cheese, 1 tablespoon bacon, salt and pepper.
2. Pour into two 2-cup baking dishes coated with cooking spray. Sprinkle with remaining cheese and bacon.
3. Bake, uncovered, at 350° for 30-35 minutes or until a knife inserted near the center comes out clean.

Turkey Florentine Sandwiches

Why not give your old turkey sandwich an upgrade? Here, the lunchtime classic becomes a dinnertime feast with a few simple tweaks.
—**KAREL REYNOLDS** RUTHERFORDTON, NC

START TO FINISH: 20 MIN.
MAKES: 2 SERVINGS

- ½ **cup sliced fresh mushrooms**
- 2 **teaspoons olive oil**
- 1 **cup fresh baby spinach**
- 2 **garlic cloves, minced**
- 4 **ounces sliced deli turkey breast**
- 2 **slices part-skim mozzarella cheese**
- 4 **slices whole wheat bread**
  Cooking spray

1. In a small nonstick skillet, saute the mushrooms in oil until they are tender. Add the spinach and garlic; cook 1 minute longer.
2. Layer the spinach mixture, turkey and cheese on two bread slices; top with remaining bread. Spritz outsides of the sandwiches with cooking spray. Cook on a panini maker or indoor grill for 4-5 minutes or until the bread is browned and cheese is melted.

Berries with Vanilla Custard for Two

What a simple, delectable way to enjoy fresh raspberries. For a change, also try the custard with strawberries or peaches.
—**SARAH VASQUES** MILFORD, NH

PREP: 20 MIN. + CHILLING
MAKES: 2 SERVINGS

- ½ **cup half-and-half cream**
- 1 **large egg yolk**
- 1 **tablespoon sugar**
- 1 **teaspoon vanilla extract**
- 1 **cup fresh raspberries**

In a small saucepan, combine the cream, egg yolk and sugar. Cook and stir over medium heat until mixture reaches 160° and is thick enough to coat the back of a spoon. Remove from the heat; stir in vanilla. Chill until serving. Serve with raspberries.

Contest Winner

Contest Winner

Ham & Egg Pita Pockets

I made these one day when the kids were running late for school and I needed a quick and healthy portable breakfast. The eggs cook quickly in the microwave, and the sandwiches are ready to eat in 10 minutes.

—**SUE OLSEN** FREMONT, CA

START TO FINISH: 10 MIN. • **MAKES:** 1 SERVING

- 2 large egg whites
- 1 large egg
- ⅛ teaspoon smoked or plain paprika
- ⅛ teaspoon freshly ground pepper
- 1 slice deli ham, chopped
- 1 green onion, sliced
- 2 tablespoons shredded reduced-fat cheddar cheese
- 2 whole wheat pita pocket halves

In a microwave-safe bowl, whisk egg whites, egg, paprika and pepper until blended; stir in ham, green onion and cheese. Microwave, covered, on high for 1 minute. Stir; cook on high 30-60 seconds longer or until the blend is almost set. Serve in pitas.

NOTE *This recipe was tested in a 1,100-watt microwave.*

FUNNEL FUN

A small funnel comes in handy for separating egg whites from the yolks. Break the egg over the funnel; the white will run through the funnel while the yolk will remain.
—**ALICE N.** REED CITY, MI

Italian Sausage Minestrone for Two

Bundle up from the cold with this no-fuss minestrone. You can substitute a can of butter beans or pinto beans for one of the cans of cannellini beans.

—**ELIZABETH RENTERIA** VANCOUVER, WA

PREP: 20 MIN. + FREEZING • **COOK:** 1¼ HOURS
MAKES: 3 CUPS

- ¼ pound bulk Italian sausage
- ⅓ cup chopped carrot
- ¼ cup chopped celery
- 3 tablespoons chopped onion
- 1 garlic cloves, minced
- 2¼ teaspoons olive oil
- 1¾ cups reduced-sodium chicken broth
- ¾ cup cannellini beans, rinsed and drained
- ¾ cup undrained fire-roasted diced tomatoes
- 1 bay leaf
- ¾ teaspoon Italian seasoning
- ¾ teaspoon tomato paste
- ¼ cup ditalini or other small pasta
  Shredded or shaved Parmesan cheese

1. In a Dutch oven, cook sausage over medium heat until no longer pink; drain.

2. In the same pan, saute the carrots, celery, onion and garlic in oil until tender. Stir in the broth, beans, tomatoes, bay leaf, Italian seasoning, tomato paste and sausage. Bring to a boil. Reduce heat; cover and simmer for 30 minutes.

3. Stir in ditalini; return to a boil. Reduce heat and cook, uncovered, for 6-8 minutes or until pasta is tender. Discard bay leaf. Serve with cheese.

Mahogany-Glazed Cornish Hens

I make this for my husband and myself for Thanksgiving dinner. It's an elegant tradition custom fit for two.
—**JEANNETTE SABO** LEXINGTON PARK, MD

PREP: 15 MIN. • **BAKE:** 20 MIN. • **MAKES:** 2 SERVINGS

- 1 Cornish game hen (20 to 24 ounces), split lengthwise
- 1 tablespoon butter
- ½ teaspoon minced fresh gingerroot
- ½ teaspoon grated orange peel
- 2 tablespoons apricot preserves
- 1 tablespoon balsamic vinegar
- 1 tablespoon reduced-sodium soy sauce
- 2 teaspoons Dijon mustard
- ¼ teaspoon salt
- ⅛ teaspoon pepper
- 1 to 1½ cups chicken broth, divided

1. Preheat oven to 450°. Place hen in a greased shallow roasting pan, skin side up. Combine butter, ginger and orange peel; rub under skin.

2. In a small bowl, whisk preserves, vinegar, soy sauce and mustard. Reserve half of the mixture for basting. Spoon remaining mixture over hen; sprinkle with salt and pepper. Pour ½ cup chicken broth into pan.

3. Roast 20-25 minutes or until a thermometer inserted in thigh reads 180°, adding broth to pan as necessary and basting with remaining glaze halfway through cooking. Serve with pan juices.

Honey Mustard Green Beans

I love fresh beans, but was getting tired of just steaming and eating them plain. So I whipped up this easy honey-mustard combination as a simple side dish.
—**CAROL TRAUPMAN-CARR** BREINIGSVILLE, PA

START TO FINISH: 20 MIN. • **MAKES:** 2 SERVINGS

- ½ pound fresh green beans, trimmed
- ¼ cup thinly sliced red onion
- 2 tablespoons spicy brown mustard
- 2 tablespoons honey
- 1 tablespoon snipped fresh dill or 1 teaspoon dill weed

1. In a large saucepan, bring 6 cups water to a boil. Add beans; cook, uncovered, 3-4 minutes or just until crisp-tender. Drain beans and immediately drop into ice water. Drain and pat dry; transfer to a small bowl.

2. In another bowl, combine onion, mustard, honey and dill. Pour over beans; toss to coat.

Day-After-Thanksgiving Turkey Stir-Fry

I work for a priest, Father Leo, who loves to cook and he shared this recipe with me. Perfect for the day after Thanksgiving or anytime there are leftovers, the dish is a fun dinner twist.

—**STEFEN LOVELACE** MARRIOTTSVILLE, MD

START TO FINISH: 30 MIN.
MAKES: 2 SERVINGS

- 1 **cup cut fresh green beans**
- 1 **small red onion, chopped**
- 1 **tablespoon peanut or canola oil**
- 1 **garlic clove, minced**
- 2 **tablespoons whole-berry cranberry sauce**
- 1 **tablespoon soy sauce**
- 1 **teaspoon white vinegar**
- ⅛ **teaspoon salt**
- ⅛ **teaspoon pepper**
- 1½ **cups cubed cooked turkey breast**
- 2 **tablespoons chopped cashews**
  Minced fresh cilantro, optional
  Hot cooked rice

1. In a large skillet, saute beans and onion in oil until tender. Add garlic; cook 1 minute longer.

2. Meanwhile, in a small bowl, combine the cranberry sauce, soy sauce, vinegar, salt and pepper; pour over bean mixture. Add the turkey; simmer, uncovered, for 4-6 minutes or until heated through. Sprinkle with cashews and, if desired, cilantro. Serve with rice.

Pork Chops with Cherry Sauce

It takes less than a half hour to create this indulgent-tasting dish. The spice rub also works well on lamb or beef.

—**KENDRA DOSS** COLORADO SPRINGS, CO

START TO FINISH: 25 MIN.
MAKES: 2 SERVINGS

- 1 **tablespoon finely chopped shallot**
- 1 **teaspoon olive oil**
- 1 **cup fresh or frozen pitted dark sweet cherries, halved**
- ⅓ **cup ruby port wine**
- 1 **teaspoon balsamic vinegar**
- ⅛ **teaspoon salt**

PORK CHOPS

- 1 **teaspoon coriander seeds, crushed**
- ¾ **teaspoon ground mustard**
- ¼ **teaspoon salt**
- ¼ **teaspoon pepper**
- 2 **bone-in pork loin chops (7 ounces each)**
- 2 **teaspoons olive oil**

1. In a small saucepan, saute shallot in oil until tender. Stir in the cherries, wine, vinegar and salt. Bring to a boil; cook until liquid is reduced by half, about 10 minutes.

2. Meanwhile, in a small bowl, combine the coriander, mustard, salt and pepper; rub over the chops. In a large skillet, cook chops in oil over medium heat for 4-5 minutes on each side or until a thermometer reads 145°. Serve with sauce.

Cucumber Dill Salad

Let this crisp, tangy salad hit the spot on warm afternoons and evenings. Sprinkling the cucumbers with salt and letting them sit draws out excess water so they stay nice and crisp.

—*TASTE OF HOME* TEST KITCHEN

PREP: 20 MIN. + CHILLING
MAKES: 3 SERVINGS

- 1 **medium cucumber, thinly sliced**
- 1½ **teaspoons kosher salt**
- ¼ **cup white vinegar**
- 2 **tablespoons snipped fresh dill**
- 4½ **teaspoons sugar**
- ¼ **teaspoon coarsely ground pepper**

1. Place cucumber slices in a colander over a plate; sprinkle with salt and toss. Let stand for 15 minutes, stirring once. Rinse and drain well.

2. In a big bowl, combine the vinegar, dill, sugar and pepper. Add cucumbers and toss to coat. Cover and refrigerate for at least 15 minutes before serving.

Mexican Shrimp Bisque

I enjoy both Cajun and Mexican cuisine, and this rich, elegant soup combines the best of both. I serve it with a crispy green salad and a glass of white wine.
—**KAREN HARRIS** LITTLETON, CO

START TO FINISH: 30 MIN.
MAKES: 3 SERVINGS

- 1 **small onion, chopped**
- 1 **tablespoon olive oil**
- 2 **garlic cloves, minced**
- 1 **tablespoon all-purpose flour**
- 1 **cup water**
- ½ **cup heavy whipping cream**
- 2 **teaspoons chicken bouillon granules**
- 1 **tablespoon chili powder**
- ½ **teaspoon ground cumin**
- ½ **teaspoon ground coriander**
- ½ **pound uncooked medium shrimp, peeled and deveined**
- ½ **cup sour cream**
    Chopped fresh cilantro and sliced avocado, optional

1. In a small saucepan, saute onion in oil until tender. Add the garlic; cook 1 minute longer. Stir in the flour until blended. Stir in water, cream, bouillon and seasonings; bring to a boil. Reduce heat; cover and simmer for 5 minutes.
2. Cut the shrimp into bite-size pieces if desired; add the shrimp to the soup.

Simmer 5-10 minutes longer or until the shrimp turn pink. Place the sour cream in a small bowl; gradually stir in ½ cup hot soup. Return all to the pan, stirring constantly. Heat through (do not boil). Top with some cilantro and avocado if desired.

Chocolate Cinnamon Toast

Are you looking for a fun dessert or snack? Cinnamon bread is toasted to perfection in a skillet, then topped with chocolate and fresh fruit. Add a small dollop of whipped cream to each slice to make it extra indulgent.
—**JEANNE AMBROSE** MILWAUKEE, WI

START TO FINISH: 10 MIN.
MAKES: 1 SERVING

- 1 **slice cinnamon bread**
- 1 **teaspoon butter, softened**
- 2 **tablespoons 60% cacao bittersweet chocolate baking chips**
    Sliced banana and strawberries, optional

Spread both sides of bread with butter. In a small skillet, toast bread over medium-high heat 2-3 minutes on each side, topping with chocolate chips after turning. Remove from heat; spread melted chocolate evenly over toast. If desired, top with fruit.

Open-Faced Egg Sandwiches

I always experiment with different herbs on my eggs, since I eat them every morning. This combination became one of my favorites!
—**VALERIE BELLEY** ST. LOUIS, MO

START TO FINISH: 15 MIN.
MAKES: 2 SERVINGS

- 4 **large egg whites**
- 2 **large eggs**
- 2 **tablespoons grated Parmesan cheese**
- 2 **teaspoons butter, softened**
- 2 **slices whole wheat bread, toasted**
- ⅛ **teaspoon dried rosemary, crushed**
- ⅛ **teaspoon pepper**

Heat a small nonstick skillet coated with cooking spray over medium-high heat. Whisk the egg whites, eggs and cheese; add them to the skillet. Cook and stir them until set. Spread butter over the toasts; top with egg mixture. Sprinkle with the rosemary and pepper. Serve immediately.

Contest Winner

SLOW COOKER

If it seems like there aren't enough hours in the day to create a comforting meal, think again! Set aside a few minutes for prep work, then go about your day and come home to a ready-made meal.

Slow Cooker Cheesy Broccoli Soup

Whenever I order soup at a restaurant, I go for the broccoli-cheese option. I put my own slow cooker to the test and made my own. It took a few tries, but now the soup is exactly how I like it.

—**KRISTEN HILLS** LAYTON, UT

PREP: 15 MIN. • **COOK:** 3 HOURS
MAKES: 4 SERVINGS

- 2 tablespoons butter
- 1 small onion, finely chopped
- 2 cups finely chopped fresh broccoli
- 3 cups reduced-sodium chicken broth
- 1 can (12 ounces) evaporated milk
- ½ teaspoon pepper
- 1 package (8 ounces) process cheese (Velveeta), cubed
- 1½ cups shredded extra-sharp cheddar cheese
- 1 cup shredded Parmesan cheese
  Additional shredded extra-sharp cheddar cheese

1. In a small skillet, heat butter over medium-high heat. Add onion; cook and stir 3-4 minutes or until tender. Transfer to a 3- or 4-qt. slow cooker. Add broccoli, broth, milk and pepper.
2. Cook, covered, on low 3-4 hours or until the broccoli is tender. Stir in the process cheese until it is melted. Add the shredded cheeses; stir until they are melted. Just before serving, stir the soup to combine. Top the servings with additional cheddar cheese.

Slow Cooker Sausage Sandwiches

This Italian sandwich started as pork chops and sausage over angel hair pasta. Now we have a handy, new slow-cooked version of a beloved family recipe.

—**DEBRA GOFORTH** NEWPORT, TN

PREP: 20 MIN. • **COOK:** 6 HOURS
MAKES: 8 SERVINGS

- 3 bone-in pork loin chops (7 ounces each)
- 4 Italian sausage links (4 ounces each)
- 1 can (28 ounces) whole plum tomatoes, undrained
- 1 can (6 ounces) tomato paste
- 1 teaspoon Italian seasoning
- 3 garlic cloves, minced
- ¼ teaspoon crushed red pepper flakes
- 1 large onion, halved and sliced
- 1 large sweet red pepper, cut into strips
- 1 large green pepper, cut into strips
- 1 jar (16 ounces) mild pickled pepper rings, drained
- 8 submarine buns, split
- 1 cup shredded Italian cheese blend

1. Place the pork chops and sausage in a 5- or 6-qt. slow cooker. Place the tomatoes, tomato paste, Italian seasoning, garlic and pepper flakes in a food processor; pulse until chunky. Pour over meats. Cook, covered, on low 4 hours.
2. Add onion and peppers to the slow cooker. Cook, covered, on low 2-3 hours longer or until pork is tender, a thermometer inserted in sausages reads 160°, and vegetables are crisp-tender. Remove pork chops and sausages from the slow cooker. Remove pork from bones; discard bones. Shred the meat with two forks and cut sausages into 2-in. pieces; return to slow cooker. Serve on buns with cheese.

Apple-Cranberry Grains

I made some changes to my diet in order to lose weight. My kids are skeptical when it comes to healthy food, but they adore these wholesome grains.

—**SHERISSE DAWE** BLACK DIAMOND, AB

PREP: 10 MIN. • **COOK:** 4 HOURS
MAKES: 10 SERVINGS

- 2 medium apples, peeled and chopped
- 1 cup sugar
- 1 cup fresh cranberries
- ½ cup wheat berries
- ½ cup quinoa, rinsed
- ½ cup oat bran
- ½ cup medium pearl barley
- ½ cup chopped walnuts
- ½ cup packed brown sugar
- 1½ to 2 teaspoons ground cinnamon
- 6 cups water
  Milk

In a 3-qt. slow cooker, combine the first 11 ingredients. Cook, covered, on low 4-5 hours or until the grains are tender. Serve with milk.
NOTE *Look for oat bran cereal near the hot cereals or in the natural foods section. Look for quinoa in the cereal, rice or organic food aisle.*

Chutney-Glazed Carrots

Carrots slow-cooked with chutney, Dijon and ginger make a zippy side for a potluck or barbecue. We love serving these carrots with grilled chicken or beef roast.

—**NANCY HEISHMAN** LAS VEGAS, NV

PREP: 15 MIN. • **COOK:** 4 HOURS
MAKES: 4 SERVINGS

- ⅓ cup mango chutney
- 2 tablespoons sugar
- 2 tablespoons minced fresh parsley
- 2 tablespoons white wine or unsweetened apple juice
- 1 tablespoon Dijon mustard
- 1 tablespoon butter, melted
- 1 garlic clove, minced
- ½ teaspoon salt
- ¼ teaspoon ground ginger
- ¼ teaspoon pepper
- 1 pound fresh carrots, cut into ¼-inch slices (about 4 cups)

1. Place the first 10 ingredients in a 3-qt. slow cooker. Add carrots; toss to combine.
2. Cook, covered, on low 4-5 hours or until the carrots are tender. Stir before serving.

Contest Winner

Sweet Onion & Red Bell Pepper Topping

When the spring Vidalia onions hit the market, I turn to this recipe. I use it on hot dogs, bruschetta, cream cheese and crackers. It's so versatile.

—**PAT HOCKETT** OCALA, FL

PREP: 20 MIN. • **COOK:** 4 HOURS
MAKES: 4 CUPS

- 4 large sweet onions, thinly sliced (about 8 cups)
- 4 large sweet red peppers, thinly sliced (about 6 cups)
- ½ cup cider vinegar
- ¼ cup packed brown sugar
- 2 tablespoons canola oil
- 2 tablespoons honey
- 2 teaspoons celery seed
- ¾ teaspoon crushed red pepper flakes
- ½ teaspoon salt

In a 5- or 6-qt. slow cooker, combine all ingredients. Cook, covered, on low 4-5 hours or until the vegetables are tender. Serve with a slotted spoon.

BBQ Chicken

Of all the recipes I make in my slow cooker, this is the best. If you like your BBQ sweet with a little touch of spice, this will be your new go-to, too.
—**YVONNE MCKIM** VANCOUVER, WA

PREP: 15 MIN. • **COOK:** 5 HOURS • **MAKES:** 12 SERVINGS

 6 chicken leg quarters, skin removed
 ¾ cup ketchup
 ½ cup orange juice
 ¼ cup packed brown sugar
 ¼ cup red wine vinegar
 ¼ cup olive oil
 4 teaspoons minced fresh parsley
 2 teaspoons Worcestershire sauce
 1 teaspoon garlic salt
 ½ teaspoon pepper
 2 tablespoons plus 2 teaspoons cornstarch
 ¼ cup water

1. Using a sharp knife, cut through the joint of each leg quarter to separate into two pieces. Place chicken in a 4-qt. slow cooker.
2. In a small bowl, mix ketchup, orange juice, brown sugar, vinegar, oil, parsley, Worcestershire sauce, garlic salt and pepper; pour over chicken. Cook, covered, on low 5-6 hours or until meat is tender.
3. Remove chicken to a serving platter; keep warm. Skim fat from cooking juices; pour into a measuring cup to measure 2 cups. Transfer to a small saucepan; bring to a boil. In a small bowl, mix cornstarch and water until smooth; stir into cooking juices. Return to a boil, stirring constantly; cook and stir 1-2 minutes or until thickened. Serve with chicken.

Old-Fashioned Dressing

Remember Grandma's delicious turkey dressing? Taste it again, combined with incredible herbs and crisp veggies, in this family-favorite recipe. You'll love the fact you can make it in your slow cooker.
—**SHERRY VINK** LACOMBE, AB

PREP: 35 MIN. • **COOK:** 3 HOURS • **MAKES:** 8 SERVINGS

 ½ cup butter, cubed
 2 celery ribs, chopped
 1 cup sliced fresh mushrooms
 1 medium onion, chopped
 ½ cup minced fresh parsley
 2 teaspoons rubbed sage
 2 teaspoons dried marjoram
 1 teaspoon dried thyme
 1 teaspoon poultry seasoning
 ½ teaspoon pepper
 ¼ teaspoon salt
 6 cups cubed day-old white bread
 6 cups cubed day-old whole wheat bread
 1 can (14½ ounces) chicken broth

1. In a large skillet, melt butter. Add the celery, mushrooms and onion; saute until tender. Stir in the seasonings. Place bread cubes in a large bowl. Stir in vegetable mixture. Add broth; toss to coat.
2. Transfer to a 3-qt. slow cooker coated with cooking spray. Cover and cook on low for 3-4 hours or until heated through.

Contest Winner

Turkey Sausage Soup with Fresh Vegetables

Our family is big on soup. This one is quick to make and very tasty, and it gives me plenty of time for fun with the family as it cooks.

—**NANCY HEISHMAN** LAS VEGAS, NV

PREP: 30 MIN. • **COOK:** 6 HOURS
MAKES: 10 SERVINGS (3½ QUARTS)

- 1 package (19½ ounces) Italian turkey sausage links, casings removed
- 3 large tomatoes, chopped
- 1 can (15 ounces) chickpeas, rinsed and drained
- 3 medium carrots, thinly sliced
- 1½ cups cut fresh green beans (1-inch pieces)
- 1 medium zucchini, quartered lengthwise and sliced
- 1 large sweet red or green pepper, chopped
- 8 green onions, chopped
- 4 cups chicken stock
- 1 can (12 ounces) tomato paste
- ½ teaspoon seasoned salt
- ⅓ cup minced fresh basil

1. In a large skillet, cook the sausage over medium heat 8-10 minutes or until no longer pink, breaking into crumbles; drain and transfer to a 6-qt. slow cooker.
2. Add tomatoes, beans, carrots, green beans, zucchini, pepper and green onions. In a large bowl, whisk stock, tomato paste and seasoned salt; pour over vegetables.
3. Cook, covered, on low 6-8 hours or until vegetables are tender. Just before serving, stir in basil.
FREEZE OPTION *Freeze cooled soup in freezer containers. To use, partially thaw in refrigerator overnight. Heat through in a saucepan, stirring occasionally and adding a little stock if necessary.*

Sweet Pepper Steak

Pepper steak is one of my favorite dishes but I was always upset with beef that was too tough. This recipe solves that problem! I've stored leftovers in one big resealable bag and also in individual portions for quick lunches.

—**JULIE RHINE** ZELIENOPLE, PA

PREP: 30 MIN. • **COOK:** 6¼ HOURS • **MAKES:** 12 SERVINGS

- 1 beef top round roast (3 pounds)
- 1 large onion, halved and sliced
- 1 large green pepper, cut into ½-inch strips
- 1 large sweet red pepper, cut into ½-inch strips
- 1 cup water
- 4 garlic cloves, minced
- ⅓ cup cornstarch
- ½ cup reduced-sodium soy sauce
- 2 teaspoons sugar
- 2 teaspoons ground ginger
- 8 cups hot cooked brown rice

1. Place roast, onion and peppers in a 5-qt. slow cooker. Add water and garlic. Cook, covered, on low 6-8 hours or until meat is tender.
2. Remove beef to a cutting board. Transfer the vegetables and cooking juices to a large saucepan. Bring to a boil. In a small bowl, mix cornstarch, soy sauce, sugar and ginger until smooth; stir into vegetable mixture. Return to a boil, stirring constantly; cook and stir 1-2 minutes or until thickened.
3. Cut beef into slices. Stir gently into sauce; heat through. Serve with rice.
FREEZE OPTION *Freeze cooled beef mixture in freezer containers. To use, partially thaw in refrigerator overnight. Heat through in a saucepan, stirring occasionally and adding a little water if necessary.*

Contest Winner

Country Ribs Dinner

This is my favorite recipe for the classic ribs dinner. It's always a treat for my family when we have this.

—ROSE INGALL MANISTEE, MI

PREP: 10 MIN. • **COOK:** 6¼ HOURS
MAKES: 4 SERVINGS

- 2 **pounds boneless country-style pork ribs**
- ½ **teaspoon salt**
- ¼ **teaspoon pepper**
- 8 **small red potatoes (about 1 pound), halved**
- 4 **medium carrots, cut into 1-inch pieces**
- 3 **celery ribs, cut into ½-inch pieces**
- 1 **medium onion, coarsely chopped**
- ¾ **cup water**
- 1 **garlic clove, crushed**
- 1 **can (10¾ ounces) condensed cream of mushroom soup, undiluted**

1. Sprinkle ribs with salt and pepper; transfer to a 4-qt. slow cooker. Add potatoes, carrots, celery, onion, water and garlic. Cook, covered, on low 6-8 hours or until meat and vegetables are tender.

2. Remove meat and vegetables; skim fat from cooking juices. Whisk the soup into the cooking juices; return meat and vegetables to slow cooker. Cook, covered, 15-30 minutes longer or until heated through.

Super Easy Country-Style Ribs

I'm a diehard rib fanatic. When we were growing up, our mother made these ribs for us all the time, and we still can't get enough of them.

—STEPHANIE LOAIZA LAYTON, UT

PREP: 10 MIN. • **COOK:** 5 HOURS
MAKES: 4 SERVINGS

- 1½ **cups ketchup**
- ½ **cup packed brown sugar**
- ½ **cup white vinegar**
- 2 **teaspoons seasoned salt**
- ½ **teaspoon liquid smoke, optional**
- 2 **pounds boneless country-style pork ribs**

1. In a 3-qt. slow cooker, mix ketchup, brown sugar, vinegar, seasoned salt and, if desired, liquid smoke. Add ribs; turn to coat. Cook, covered, on low 5-6 hours or until meat is tender.

2. Remove pork to a serving plate. Skim fat from cooking liquid. If desired, transfer to a small saucepan to thicken. Bring to a boil; cook 12-15 minutes or until the sauce is reduced to 1½ cups. Serve with ribs.

TO MAKE AHEAD *Using a large resealable plastic freezer bag, combine ketchup, brown sugar, vinegar, seasoned salt and, if desired, liquid smoke. Add pork; seal bag and freeze. To use, place the filled freezer bag in refrigerator 48 hours or until ribs are completely thawed. Cook as directed.*

Slow Cooker Tamale Pie

Canned beans and corn bread/muffin mix speed up the prep on this crowd-pleasing main dish. It's perfect for busy evenings.

—JILL POKRIVKA YORK, PA

PREP: 25 MIN. • **COOK:** 7 HOURS
MAKES: 8 SERVINGS

- 1 pound ground beef
- 1 teaspoon ground cumin
- ½ teaspoon salt
- ½ teaspoon chili powder
- ¼ teaspoon pepper
- 1 can (15 ounces) black beans, rinsed and drained
- 1 can (14½ ounces) diced tomatoes with mild green chilies, undrained
- 1 can (11 ounces) whole kernel corn, drained
- 1 can (10 ounces) enchilada sauce
- 2 green onions, chopped
- ¼ cup minced fresh cilantro
- 1 package (8½ ounces) corn bread/ muffin mix
- 2 large eggs
- 1 cup shredded Mexican cheese blend
    Sour cream and additional minced fresh cilantro, optional

1. In a large skillet, cook beef over medium heat until no longer pink; drain. Stir in cumin, salt, chili powder and pepper.

2. Transfer to a 4-qt. slow cooker; stir in the beans, tomatoes, corn, enchilada sauce, onions and cilantro. Cover and cook on low for 6-8 hours or until heated through.

3. In a small bowl, combine muffin mix and eggs; spoon over the meat mixture. Cover and cook 1 hour longer or until a toothpick inserted near the center comes out clean.

4. Sprinkle with cheese; cover and let stand for 5 minutes. Serve with sour cream and additional cilantro if desired.

Zesty Italian Beef Sandwiches

It's so easy to build a sandwich when you pile on the shredded beef, pickles and smoked provolone. Can't find smoked provolone? I use regular, too.

—CRYSTAL SCHLUETER NORTHGLENN, CO

PREP: 15 MIN. • **COOK:** 8 HOURS
MAKES: 6 SERVINGS

- 1 boneless beef chuck roast (3 to 4 pounds)
- 1 can (10½ ounces) condensed French onion soup, undiluted
- ½ cup cider vinegar
- 2 tablespoons reduced-sodium soy sauce
- 1 tablespoon brown sugar
- ½ cup mayonnaise
- 1 tablespoon horseradish mustard or spicy brown mustard
- 1 tablespoon chili garlic sauce
- 6 Italian rolls, split
- 6 thin slices red onion
- 18 sweet pickle slices
- 6 slices smoked provolone cheese

1. Place roast in a 5- or 6-qt. slow cooker. In a small bowl, mix soup, vinegar, soy sauce and brown sugar; pour over roast. Cook, covered, on low 8-10 hours or until meat is tender.

2. Remove roast; cool slightly. Shred meat with two forks. Return meat to slow cooker; heat through. In a small bowl, mix mayonnaise, mustard and chili sauce; spread on roll bottoms. Layer with onion, pickles, shredded beef and cheese. Replace tops.

Contest Winner

TOASTY DESSERTS

No need to heat up the house with the oven—just flip the switch on your slow cooker.
Slow-cooked desserts are just as decadent and satisfying, without much time in the kitchen!

Slow Cooker Baked Apples

On a cool fall day, coming home to this dessert is a healthy double dose of nutrition and just plain wonderful.

—**EVANGELINE BRADFORD** ERLANGER, KY

PREP: 25 MIN. • **COOK:** 4 HOURS
MAKES: 6 SERVINGS

- 6 **medium tart apples**
- ½ **cup raisins**
- ⅓ **cup packed brown sugar**
- 1 **tablespoon grated orange peel**
- 1 **cup water**
- 3 **tablespoons thawed orange juice concentrate**
- 2 **tablespoons butter**

1. Core the apples and peel the top third of each if desired. Combine the raisins, brown sugar and orange peel; spoon into the apples. Place in a 5-qt. slow cooker.
2. Pour water around apples. Drizzle with orange juice concentrate. Dot with butter. Cover and cook on low for 4-5 hours or until apples are tender.

Gooey Peanut Butter-Chocolate Cake

Here in Wisconsin, winter weather is extreme. A hot dessert is just the thing to warm us up. This chocolaty delight gets its crunch from a sprinkling of peanuts.

—**LISA ERICKSON** RIPON, WI

PREP: 20 MIN. • **COOK:** 2 HOURS
MAKES: 8 SERVINGS

- 1¾ **cups sugar, divided**
- 1 **cup 2% milk**
- ¾ **cup creamy peanut butter**
- 3 **tablespoons canola oil**
- 2 **cups all-purpose flour**
- ¾ **cup baking cocoa, divided**
- 3 **teaspoons baking powder**
- 2 **cups boiling water**
  Chopped salted peanuts, optional

1. In a large bowl, beat 1 cup sugar, milk, peanut butter and oil until they are well blended. In another bowl, whisk the flour, ½ cup cocoa and baking powder; gradually beat into the peanut butter mixture (the batter will be thick). Transfer to a greased 5-qt. slow cooker.
2. In a small bowl, mix remaining sugar and cocoa. Stir in water. Pour over batter (do not stir).
3. Cook, covered, on high for 2 to 2½ hours or until a toothpick inserted in cake portion comes out with moist crumbs. If desired, sprinkle with peanuts. Serve warm.

Slow-Cooked Blueberry Grunt

If you love blueberries, then you can't go wrong with this easy dessert. For a special treat, serve it warm with vanilla ice cream.
—CLEO GONSKE REDDING, CA

PREP: 20 MIN. • **COOK:** 2½ HOURS
MAKES: 6 SERVINGS

- 4 cups fresh or frozen blueberries
- ¾ cup sugar
- ½ cup water
- 1 teaspoon almond extract

DUMPLINGS
- 2 cups all-purpose flour
- 4 teaspoons baking powder
- 1 teaspoon sugar
- ½ teaspoon salt
- 1 tablespoon cold butter
- 1 tablespoon shortening
- ¾ cup 2% milk
  Vanilla ice cream, optional

1. Place blueberries, sugar, water and extract in a 3-qt. slow cooker; stir to combine. Cook, covered, on high 2-3 hours or until bubbly.
2. For the dumplings, in a small bowl, whisk flour, baking powder, sugar and salt. Cut in butter and shortening until crumbly. Add milk; stir just until a soft dough forms.
3. Drop dough by tablespoonfuls on top of hot blueberry mixture. Cook, covered, 30 minutes longer or until a toothpick inserted in the center of the dumplings comes out clean. If desired, serve warm with ice cream.

Slow Cooker Candied Nuts

I like giving spiced nuts as holiday gifts. This slow cooker recipe with ginger and cinnamon is so good, you just might use it all year long.
—YVONNE STARLIN WESTMORELAND, TN

PREP: 10 MIN. • **COOK:** 2 HOURS
MAKES: 4 CUPS

- ½ cup butter, melted
- ½ cup confectioners' sugar
- 1½ teaspoons ground cinnamon
- ¼ teaspoon ground ginger
- ¼ teaspoon ground allspice
- 1½ cups pecan halves
- 1½ cups walnut halves
- 1 cup unblanched almonds

1. In a greased 3-qt. slow cooker, mix butter, confectioners' sugar and spices. Add nuts; toss to coat. Cook, covered, on low 2-3 hours or until nuts are crisp, stirring once.
2. Transfer nuts to waxed paper to cool completely. Store in an airtight container.

Tomato-Basil Steak

I use basil and bell peppers from my herb and vegetable garden to make this dish. It's so rich and delicious.

—**SHERRY LITTLE** SHERWOOD, AR

PREP: 15 MIN. • **COOK:** 6 HOURS
MAKES: 4 SERVINGS

- 1¼ pounds boneless beef shoulder top blade or flat iron steaks
- ½ pound whole fresh mushrooms, quartered
- 1 medium sweet yellow pepper, julienned
- 1 can (14½ ounces) stewed tomatoes, undrained
- 1 can (8 ounces) tomato sauce
- 1 envelope onion soup mix
- 2 tablespoons minced fresh basil
  Hot cooked rice

1. Place the steaks in a 4-qt. slow cooker. Add the mushrooms and pepper. In a small bowl, mix the tomatoes, tomato sauce, soup mix and basil; pour over the top.
2. Cook, covered, on low 6-8 hours or until beef and vegetables are tender. Serve with rice.

Contest Winner

Slow Cooker Tropical Pork Chops

Pork and fruit go so nicely together. And when you add fresh herbs, you get this fresh, light and bright main dish that everyone loves.

—**ROXANNE CHAN** ALBANY, CA

PREP: 15 MIN. • **COOK:** 3 HOURS
MAKES: 4 SERVINGS

- 2 jars (23½ ounces each) mixed tropical fruit, drained and chopped
- ¾ cup thawed limeade concentrate
- ¼ cup sweet chili sauce
- 1 garlic clove, minced
- 1 teaspoon minced fresh gingerroot
- 4 bone-in pork loin chops (¾ inch thick and 5 ounces each)
- 1 green onion, finely chopped
- 2 tablespoons minced fresh cilantro
- 2 tablespoons minced fresh mint
- 2 tablespoons slivered almonds, toasted

- 2 tablespoons finely chopped crystallized ginger, optional
- ½ teaspoon grated lime peel

1. In a 3-qt. slow cooker, combine the first five ingredients. Add pork, arranging chops to sit snugly in fruit mixture. Cook, covered, on low 3-4 hours or until meat is tender (a thermometer inserted in pork should read at least 145°).
2. In a small bowl, mix remaining ingredients. To serve, remove pork chops from slow cooker. Using a slotted spoon, serve fruit over pork. Sprinkle with herb mixture.
NOTE *To toast the nuts, place them in a dry nonstick skillet and heat over low heat until they are lightly browned, stirring occasionally.*

Sweet & Smoky Pulled Pork Sandwiches

These simple pork sandwiches taste like something that you'd order from a local barbecue joint. The tender meat basically shreds itself when it's done cooking. It's definitely my favorite pulled pork sandwich of all time.
—LAUREN ADAMSON LAYTON, UT

PREP: 15 MIN. • **COOK:** 8 HOURS
MAKES: 10 SERVINGS

- ⅓ cup liquid smoke
- 3 tablespoons paprika
- 3 teaspoons salt
- 3 teaspoons pepper
- 1 teaspoon garlic powder
- 1 teaspoon ground mustard
- 1 boneless pork shoulder butt roast (3 to 4 pounds)
- 1 bottle (18 ounces) barbecue sauce
- 10 hamburger buns, split

1. In a small bowl, whisk the first six ingredients; rub over roast. Place the roast in a 5- or 6-qt. slow cooker. Cook, covered, on low 8-10 hours or until the meat is tender.

2. Remove roast; cool slightly. Discard the cooking juices. Shred the pork with two forks; return to slow cooker. Stir in barbecue sauce; heat through. Serve on buns.

TO MAKE AHEAD *In a small bowl, whisk the first six ingredients; rub over roast. Place roast in a large resealable plastic freezer bag; seal bag and freeze. To use, place the roast in a refrigerator 48 hours or until completely thawed. Cook and serve as directed.*

FREEZE OPTION *Freeze the cooled meat mixture in freezer containers. To use, partially thaw in refrigerator overnight. Heat mixture through in a saucepan, stirring occasionally and adding a little water if necessary.*

Contest Winner

Green Chili Creamed Corn

When hosting big meals, I'd sometimes run out of burners. Then I realized my slow cooker could help by simmering corn and green chilies with pickled jalapenos.
—PAT DAZIS CHARLOTTE, NC

PREP: 10 MIN. • **COOK:** 3 HOURS
MAKES: 8 SERVINGS

- 6 cups fresh or frozen corn (about 30 ounces), thawed
- 1 package (8 ounces) cream cheese, cubed
- 1 jar (4 ounces) diced pimientos, drained
- 1 can (4 ounces) chopped green chilies
- ½ cup vegetable broth
- ¼ cup butter, cubed
- ¼ cup pickled jalapeno slices, coarsely chopped
- 1 tablespoon sugar
- ⅛ teaspoon crushed red pepper flakes

In a 3- or 4-qt. slow cooker, combine all ingredients. Cook, covered, on low 2½ to 3 hours or until heated through. Stir just before serving.

Apple-Cinnamon Pork Loin

I love to make this slow-cooked dish for chilly fall dinners with my family—the delightful apple-cinnamon aroma fills our entire house. The pork roast tastes even better served with buttery homemade mashed potatoes.

—RACHEL SCHULTZ LANSING, MI

PREP: 20 MIN. • **COOK:** 6 HOURS • **MAKES:** 6 SERVINGS

- 1 **boneless pork loin roast (2 to 3 pounds)**
- ½ **teaspoon salt**
- ¼ **teaspoon pepper**
- 1 **tablespoon canola oil**
- 3 **medium apples, peeled and sliced, divided**
- ¼ **cup honey**
- 1 **small red onion, halved and sliced**
- 1 **tablespoon ground cinnamon**
  Minced fresh parsley, optional

1. Sprinkle roast with salt and pepper. In a large skillet, brown roast in oil on all sides; cool slightly. With a paring knife, cut about sixteen 3-in.-deep slits in sides of roast; insert one apple slice into each slit.

2. Place half of the remaining apples in a 4-qt. slow cooker. Place roast over apples. Drizzle with honey; top with onion and remaining apples. Sprinkle with cinnamon.

3. Cover and cook on low for 6-8 hours or until meat is tender. Remove pork and apple mixture; keep warm.

4. Transfer cooking juices to a small saucepan. Bring to a boil; cook until liquid is reduced by half. Serve with pork and apple mixture. Sprinkle with parsley if desired.

Slow Cooker Turkey Chili

I love this recipe because I can prepare it in the morning and a wholesome dinner is ready when I get home in the evening. And you can make a big batch to freeze!
—**TERRI CRANDALL** GARDNERVILLE, NV

PREP: 30 MIN. • **COOK:** 7¼ HOURS
MAKES: 8 SERVINGS (2¾ QUARTS)

- 2 tablespoons olive oil
- 1½ pounds ground turkey
- 1 medium onion, chopped
- 2 tablespoons ground ancho chili pepper
- 1 tablespoon chili powder
- 1½ teaspoons salt
- 1½ teaspoons ground cumin
- 1½ teaspoons paprika
- 2 cans (14½ ounces each) fire-roasted diced tomatoes, undrained
- 1 medium sweet yellow pepper, chopped
- 1 medium sweet red pepper, chopped
- 1 can (4 ounces) chopped green chilies
- 1 garlic clove, minced
- 1 cup brewed coffee
- ¾ cup dry red wine or chicken broth
- 1 can (16 ounces) kidney beans, rinsed and drained
- 1 can (15 ounces) white kidney or cannellini beans, rinsed and drained
  Sliced avocado and chopped green onions

1. In a large skillet, heat oil over medium heat. Add turkey and onion; cook 8-10 minutes or until meat is no longer pink, breaking up turkey into crumbles.
2. Transfer to a 5-qt. slow cooker; stir in the seasonings. Add tomatoes, sweet peppers, chilies and garlic; stir in the coffee and wine.
3. Cook, covered, on low 7-9 hours. Stir in beans; cook 15-20 minutes longer or until heated through. Top servings with avocado and green onions.

FREEZE OPTION *Freeze cooled chili in freezer containers. To use, partially thaw in the refrigerator overnight. Heat through in a saucepan, stirring occasionally and adding broth or water if necessary.*

Maryland-Style Crab Soup

For a different take on vegetable soup, give this recipe a try. It incorporates the best of a vegetable soup and adds flavorful crab. Whole crabs can be cleaned and broken into pieces for the soup, which is my personal preference. I serve the dish with saltine crackers and cold beer.
—**FREELOVE KNOTT** PALM BAY, FL

PREP: 20 MIN. • **COOK:** 6¼ HOURS • **MAKES:** 8 SERVINGS (3 QUARTS)

- 2 cans (14½ ounces each) diced tomatoes with green peppers and onions, undrained
- 2 cups water
- 1½ pounds potatoes, cut into ½-inch cubes (about 5 cups)
- 2 cups cubed peeled rutabaga
- 2 cups chopped cabbage
- 1 medium onion, finely chopped
- 1 medium carrot, sliced
- ½ cup frozen corn, thawed
- ½ cup frozen lima beans, thawed
- ½ cup frozen peas, thawed
- ½ cup cut fresh green beans (1-inch pieces)
- 4 teaspoons seafood seasoning
- 1 teaspoon celery seed
- 1 vegetable bouillon cube
- ¼ teaspoon salt
- ¼ teaspoon pepper
- 1 pound fresh or lump crabmeat, drained

1. In a 6-qt. slow cooker, combine first 16 ingredients. Cook, covered, on low 6-8 hours or until vegetables are tender.
2. Stir in crab. Cook, covered, on low 15 minutes longer or until heated through.
NOTE *This recipe was prepared with Knorr vegetable bouillon.*

Slow Cooker Rotisserie-Style Chicken

You wouldn't believe this golden brown chicken was made in the slow cooker. Packed with flavor, the meat is moist, the carrots are tender, and the juices would make a nice gravy.
—**TASTE OF HOME** TEST KITCHEN

PREP: 30 MIN. • **COOK:** 6 HOURS + STANDING
MAKES: 6 SERVINGS

- 4 teaspoons seasoned salt
- 4 teaspoons poultry seasoning
- 1 tablespoon paprika
- 1½ teaspoons onion powder
- 1½ teaspoons brown sugar
- 1½ teaspoons salt-free lemon-pepper seasoning
- ¾ teaspoon garlic powder
- 1 broiler/fryer chicken (4 pounds)
- 1 pound carrots, halved lengthwise and cut into 1½-inch lengths
- 2 large onions, chopped
- 2 tablespoons cornstarch

1. In a small bowl, combine the first seven ingredients. Carefully loosen skin from chicken breast; rub 1 tablespoon spice mixture under the skin. Rub remaining spice mixture over chicken. In another bowl, toss carrots and onions with cornstarch; transfer to a 6-qt. slow cooker. Place chicken on vegetables.
2. Cover and cook on low for 6-7 hours or until a thermometer inserted in thigh reads 180°. Remove chicken and vegetables to a serving platter; cover and let stand for 15 minutes before carving. Skim fat from cooking juices. Serve with chicken and vegetables.

Autumn Slow-Cooked Beef Stew

If any dish could taste like a special occasion, it's this one with beef, pears, walnuts and sweet dried apricots. We recommend a leafy salad and rolls to complete the masterpiece.
—**AMY DODSON** DURANGO, CO

PREP: 35 MIN. • **COOK:** 6 HOURS
MAKES: 8 SERVINGS

- 2 pounds boneless beef chuck roast, cubed
- ½ teaspoon garlic salt
- ½ teaspoon pepper
- 2 tablespoons olive oil
- 2 cups dry red wine or reduced-sodium beef broth
- 1 cup reduced-sodium beef broth
- 4 garlic cloves, minced
- 1 teaspoon rubbed sage
- 1 teaspoon dried thyme
- ½ teaspoon salt
- 2½ pounds small red potatoes (about 20)
- 4 medium carrots, cut into 1-inch pieces
- 1 large onion, halved and sliced
- 2 medium pears, quartered
- 1 cup walnut halves
- 1 cup dried apricots
- 2 tablespoons cornstarch
- 3 tablespoons cold water

1. Sprinkle beef with garlic salt and pepper. In a large skillet, heat oil over medium-high heat. Brown beef in batches. Remove with a slotted spoon; transfer to a 6-qt. slow cooker.
2. In a large bowl, combine wine, broth, garlic, sage, thyme and salt; pour over beef. Top with potatoes, carrots, onion, pears, walnuts and apricots. Cook, covered, on low 6-8 hours or until meat is tender; skim fat.
3. In a small bowl, mix cornstarch and water until smooth; gradually stir into stew. Cook, covered, on high 20-30 minutes or until sauce is thickened.

> **TWIST ON BEEF STEW**
> To add an extra flavor layer to my beef stew when I make it in the slow cooker, I stir in a can of tomato soup.
> —**CAROL F.** LANDERS, CA

Caribbean Beef Short Ribs

The short ribs, rum and fruit together make this feel like an exotic Caribbean dish. When removing the mixture from the slow cooker, take out the fruit first and place in a separate bowl from the meat to avoid coating it with the brown sauce.
—**LOANNE CHIU** FORT WORTH, TX

PREP: 30 MIN. • **COOK:** 5½ HOURS
MAKES: 8 SERVINGS

- 3 pounds boneless beef short ribs, cut into 1½-inch pieces
- ¼ cup olive oil
- ⅔ cup thawed pineapple juice concentrate
- ⅔ cup reduced-sodium soy sauce
- ½ cup water
- ⅓ cup rum
- ⅓ cup honey
- 2 tablespoons minced fresh gingerroot
- 6 garlic cloves, minced
- 2 teaspoons pepper
- 1 teaspoon ground allspice
- ½ teaspoon salt
- 2 large sweet red peppers, chopped
- 2 cups cubed fresh pineapple
- 2 cups cubed peeled mango
- 6 green onions, cut into 1-inch pieces
- 2 tablespoons cornstarch
- 2 tablespoons cold water
  Lettuce leaves

1. In a large skillet, brown the ribs in oil in batches on all sides. Transfer to a 4-qt. slow cooker.
2. Add pineapple juice concentrate, soy sauce, water, rum, honey, ginger, garlic, pepper, allspice and salt to the skillet. Bring to a boil; reduce heat and simmer for 5 minutes. Pour over ribs.
3. Cover and cook dish on low for 5-6 hours or until meat is tender. Stir in red peppers. Top with the pineapple, mango and onions (do not stir). Cover and cook 30 minutes longer or until heated through.
4. Remove beef mixture to a large bowl; keep warm. Transfer cooking juices to a small saucepan. Combine the cornstarch and cold water until smooth; gradually stir into pan. Bring to a boil; cook and stir for 2 minutes or until thickened. Serve beef mixture on lettuce; drizzle with gravy.

Pineapple-Dijon Ham Sandwiches

My kids like ham, but it's a challenge to come up with different ways to prepare it. I like the combination of ham and pineapple, so I decided to throw it in the slow cooker. The result was amazing. Even my two youngest children ate their sandwiches right up.
—**CAMILLE BECKSTRAND** LAYTON, UT

PREP: 20 MIN. • **COOK:** 3 HOURS
MAKES: 10 SERVINGS

- 2 pounds fully cooked ham, cut into ½-inch cubes
- 1 can (20 ounces) crushed pineapple, undrained
- 1 medium green pepper, finely chopped
- ¾ cup packed brown sugar
- ¼ cup finely chopped onion
- ¼ cup Dijon mustard
- 1 tablespoon dried minced onion
- 10 hamburger buns, split
- 10 slices Swiss cheese
  Additional Dijon mustard, optional

1. In a greased 4-qt. slow cooker, combine the first seven ingredients. Cook, covered, on low 3-4 hours or until heated through.
2. Preheat broiler. Place bun bottoms and tops on baking sheets, cut side up. Using a slotted spoon, place the ham mixture on bottoms; top with cheese. Broil 3-4 in. from heat 1-2 minutes or until cheese is melted and tops are toasted. Replace tops. If desired, serve with additional mustard.

Contest Winner

COOKIES, BARS & CANDIES

You know what turns a day around instantly? Baking up a batch or two of these goodies! Surprise someone you love with a plate full of sweetness—we won't tell if you snag a few for yourself.

Raspberry Cream Sugar Cookies

We make sugar cookies and fill them with a tangy raspberry cream cheese. They taste best after they've been refrigerated for at least 45 minutes.

—**HEIDI FARNWORTH** RIVERTON, UT

PREP: 10 MIN. + CHILLING
BAKE: 10 MIN./BATCH + COOLING
MAKES: ABOUT 1½ DOZEN

- ½ **cup white baking chips**
- ¼ **cup heavy whipping cream**
- 6 **ounces cream cheese, softened**
- ¼ **cup red raspberry preserves**
- 1 **package sugar cookie mix**
- ½ **cup butter, softened**
- 1 **large egg**

1. Preheat the oven to 350°. In a microwave, melt baking chips with cream; stir until smooth. In a large bowl, beat cream cheese and preserves until blended. Add the melted baking chip mixture; beat until smooth. Refrigerate until assembling.

2. In a large bowl, mix cookie mix, butter and egg until blended. Shape into 1-in. balls; place 2 in. apart on ungreased baking sheets. Bake 7-9 minutes or until edges are light brown. Cool on pans 5 minutes. Remove to wire racks to cool completely.

3. Spread 1 tablespoon filling on the bottoms of half of the cookies; cover with remaining cookies. Refrigerate in an airtight container.

Contest Winner

Honey-Pecan Squares

When we left Texas to head north, a kind neighbor gave me pecans from his trees. I like to send these nutty squares back to him, and he's always happy to receive them.
—**LORRAINE CALAND** SHUNIAH, ON

PREP: 15 MIN. • **BAKE:** 30 MIN.
MAKES: 2 DOZEN

- 1 **cup unsalted butter, softened**
- ¾ **cup packed dark brown sugar**
- ½ **teaspoon salt**
- 3 **cups all-purpose flour**

FILLING
- ½ **cup unsalted butter, cubed**
- ½ **cup packed dark brown sugar**
- ⅓ **cup honey**
- 2 **tablespoons sugar**
- 2 **tablespoons heavy whipping cream**
- ¼ **teaspoon salt**
- 2 **cups chopped pecans, toasted**
- ½ **teaspoon maple flavoring or vanilla extract**

1. Preheat the oven to 350°. Line a 13x9-in. baking pan with parchment paper, letting the ends extend up the sides of the pan. In a large bowl, cream the butter, brown sugar and salt until light and fluffy. Gradually beat in the flour. Press onto the bottom of the prepared pan. Bake 16-20 minutes or until lightly browned.

2. In a small saucepan, combine first six filling ingredients; bring to a boil. Cook 1 minute. Remove from heat; stir in pecans and maple flavoring. Pour over the crust.

3. Bake 10-15 minutes or until bubbly. Cool in pan on a wire rack. Lifting with parchment paper, transfer to a cutting board; cut into bars.

NOTE *To toast nuts, bake in a shallow pan in a 350° oven for 5-10 minutes or cook in a skillet over low heat until lightly browned, stirring occasionally.*

Mocha Truffles

Nothing compares to the melt-in-your-mouth flavor of these truffles...or to the simplicity of the recipe. Whenever I make them for my family or friends, they're quickly devoured. No one has to know how easy they are to prepare!
—STACY ABELL OLATHE, KS

PREP: 25 MIN. + CHILLING
MAKES: ABOUT 5½ DOZEN

- 2 packages (12 ounces each) semisweet chocolate chips
- 1 package (8 ounces) cream cheese, softened
- 3 tablespoons instant coffee granules
- 2 teaspoons water
- 1 pound dark chocolate candy coating, coarsely chopped
  White candy coating, optional

1. In a microwave-safe bowl, melt chocolate chips; stir until smooth. Beat in cream cheese. Dissolve coffee in water; add to cream cheese and beat until smooth.

2. Chill until firm enough to shape. Shape into 1-in. balls and place on waxed paper-lined baking sheet. Chill for 1-2 hours or until firm.

3. In a microwave, melt the chocolate coating; stir until smooth. Dip balls in chocolate; allow the excess to drip off. Place on waxed paper; let stand until set. Melt white coating and drizzle over truffles if desired.

NOTE *Dark, white or milk chocolate candy coating is found in the baking section of most grocery stores. It is sometime labeled almond bark or confectionery coating and is often sold in bulk packages (of 1 to 1½ pounds). A substitute for 6 ounces chocolate coating would be 1 cup (6 ounces) semisweet, dark or white chocolate chips and 1 tablespoon shortening melted together.*

FREEZE OPTION *Truffles can be frozen for several months before dipping in chocolate. Thaw in the refrigerator before dipping.*

Easy 3-Ingredient Shortbread Cookies

These buttery cookies are so simple to make, with only a few ingredients.
—PATRICIA PRESCOTT MANCHESTER, NH

PREP: 10 MIN. • **BAKE:** 30 MIN. + COOLING
MAKES: 16 COOKIES

- 1 cup unsalted butter, softened
- ½ cup sugar
- 2 cups all-purpose flour
  Confectioners' sugar, optional

1. Preheat oven to 325°. Cream the butter and sugar until light and fluffy. Gradually beat in flour. Press dough into an ungreased 9-in. square baking pan. Prick with a fork.

2. Bake until the shortbread is light brown, for 30-35 minutes. Cut into squares while warm. Cool completely on a wire rack. If desired, dust with confectioners' sugar.

Contest Winner

KEEP COOKIES APART

When storing cookies, be sure to keep crisp and soft cookies in separate containers. If stored together, the moisture from the soft cookies can cause the crisp ones to lose their crunch.

Almond Crispies

The triple almonds punch (almond extract, ground almonds and blanched almonds) make the cookies extra tasty, but I sometimes make them with toasted pecans and place a pecan half in the center of each cookie.
—**TRISHA KRUSE** EAGLE, ID

PREP: 20 MIN. + CHILLING • **BAKE:** 20 MIN./BATCH
MAKES: 3 DOZEN

- 3 tablespoons plus 1 cup sugar, divided
- ⅛ teaspoon ground cinnamon
- ⅓ cup butter, softened
- 1 large egg
- ¼ cup fat-free milk
- ½ teaspoon almond extract
- ½ teaspoon vanilla extract
- 2½ cups all-purpose flour
- ¼ cup ground almonds
- ⅛ teaspoon salt
- 36 blanched almonds

1. In a small bowl, combine 3 tablespoons sugar and the cinnamon; set aside.
2. In a large bowl, beat butter and remaining sugar until crumbly. Beat in egg, milk and extracts. Combine flour, ground almonds and salt; add to the creamed mixture and mix well. Cover and refrigerate for at least 1 hour.
3. Roll into 1-in. balls. Place 2 in. apart on ungreased baking sheets. Coat bottom of glass with cooking spray, then dip in cinnamon-sugar mixture. Flatten cookies with prepared glass, redipping in cinnamon-sugar mixture as needed. Top each cookie with an almond.
4. Bake at 325° for 16-18 minutes or until lightly browned. Remove to wire racks.

Sacher Torte Squares

Sacher torte is a classic Viennese cake that requires several steps. My squares give you the classic apricot and chocolate taste.
—**ARLENE ERLBACH** MORTON GROVE, IL

PREP: 30 MIN. • **BAKE:** 30 MIN. + CHILLING • **MAKES:** 20 SERVINGS

- 1 package devil's food cake mix (regular size)
- 2 cans (12 ounces each) apricot cake and pastry filling
- 3 large eggs
- 2 teaspoons vanilla extract
- 1 cup (6 ounces) dark chocolate chips

TOPPINGS
- ½ cup apricot preserves
- 2 teaspoons vanilla extract
- ⅓ cup butter, cubed
- 1 cup sugar
- 1 cup heavy whipping cream
- 1 cup (6 ounces) dark chocolate chips
- ¼ cup sliced almonds

1. Preheat oven to 350°. Grease a 13x9-in. baking pan.
2. In a large bowl, combine cake mix, apricot filling, eggs and vanilla; beat on low speed 30 seconds. Beat on medium 2 minutes. Fold in chocolate chips. Transfer to prepared pan. Bake 30-35 minutes or until a toothpick inserted in center comes out clean.
3. Remove the pan from oven and place on a wire rack. In a small bowl, mix preserves and vanilla; spread over warm cake.
4. In a small saucepan, combine butter, sugar and cream; bring to a boil, stirring to dissolve sugar. Remove from the heat; stir in chocolate chips until melted. Spread over cake; sprinkle with almonds. Refrigerate until set, about 1 hour.

Frosted Malted Milk Cookies

My family loves anything made with malt or chocolate malted milk balls, so these cookies are one of their favorites!

—NANCY FOUST STONEBORO, PA

PREP: 40 MIN. • **BAKE:** 10 MIN./BATCH + COOLING • **MAKES:** 4 DOZEN

- 1 cup butter, softened
- 2 cups packed brown sugar
- 2 large eggs
- ⅓ cup sour cream
- 2 teaspoons vanilla extract
- 4¾ cups all-purpose flour
- ¾ cup malted milk powder
- 2 teaspoons baking powder
- ½ teaspoon baking soda
- ½ teaspoon salt

FROSTING

- 3 cups confectioners' sugar
- ½ cup malted milk powder
- ⅓ cup butter, softened
- 1½ teaspoons vanilla extract
- 3 to 4 tablespoons 2% milk
- 2 cups coarsely chopped malted milk balls

1. Preheat oven to 350°. In a large bowl, cream butter and brown sugar until light and fluffy. Beat in eggs, sour cream and vanilla. In another bowl, whisk the flour, malted milk powder, baking powder, baking soda and salt; gradually beat into creamed mixture.

2. Divide dough into three portions. On a lightly floured surface, roll each portion of dough to ¼-in. thickness. Cut with a floured 2½-in. round cookie cutter. Place 2 in. apart on parchment paper-lined baking sheets.

3. Bake 10-12 minutes or until the edges are light brown. Remove from pans to wire racks to cool completely.

4. For frosting, in a bowl, beat confectioners' sugar, malted milk powder, butter, vanilla and enough milk to reach a spreading consistency. Spread over cookies. Sprinkle with chopped candies.

S'more Sandwich Cookies

Capture the taste of campfire s'mores in your own kitchen. Melting the marshmallow centers in the microwave makes them simple to assemble.

—ABBY METZGER LARCHWOOD, IA

PREP: 25 MIN. • **BAKE:** 10 MIN. + COOLING • **MAKES:** ABOUT 2 DOZEN

- ¾ cup butter, softened
- ½ cup sugar
- ½ cup packed brown sugar
- 1 large egg
- 2 tablespoons milk
- 1 teaspoon vanilla extract
- 1¼ cups all-purpose flour
- 1¼ cups graham cracker crumbs (about 20 squares)
- ½ teaspoon baking soda
- ¼ teaspoon salt
- ⅛ teaspoon ground cinnamon
- 2 cups (12 ounces) semisweet chocolate chips
- 24 to 28 large marshmallows

1. In a large bowl, cream the butter and sugars until light and fluffy. Beat in egg, milk and vanilla. Combine flour, graham cracker crumbs, baking soda, salt and cinnamon; gradually add to creamed mixture and mix well. Stir in chocolate chips.

2. Drop by tablespoonfuls 2 in. apart onto ungreased baking sheets. Bake at 375° for 8-10 minutes or until golden brown. Remove to wire racks to cool.

3. Place four cookies bottom side up on a microwave-safe plate; top each of them with a marshmallow. Microwave, uncovered, on high for 10-15 seconds or until marshmallows begin to puff (do not overcook). Top each with another cookie. Repeat.

NOTE *This recipe was tested in a 1,100-watt microwave.*

Contest Winner

Pecan Toffee Fudge

My fudge is always popular wherever I take it and makes great gifts for loved ones and friends. The creaminess and toffee bits make it a hit with everyone. And it's so easy, even young children can help make it—with a little supervision!

—DIANE WILLEY BOZMAN, MD

PREP: 20 MIN. + CHILLING
MAKES: 2½ POUNDS

- 1 teaspoon butter
- 1 package (8 ounces) cream cheese, softened
- 3¾ cups confectioners' sugar
- 6 ounces unsweetened chocolate, melted and cooled
- ¼ teaspoon almond extract
    Dash salt
- ¼ cup coarsely chopped pecans
- ¼ cup English toffee bits

1. Line a 9-in. square pan with foil and grease the foil with butter; set aside. In a large bowl, beat cream cheese until fluffy. Gradually beat in confectioners' sugar. Beat in the melted chocolate, extract and salt until smooth. Stir in pecans and toffee bits.

2. Spread into prepared pan. Cover and refrigerate overnight or until firm. Using foil, lift fudge out of the pan. Gently peel off foil; cut fudge into 1-in. squares. Store in an airtight container in the refrigerator.

Contest Winner

Nutty Pie-Crust Cookies

I like Italian cream cake, so I used it as inspiration for this cookie recipe. The splash of orange liqueur in the filling makes it special.

—SONJI MCCARTY-ONEZINE BEAUMONT, TX

PREP: 15 MIN. + CHILLING
BAKE: 10 MIN./BATCH + COOLING
MAKES: ABOUT 3 DOZEN

- 1 cup butter, softened
- 1¾ cups all-purpose flour
- ¼ cup confectioners' sugar
- ⅛ teaspoon salt
- ⅓ cup heavy whipping cream

FILLING

- ½ cup finely chopped pecans, toasted
- ½ cup flaked coconut, toasted
- ½ cup butter, softened
- ½ cup cream cheese, softened
- ⅛ teaspoon salt
- 2 teaspoons orange liqueur, optional
- ¾ cup confectioners' sugar

1. In a large bowl, beat butter, flour, confectioners' sugar and salt until crumbly. Beat in cream. Divide dough in half. Shape each into a disk; wrap in plastic. Refrigerate 30 minutes or until firm enough to roll.

2. Preheat oven to 350°. On a lightly floured surface, roll each portion of dough to ¼-in. thickness. Cut dough with a floured 1½-in. round cookie cutter. Place 1 in. apart on ungreased baking sheets.

3. Bake 10-12 minutes or until the edges begin to brown. Cool on pans 2 minutes. Remove to wire racks to cool completely.

4. Place pecans and coconut in a small bowl; toss to combine. Reserve ½ cup coconut mixture. In another bowl, beat butter, cream cheese, salt and, if desired, liqueur until creamy. Gradually beat in the confectioners' sugar until smooth. Fold in remaining coconut mixture. Spread over the bottoms of half of the cookies; cover with remaining cookies. Place the reserved coconut mixture in a shallow bowl. Roll the sides of the cookies in coconut mixture.

FREEZE OPTION *Transfer wrapped disks to a resealable plastic freezer bag; freeze. To use, thaw the dough in refrigerator until it is soft enough to roll. Prepare, bake and fill cookies as directed.*

Chocolate Buttermilk Squares

Every time I take a pan of these squares to a potluck, it comes back clean! At home, they vanish as fast as I make them.

—**CLARICE BAKER** STROMSBURG, NE

PREP: 20 MIN. • **BAKE:** 20 MIN.
MAKES: 15 SERVINGS

- 1 cup butter, cubed
- ¼ cup baking cocoa
- 1 cup water
- 2 cups all-purpose flour
- 2 cups sugar
- 1 teaspoon baking soda
- ½ teaspoon salt
- ½ cup buttermilk
- 2 large eggs, beaten
- 1 teaspoon vanilla extract
- 3 to 4 drops red food coloring, optional

FROSTING
- ½ cup butter, cubed
- ¼ cup baking cocoa
- ¼ cup buttermilk
- 3¾ cups confectioners' sugar
- 1 teaspoon vanilla extract
    Dash salt
- ¾ cup chopped almonds, optional

1. In a large saucepan, bring butter, cocoa and water just to a boil. Cool.
2. Meanwhile, in a large bowl, combine flour, sugar, baking soda and salt. Add the cocoa mixture and buttermilk; mix it well. Beat in the eggs, vanilla and, if desired, food coloring. Pour into a greased and floured 15x10x1-in. baking pan.
3. Bake at 350° for 20 minutes. To make the frosting, melt the butter with cocoa and buttermilk. Stir in confectioners' sugar, vanilla and salt. Spread over the warm cake. Garnish with nuts if desired.

Contest Winner

Aunt Myrtle's Coconut Oat Cookies

These cookies are the stuff of happy memories. Coconut and oatmeal give them rich flavor and texture. Store them in your best cookie jar.

—**CATHERINE CASSIDY** MILWAUKEE, WI

PREP: 30 MIN. • **BAKE:** 10 MIN./BATCH
MAKES: ABOUT 5 DOZEN

- 1 cup butter, softened
- 1 cup packed brown sugar
- 2 large eggs
- 2 teaspoons vanilla extract
- 2⅓ cups all-purpose flour
- 1 teaspoon salt
- 1 teaspoon baking soda
- ¾ teaspoon baking powder
- 2 cups flaked coconut
- 1 cup old-fashioned or quick-cooking oats
- ¾ cup chopped walnuts, toasted

1. Preheat oven to 375°. In a large bowl, cream butter and brown sugar until light and fluffy. Beat in eggs and vanilla. In another bowl, whisk flour, salt, baking soda and baking powder; gradually beat into creamed mixture. Stir in coconut, oats and walnuts.
2. Drop dough by tablespoonfuls 2 in. apart onto ungreased baking sheets. Bake 8-10 minutes or until light brown. Remove from pans to wire racks to cool.
NOTE *To toast nuts, bake in a shallow pan in a 350° oven for 5-10 minutes or cook in a skillet over low heat until lightly browned, stirring occasionally.*

BIT OF A CRUNCH

Have a bake sale, party or holiday get-together coming up? Get a little nutty or crunchy.
Sweet treats like these won't last long, so you may want to double up!

Nutty Chocolate Peanut Clusters

I am always surprised at just how simple these chocolaty nut clusters are to make. They're a great treat to bring out after a meal or for a party.

—CHRISTINE EILERTS JONES, OK

PREP: 10 MIN. + CHILLING • **COOK:** 10 MIN.
MAKES: 2¾ POUNDS

- 1 pound white candy coating, chopped
- 2 cups (12 ounces) semisweet chocolate chips
- 1 jar (16 ounces) dry roasted peanuts

1. In a double boiler or metal bowl over hot water, melt candy coating and chocolate chips; stir until smooth. Remove from heat; stir in peanuts.
2. Drop by rounded teaspoonfuls onto waxed paper-lined baking sheets. Refrigerate for 10-15 minutes or until set. Store in airtight containers.

Butterfinger Cookie Bars

My boys went through a phase where they loved Butterfingers and wanted them in all kinds of desserts. We experimented with different recipes; this one was voted the best of the bunch.

—BARBARA LEIGHTY SIMI VALLEY, CA

PREP: 20 MIN. • **BAKE:** 25 MIN. + COOLING
MAKES: 3 DOZEN

- 1 package dark chocolate cake mix (regular size)
- 1 cup all-purpose flour
- 1 package (3.9 ounces) instant chocolate pudding mix
- 1 tablespoon baking cocoa
- ½ cup 2% milk
- ⅓ cup canola oil
- ⅓ cup butter, melted
- 2 large eggs, divided use
- 6 Butterfinger candy bars (2.1 ounces each), divided
- 1½ cups chunky peanut butter
- 1 teaspoon vanilla extract
- 1½ cups semisweet chocolate chips, divided

1. Preheat oven to 350°. In a large bowl, combine the cake mix, flour, pudding mix and cocoa. In another bowl, whisk milk, oil, butter and 1 egg until blended. Add to dry ingredients; stir just until moistened. Press half of the mixture into a greased 15x10x1-in. baking pan. Bake 10 minutes.
2. Meanwhile, chop two candy bars. Stir the peanut butter, vanilla and remaining egg into remaining cake mix mixture. Fold in chopped bars and 1 cup chocolate chips.
3. Chop three additional candy bars; sprinkle over warm crust and press down gently. Cover with cake mix mixture; press down firmly with a metal spatula. Crush the remaining candy bar; sprinkle crushed bar and remaining chocolate chips over top.
4. Bake 25-30 minutes or until a toothpick inserted in center comes out clean. Cool on a wire rack. Cut into bars. Store in an airtight container.

Coconut-Macadamia Biscotti

I created this recipe after my husband and I returned from our first trip to Hawaii. Dipping these tropical treats in a good cup of coffee brings us right back to the wonderful memories we made there.

—SHANNON KOENE BLACKSBURG, VA

PREP: 20 MIN. • **BAKE:** 55 MIN. + STANDING
MAKES: ABOUT 2½ DOZEN

- 6 tablespoons butter, softened
- ¾ cup sugar
- ⅓ cup canola oil
- 3 large eggs
- 2 teaspoons vanilla extract
- 1 teaspoon coconut extract
- 3¼ cups all-purpose flour
- 1¾ teaspoons baking powder
- ¼ teaspoon salt
- 1 cup flaked coconut, toasted and finely chopped
- 1 cup macadamia nuts, coarsely chopped
- 2 cups (12 ounces) semisweet chocolate chips
- 2 tablespoons shortening

1. Preheat oven to 350°. In a large bowl, beat the butter, sugar and oil until they are blended. Beat in the eggs and extracts. In another bowl, whisk the flour, baking powder and salt; gradually beat into the creamed mixture. Stir in coconut and nuts.

2. Divide the dough in half. Using parchment paper-lined baking sheets, shape each of the halves into an 8x3-in. rectangle. Bake about 25 minutes or until set.

3. Place the pans on wire racks. When cool enough to handle, transfer baked rectangles to a cutting board. Using a serrated knife, cut crosswise into ½-in. slices. Return to the pans, cut side down.

4. Bake 15-18 minutes on each side or until golden brown. Remove from pans to wire racks to cool completely.

5. In a microwave, melt chocolate chips and shortening; stir until smooth. Dip each cookie halfway into mixture; allow excess to drip. Place on waxed paper until set. Store in an airtight container.

Chocolate-Covered Peanut Butter & Pretzel Truffles

Chocolate, peanut butter and pretzels create an irresistible truffle. It's a special indulgence for the holidays.

—ASHLEY WISNIEWSKI CHAMPAIGN, IL

PREP: 40 MIN. + CHILLING • **MAKES:** 3 DOZEN

- 1¾ cups creamy peanut butter, divided
- ⅓ cup confectioners' sugar
- ¼ cup packed brown sugar
- 2 tablespoons butter, softened
- ⅛ teaspoon salt
- 3¼ cups crushed pretzels, divided
- 3 cups (18 ounces) semisweet chocolate chips
- 3 tablespoons shortening

1. In a large bowl, beat 1½ cups peanut butter, confectioners' sugar, brown sugar, butter and salt until blended. Stir in 3 cups pretzels.

2. Shape pretzel mixture into 1-in. balls; transfer to waxed paper-lined baking sheets. Refrigerate at least 30 minutes or until firm.

3. In a microwave, melt chocolate chips and shortening; stir until smooth. Dip truffles in chocolate; allow excess to drip off. Return to baking sheets.

4. Microwave remaining peanut butter on high for 30-45 seconds or until melted. Drizzle over truffles; sprinkle with remaining pretzels. Refrigerate until set. Store between layers of waxed paper in an airtight container in the refrigerator.

Cardamom-Blackberry Linzer Cookies

When you bite into one of these cookies, it's like you're enjoying a miniature version of the Austrian classic, the Linzer torte. The cardamom goes well with the jam.

—**CHRISTIANNA GOZZI** ASTORIA, NY

PREP: 50 MIN. + CHILLING • **BAKE:** 10 MIN./BATCH + COOLING
MAKES: ABOUT 2 DOZEN

- 2 cups all-purpose flour
- 1 cup salted roasted almonds
- 2 to 3 teaspoons ground cardamom
- ¼ teaspoon salt
- 1 cup unsalted butter, softened
- ½ cup plus 1 teaspoon sugar, divided
- 1 large egg
- 1 jar (10 ounces) seedless blackberry spreadable fruit
- 1 tablespoon lemon juice
- 3 tablespoons confectioners' sugar

1. In a food processor, combine ½ cup flour and almonds; pulse until almonds are finely ground. Add cardamom, salt and remaining flour; pulse until combined.
2. In a large bowl, cream butter and ½ cup sugar until light and fluffy. Beat in egg. Gradually beat in the flour mixture. Divide dough in half. Shape each into a disk; wrap in plastic. Refrigerate 1 hour or until firm enough to roll.
3. Preheat oven to 350°. On a lightly floured surface, roll each portion to ⅛-in. thickness. Cut with a floured 2-in. round cookie cutter. Using a floured 1-in. round cookie cutter, cut out the centers of half the cookies. Place solid and window cookies 1 in. apart on greased baking sheets.
4. Bake 10-12 minutes or until light brown. Remove from pans to wire racks to cool completely.
5. In a small bowl, mix spreadable fruit, lemon juice and remaining sugar. Spread filling on bottoms of solid cookies; top with window cookies. Dust with confectioners' sugar.

Macadamia Sunshine Bars

Your guests will be delighted with my bars. They are packed with nuts and dried fruit. When you take a bite of this treat it's like a mini-vacation to a Polynesian paradise.

—**JEANNE HOLT** MENDOTA HEIGHTS, MN

PREP: 20 MIN. • **BAKE:** 35 MIN. + COOLING • **MAKES:** 2 DOZEN

- 1 package lemon cake mix (regular size)
- ⅔ cup packed light brown sugar
- ½ teaspoon Chinese five-spice powder
- ¾ cup butter, melted
- 2 large eggs
- 4½ teaspoons thawed pineapple-orange juice concentrate
- 2 teaspoons grated orange peel
- 2 teaspoons grated lemon peel
- ½ teaspoon vanilla extract
- 2 jars (3 ounces each) macadamia nuts, coarsely chopped
- ⅔ cup coarsely chopped shelled pistachios
- ⅔ cup chopped dried pineapple
- ⅔ cup chopped dried mangoes
- ⅓ cup flaked coconut, toasted
- **GLAZE**
- 1¼ cups confectioners' sugar
- 1½ teaspoons thawed pineapple-orange juice concentrate
- 4 to 5 teaspoons water

1. In large bowl, combine the cake mix, brown sugar and spice powder. Add the butter, eggs, juice concentrate, orange and lemon peels and vanilla; beat on medium speed for 2 minutes. Stir in the nuts, dried fruits and coconut.
2. Spread into a greased 13x9-in. baking pan. Bake at 350° for 35-40 minutes or until a toothpick inserted near the center comes out clean. Cool completely on a wire rack.
3. Combine the confectioners' sugar, juice concentrate and enough water to reach desired consistency; drizzle over top. Cut into bars.

Contest Winner

Cranberry Cookies with Browned Butter Glaze

I won a baking contest with these soft, glazed cookies, which are so easy to make. The fresh cranberries make them perfect for the holidays or other special occasions.

—**LAURIE CORNETT** CHARLEVOIX, MI

PREP: 40 MIN. • **BAKE:** 10 MIN./BATCH + COOLING
MAKES: ABOUT 4½ DOZEN

- ½ cup butter, softened
- 1 cup sugar
- ¾ cup packed brown sugar
- 1 large egg
- 2 tablespoons orange juice
- 3 cups all-purpose flour
- 1 teaspoon baking powder
- ½ teaspoon salt
- ¼ teaspoon baking soda
- ¼ cup 2% milk
- 2½ cups coarsely chopped fresh cranberries
- 1 cup white baking chips
- 1 cup chopped pecans or walnuts

GLAZE

- ⅓ cup butter, cubed
- 2 cups confectioners' sugar
- 1½ teaspoons vanilla extract
- 3 to 4 tablespoons water

1. Preheat oven to 375°. In a large bowl, cream butter and sugars until light and fluffy. Beat in egg and orange juice. In another bowl, whisk flour, baking powder, salt and baking soda; add to creamed mixture alternately with milk. Stir in cranberries, baking chips and pecans.
2. Drop dough by level tablespoonfuls 1 in. apart onto greased baking sheets. Bake 10-12 minutes or until light brown. Remove from pans to wire racks to cool completely.
3. For glaze, in a small heavy saucepan, melt butter over medium heat. Heat 5-7 minutes or until golden brown,

stirring constantly. Remove from heat. Stir in confectioners' sugar, vanilla and enough water to reach a drizzling consistency. Drizzle over cookies. Let stand until set.

Coconut-Almond Cookie Bark

As kids, my friends and I sandwiched Almond Joys between cookies. For our high school reunion, I re-created the idea with a tasty cookie version that breaks apart like chocolate bark.

—**FAITH CROMWELL** SAN FRANCISCO, CA

PREP: 25 MIN. + COOLING • **BAKE:** 25 MIN. + COOLING
MAKES: ABOUT 2 POUNDS

- 1 cup butter, cubed
- ½ cup sugar
- ½ cup packed brown sugar
- 1 large egg
- ¾ teaspoon almond extract
- 2 cups all-purpose flour
- ¾ teaspoon salt
- 1¼ cups flaked coconut, divided
- 1½ cups milk chocolate chips, divided
- ⅓ cup sliced almonds, toasted

1. Preheat oven to 375°. In a small heavy saucepan, melt the butter over medium heat. Heat 6-8 minutes or until golden brown, stirring constantly. Transfer to a large bowl; cool for 15 minutes.
2. Whisk in sugars, egg and extract until smooth. In another bowl, whisk flour and salt; stir into the sugar mixture. Fold in 1 cup coconut and ¾ cup chocolate chips. Press into an ungreased 15x10x1-in. baking pan. Bake 24-28 minutes or until golden brown.
3. Transfer pan to a wire rack; sprinkle with remaining chocolate chips. Toast remaining coconut. Spread chocolate chips evenly over cookie. Sprinkle with remaining coconut; top with almonds. Cool completely in pan on a wire rack.
4. Refrigerate 15 minutes or until chocolate is set. Break cookie into pieces.

Molasses Crackle Cookies

You can treat yourself to one or two of my crackle cookies without any guilt. Most molasses cookies are loaded with butter and have way too much sugar, but not mine. You would never know these are so low in fat.

—JEAN ECOS HARTLAND, WI

PREP: 20 MIN. + CHILLING
BAKE: 10 MIN./BATCH
MAKES: 2½ DOZEN

- ⅔ cup sugar
- ¼ cup canola oil
- 1 large egg
- ⅓ cup molasses
- 2 cups white whole wheat flour
- 1½ teaspoons baking soda
- 1 teaspoon ground cinnamon
- ½ teaspoon salt
- ¼ teaspoon ground ginger
- ¼ teaspoon ground cloves
- 1 tablespoon confectioners' sugar

1. In a small bowl, beat the sugar and oil until blended. Beat in the egg and molasses. Combine the flour, baking soda, cinnamon, salt, ginger and cloves; gradually add to the sugar mixture and mix well. Cover and refrigerate at least 2 hours.

2. Preheat oven to 350°. Shape dough into 1-in. balls; roll in confectioners' sugar. Place them 2 in. apart on baking sheets coated with cooking spray; flatten slightly. Bake 7-9 minutes or until set. Remove to wire racks to cool.

Contest Winner

Ginger & Maple Macadamia Nut Cookies

The pop of ginger flavor in this spiced cookie reminds me of the traditional German lebkuchen. Add colored sprinkles for extra sparkle.

—THOMAS FAGLON SOMERSET, NJ

PREP: 45 MIN. + CHILLING
BAKE: 10 MIN./BATCH + COOLING
MAKES: ABOUT 7 DOZEN

- 1½ cups butter, softened
- ½ cup sugar
- ¾ cup maple syrup
- 4 cups all-purpose flour
- 3 teaspoons ground ginger
- 3 teaspoons ground cinnamon
- 1 teaspoon ground allspice
- ½ teaspoon ground cloves
- 1½ teaspoons salt
- 1½ teaspoons baking soda
- 1½ cups finely chopped macadamia nuts
- 24 ounces dark chocolate candy coating, melted
- ⅓ cup finely chopped crystallized ginger

1. In a large bowl, cream butter and sugar until light and fluffy. Gradually beat in syrup. In another bowl, whisk flour, spices, salt and baking soda; gradually beat into creamed mixture. Stir in nuts.

2. Divide dough in half; shape each into a 12-in.-long roll. Wrap in plastic wrap; refrigerate 2 hours or until firm.

3. Preheat oven to 350°. Unwrap and cut dough crosswise into ¼-in. slices. Place 1 in. apart on ungreased baking sheets. Bake 8-10 minutes or until set. Cool on pans 2 minutes. Remove to wire racks to cool completely.

4. Dip each cookie halfway into the melted candy coating; allow excess to drip off. Place on waxed paper-lined baking sheets; sprinkle cookies with crystallized ginger. Refrigerate them until set.

DIY ALLSPICE

Out of allspice? No problem! You can make your own: For one teaspoon of allspice, mix ½ teaspoon ground cinnamon and ½ teaspoon ground cloves.

Chocolate-Dipped Strawberry Meringue Roses

Eat these as is, or crush them into a bowl of strawberries and whipped cream. Readers of my blog, *utry.it,* went nuts when I posted that idea!

—AMY TONG ANAHEIM, CA

PREP: 25 MIN. • **BAKE:** 40 MIN. + COOLING
MAKES: 3½ DOZEN

- 3 large egg whites
- ¼ cup sugar
- ¼ cup freeze-dried strawberries
- 1 package (3 ounces) strawberry gelatin
- ½ teaspoon vanilla extract, optional
- 1 cup 60% cacao bittersweet chocolate baking chips, melted

1. Place egg whites in a large bowl; let stand at room temperature 30 minutes. Preheat oven to 225°.
2. Place sugar and strawberries in a food processor; process until powdery. Add gelatin; pulse to blend.
3. Beat the egg whites on medium speed until foamy, adding vanilla if desired. Gradually add gelatin mixture, 1 tablespoon at a time, beating on high after each addition until sugar is dissolved. Continue beating until stiff glossy peaks form.
4. Cut a small hole in the tip of a pastry bag or in a corner of a food-safe plastic bag; insert a #1M star tip. Transfer meringue to bag. Pipe 2-in. roses 1½ in. apart onto parchment paper-lined baking sheets.
5. Bake 40-45 minutes or until set and dry. Turn off oven (do not open oven door); leave meringues in oven 1½ hours. Remove from oven; cool completely on baking sheets.
6. Remove meringues from paper. Dip bottoms in melted chocolate; allow excess to drip off. Place on waxed paper; let stand until set, about 45 minutes. Store in an airtight container at room temperature.

Contest Winner

Ultimate Double Chocolate Brownies

We live in the city, but just a block away we can see cattle grazing in a grassy green pasture, a sight I never tire of. As someone who grew up in the country, I love this type of home-style recipe.

—CAROL PREWETT CHEYENNE, WY

PREP: 15 MIN. • **BAKE:** 35 MIN.
MAKES: 3 DOZEN

- ¾ cup baking cocoa
- ½ teaspoon baking soda
- ⅔ cup butter, melted, divided
- ½ cup boiling water
- 2 cups sugar
- 2 large eggs
- 1⅓ cups all-purpose flour
- 1 teaspoon vanilla extract
- ¼ teaspoon salt
- ½ cup coarsely chopped pecans
- 2 cups (12 ounces) semisweet chocolate chunks

1. Preheat the oven to 350°. In a large bowl, combine cocoa and baking soda; blend ⅓ cup melted butter. Add the boiling water; stir until well blended. Stir in the sugar, eggs and remaining butter. Add flour, vanilla and salt. Stir in pecans and chocolate chunks.
2. Pour into a greased 13x9-in. baking pan. Bake 35-40 minutes or until the brownies begin to pull away from sides of pan. Cool.

Peanut Pretzel Toffee Bark

My toffee has been a traditional must-make treat for my family and friends for over 40 years. My toffee was my dad's favorite candy and each time I make it, I think of him.

—**BARBARA ESTABROOK** RHINELANDER, WI

PREP: 10 MIN. • **COOK:** 15 MIN. + CHILLING • **MAKES:** 1½ POUNDS

- 2 teaspoons plus 1 cup butter, divided
- ⅔ cup honey-roasted peanuts, coarsely chopped
- ½ cup miniature pretzels, coarsely chopped
- 1 cup sugar
- 2 tablespoons water
- 2 tablespoons honey
- 1 cup (6 ounces) 60% cacao bittersweet chocolate baking chips
  Sea salt, optional

1. Line bottom of a greased 9-in. square baking pan with foil; grease foil with 2 teaspoons butter. Sprinkle peanuts and pretzels onto foil.

2. In a large heavy saucepan, combine sugar, water, honey and remaining butter; bring to a boil over medium-high heat, stirring constantly. Cook 4 minutes without stirring. Stirring constantly, cook 2-3 minutes longer or until mixture is caramel-colored (a candy thermometer should read 300° for hard-crack stage). Remove from the heat. Immediately pour over peanuts and pretzels.

3. Sprinkle with chocolate chips; let stand until chocolate begins to melt. Spread evenly. If desired, sprinkle with salt. Cool 15 minutes at room temperature. Refrigerate until set, about 30 minutes.

4. Break toffee into pieces. Store between layers of waxed paper in an airtight container.

Creamy Orange Caramels

Each Christmas I teach myself a new candy recipe. Last year I started with my caramel recipe and added a splash of orange extract for fun. This year I might try buttered rum extract.

—**SHELLY BEVINGTON** HERMISTON, OR

PREP: 10 MIN. • **COOK:** 30 MIN. + STANDING
MAKES: ABOUT 2½ POUNDS (80 PIECES)

- 1 teaspoon plus 1 cup butter, divided
- 2 cups sugar
- 1 cup light corn syrup
- 1 can (14 ounces) sweetened condensed milk
- 1 teaspoon orange extract
- 1 teaspoon vanilla extract

1. Line an 11x7-in. dish with foil, then grease the foil with 1 teaspoon butter.

2. In a large heavy saucepan, combine sugar, corn syrup and remaining butter. Bring to a boil over medium heat, stirring constantly. Reduce heat to medium-low; boil gently, without stirring, for 4 minutes.

3. Remove from the heat; gradually stir in milk. Cook and stir until a candy thermometer reads 244° (firm-ball stage). Remove from the heat; stir in extracts. Immediately pour into prepared dish (do not scrape saucepan). Let it stand until firm.

4. Using foil, lift out candy; remove foil. Using a buttered knife, cut caramel into 1x¾-in. pieces. Wrap individually in waxed paper; twist ends.

NOTE *We recommend that you test your candy thermometer before each use by bringing water to a boil; the thermometer should read 212°. Adjust your recipe temperature up or down based on your test.*

Cappuccino Brownies

There's something magical in coffee that intensifies the flavor of chocolate. These three-layer wonders freeze well, but somehow most of them disappear before they reach the freezer.

—**SUSIE JONES** BUHL, ID

PREP: 30 MIN. + CHILLING • **BAKE:** 25 MIN. + COOLING
MAKES: 2 DOZEN

- 8 **ounces bittersweet chocolate, chopped**
- ¾ **cup butter, cut up**
- 2 **tablespoons instant coffee granules**
- 1 **tablespoon hot water**
- 4 **large eggs**
- 1½ **cups sugar**
- 2 **teaspoons vanilla extract**
- 1 **cup all-purpose flour**
- ½ **teaspoon salt**
- 1 **cup chopped walnuts**

TOPPING
- 1 **package (8 ounces) cream cheese, softened**
- 6 **tablespoons butter, softened**
- 1½ **cups confectioners' sugar**
- 1 **teaspoon ground cinnamon**
- 1 **teaspoon vanilla extract**

GLAZE
- 4 **teaspoons instant coffee granules**

- 1 **tablespoon hot water**
- 5 **ounces bittersweet chocolate, chopped**
- 2 **tablespoons butter**
- ½ **cup heavy whipping cream**

1. Preheat oven to 350°. In a microwave, melt chocolate and butter; stir until smooth. Cool slightly. Dissolve coffee granules in hot water. In a large bowl, beat eggs and sugar. Stir in vanilla, chocolate mixture and the coffee mixture. Combine flour and salt; gradually add to the chocolate mixture until blended. Fold in walnuts.

2. Transfer to a greased and floured 13x9-in. baking pan. Bake 25-30 minutes or until a toothpick inserted near the center comes out clean. Cool completely on a wire rack.

3. For topping, in a large bowl, beat cream cheese and butter until blended. Add confectioners' sugar, cinnamon and vanilla; beat on low speed until combined. Spread over bars. Refrigerate until firm, about 1 hour.

4. For glaze, dissolve coffee granules in hot water. In a microwave, melt chocolate and butter; cool slightly. Stir in cream and coffee mixture. Spread over cream cheese layer. Let stand until set. Cut into bars. Refrigerate leftovers.

 FREEZE OPTION *Securely wrap and freeze cooled brownies in plastic wrap and foil. To use, thaw at room temperature.*

DAZZLING DESSERTS

It's finally time for what we all want—dessert! Here's your chance to truly wow loved ones with a bit of after-dinner or snacktime sweetness. These down-home desserts are the best of the best!

Triple Fruit Freeze

These pops won't turn your tongue blue or neon green like many store-bought pops because they're made with fresh grapes, blueberries and kiwifruit. What could be better?

—COLLEEN LUDOVICE WAUWATOSA, WI

PREP: 20 MIN. + FREEZING
MAKES: 10 POPS

- 1 **cup sliced peeled kiwifruit (about 3 medium)**
- 1 **cup water, divided**
- 2 **tablespoons sugar, divided**
- 10 **plastic or paper cups (3 ounces each) and wooden pop sticks**
- 1 **cup fresh blueberries or frozen unsweetened blueberries**
- ½ **cup seedless red grapes**
- ½ **cup red grape juice**

1. Place kiwifruit, ½ cup water and 1 tablespoon sugar in a food processor; pulse until combined. Divide among cups. Top cups with foil and insert sticks through foil. Freeze until firm, about 2 hours.
2. Place blueberries and remaining water and sugar in food processor; pulse until combined. Spoon over kiwi layer. Freeze, covered, until firm, about 2 hours.
3. Wipe food processor clean. Repeat with grapes and grape juice. Spoon over blueberry layer. Freeze, covered, until firm.

Peach Cream Puffs

On a sizzling day, we crave something light, airy and cool. Nothing says summer like cream puffs stuffed with peaches and whipped cream.

—ANGELA BENEDICT DUNBAR, WV

PREP: 55 MIN. + COOLING
BAKE: 25 MIN. + COOLING
MAKES: 16 SERVINGS

- 1 **cup water**
- ½ **cup butter, cubed**
- ⅛ **teaspoon salt**
- 1 **cup all-purpose flour**
- 4 **large eggs**

FILLING
- 4 **medium peaches, peeled and cubed (about 3 cups)**
- ½ **cup sugar**
- ½ **cup water**
- ½ **cup peach schnapps liqueur or peach nectar**
- ½ **teaspoon ground cinnamon**
- ¼ **teaspoon ground nutmeg**

WHIPPED CREAM
- 2 **cups heavy whipping cream**
- ½ **cup confectioners' sugar**
- 3 **tablespoons peach schnapps liqueur, optional**
   Additional confectioners' sugar

1. Preheat oven to 400°. In a large saucepan, bring water, butter and salt to a rolling boil. Add flour all at once and beat until blended. Cook mixture over medium heat, stirring vigorously until it pulls away from the sides of the pan and forms a ball. Transfer dough to a large bowl; let stand 5 minutes.
2. Add eggs, one at a time, beating well after each addition until smooth. Continue beating until mixture is smooth and shiny.
3. Cut a ½-in. hole in tip of a pastry bag or in a corner of a food-safe plastic bag. Transfer the dough to bag; pipe sixteen 2-in. mounds 3 in. apart onto parchment paper-lined baking sheets.
4. Bake on a lower oven rack 25-30 minutes or until puffed, very firm and golden brown. Pierce side of each puff with tip of a knife to allow steam to escape. Cool completely on wire racks.
5. Meanwhile, in a large saucepan, combine the filling ingredients; bring to a boil, stirring occasionally. Reduce the heat; simmer, uncovered, for about 25-30 minutes or until the mixture is slightly thickened and the peaches are tender. Cool completely.
6. In a bowl, beat cream until it begins to thicken. Add confectioners' sugar and, if desired, peach schnapps; beat until soft peaks form.
7. Cut top third off each cream puff. Pull out and discard soft dough from inside tops and bottoms.
8. To serve, spoon 2 tablespoons whipped cream into each bottom; top with 2 tablespoons filling and 2 tablespoons additional whipped cream. Replace tops. Dust with additional confectioners' sugar.

Winning Rhubarb-Strawberry Pie

While being raised on a farm, I often ate rhubarb, so it's natural for me to use it in a pie. I prefer to use lard for the flaky pie crust and thin, red rhubarb stalks for the filling. These two little secrets helped this recipe achieve top honors at the 2013 Iowa State Fair.

—MARIANNE CARLSON JEFFERSON, IA

PREP: 50 MIN. + CHILLING
BAKE: 65 MIN. + COOLING
MAKES: 8 SERVINGS

- 1 large egg
- 4 to 5 tablespoons ice water, divided
- ¾ teaspoon white vinegar
- 2¼ cups all-purpose flour
- ¾ teaspoon salt
- ¾ cup cold lard

FILLING
- 1¼ cups sugar
- 6 tablespoons quick-cooking tapioca
- 3 cups sliced fresh or frozen rhubarb, thawed
- 3 cups halved fresh strawberries
- 3 tablespoons butter
- 1 tablespoon 2% milk
    Coarse sugar

1. In a small bowl, whisk the large egg, 4 tablespoons ice water and vinegar until blended. In a large bowl, mix the flour and salt; cut in the lard until crumbly. Gradually add egg mixture, tossing with a fork, until dough holds together when pressed. If the mixture is too dry, slowly add additional ice water, a teaspoon at a time, just until mixture comes together.

2. Divide the dough in half. Shape each into a disk; wrap in plastic wrap. Refrigerate 1 hour or overnight.

3. Preheat oven to 400°. In a bowl, mix sugar and tapioca. Add rhubarb and strawberries; toss to coat evenly. Let stand 15 minutes.

4. On a lightly floured surface, roll one half of dough to a ⅛-in.-thick circle; transfer to a 9-in. pie plate. Trim the pastry even with rim.

5. Add the filling; dot with butter. Roll the remaining dough to a ⅛-in.-thick circle. Place over filling. Trim, seal and flute edge. Cut slits in top. Brush milk over the pastry; sprinkle with coarse sugar. Place the pie on a baking sheet; bake 20 minutes.

6. Reduce oven setting to 350°. Bake 45-55 minutes or until crust is golden brown and filling is bubbly. Cool pie on a wire rack.

NOTE *If using frozen rhubarb, measure rhubarb while still frozen, then thaw completely. Drain in a colander, but do not press liquid out.*

No-Bake Oreo Cheesecake

I made 20 of these crowd-pleasing desserts in all different sizes for my wedding, and they were a big hit.

—LEANNE STINSON CARNDUFF, SK

PREP: 40 MIN. + CHILLING
MAKES: 8 SERVINGS

- 24 Oreo cookies, crushed
- 6 tablespoons butter, melted

FILLING
- 1 envelope unflavored gelatin
- ¼ cup cold water
- 1 package (8 ounces) cream cheese, softened
- ½ cup sugar
- ¾ cup 2% milk
- 1 cup whipped topping
- 10 Oreo cookies, coarsely chopped

1. In a small bowl, mix the crushed cookies and butter. Press onto the bottom of a greased 9-in. springform pan. Refrigerate until ready to use.

2. In a small saucepan, sprinkle the gelatin over cold water; let it stand 1 minute. Heat and stir over low heat until gelatin is completely dissolved. Let stand 5 minutes.

3. In a large bowl, beat cream cheese and sugar until smooth; gradually add milk. Beat in the gelatin mixture. Fold in the whipped topping and chopped cookies. Spoon over crust.

4. Refrigerate, covered, overnight. Loosen sides of cheesecake with a knife; remove rim from pan.

Contest Winner

Cranberry-Orange Crumb Tart

After my sister took the family to the local cranberry festival, my mom bet me that I couldn't make a holiday pie out of cranberries and oranges. Considering the pie was gone before the holidays arrived, I think I won!

—**HEATHER CUNNINGHAM** WHITMAN, MA

PREP: 35 MIN. + STANDING • **BAKE:** 10 MIN. + COOLING
MAKES: 12 SERVINGS

- 2 cups crushed cinnamon graham crackers (about 14 whole crackers), divided
- ½ cup sugar, divided
- 6 tablespoons butter, melted
- ¼ cup all-purpose flour
- ¼ cup packed brown sugar
- ¼ cup cold butter, cubed

FILLING
- 1 large navel orange
- 1 cup sugar
- 3 tablespoons quick-cooking tapioca
- ¼ teaspoon baking soda
- ¼ teaspoon ground cinnamon
- ⅛ teaspoon ground allspice
- 4 cups fresh or frozen cranberries, thawed
- 2 tablespoons brandy or cranberry juice

1. Preheat the oven to 375°. In a small bowl, mix 1¾ cups crushed crackers and ¼ cup sugar; stir in the melted butter. Press onto bottom and up sides of an ungreased 11-in. fluted tart pan with removable bottom. Bake 7-8 minutes or until edges are lightly browned. Cool on a wire rack.
2. For topping, in a small bowl, mix flour, brown sugar, and remaining crushed crackers and sugar; cut in cold butter until crumbly. Refrigerate while preparing filling.
3. Finely grate enough peel from the orange to measure 1 tablespoon. Cut a thin slice from the top and bottom of the orange; stand orange upright on a cutting board. Cut off peel and outer membrane, starting from the top. Holding orange over a bowl to catch juices, remove orange sections by cutting along the membrane. Squeeze membrane to reserve additional juice.
4. In a large saucepan, mix sugar, tapioca, baking soda, cinnamon and allspice. Add cranberries, brandy, grated peel and reserved juice; toss to coat. Let stand 15 minutes. Preheat oven to 425°.
5. Bring cranberry mixture to a full boil, stirring constantly. Add orange sections; heat through. Pour into crust; sprinkle with topping. Bake 10-15 minutes or until topping is golden brown. Cool on a wire rack.

Cinnamon-Toast Blueberry Bakes

What a treat! These little toast cups dotted with blueberries are so yummy served warm from the oven.

—**CLAIRE L. WATSON** CAPE GIRARDEAU, MO

START TO FINISH: 30 MIN. • **MAKES:** 4 SERVINGS

- 6 tablespoons butter, melted
- 3 tablespoons sugar
- ½ teaspoon ground cinnamon
- 4 slices whole wheat bread, cut into ½-inch cubes
- 1 cup fresh or frozen blueberries
- ¼ cup packed brown sugar
- 2 teaspoons lemon juice

1. In a large bowl, combine butter, sugar and cinnamon. Add bread cubes; toss to coat. In a small bowl, combine the remaining ingredients; toss to coat.
2. Place half of bread mixture in four 8-oz. ramekins. Layer with blueberry mixture and remaining bread mixture. Bake, uncovered, at 350° for 15-20 minutes or until crisp and heated through.

Mrs. Thompson's Carrot Cake

I received this recipe from the mother of a patient I cared for back in 1972 in St. Paul, Minnesota. It was, and still is, the best carrot cake I have ever tasted.

—**BECKY WACHOB** LARAMIE, WY

PREP: 30 MIN. • **BAKE:** 35 MIN. • **MAKES:** 15 SERVINGS

- 3 **cups shredded carrots**
- 1 **can (20 ounces) crushed pineapple, well drained**
- 2 **cups sugar**
- 1 **cup canola oil**
- 4 **large eggs**
- 2 **cups all-purpose flour**
- 2 **teaspoons baking soda**
- 2 **teaspoons ground cinnamon**

FROSTING
- 1 **package (8 ounces) cream cheese, softened**
- ¼ **cup butter, softened**
- 2 **teaspoons vanilla extract**
- 3¾ **cups confectioners' sugar**

1. In a large bowl, beat the first five ingredients until well blended. In another bowl, mix the flour, baking soda and cinnamon; gradually beat into carrot mixture.
2. Transfer to a greased 13x9-in. baking pan. Bake at 350° for 35-40 minutes or until a toothpick inserted in center comes out clean. Cool completely in pan on a wire rack.
3. For frosting, in a large bowl, beat the cream cheese, butter and vanilla until they are blended. Gradually beat in the confectioners' sugar until smooth. Spread over cake. Cover and refrigerate the leftovers.

Favorite Blackberry Cobbler

I love to pull our home-grown blackberries out of the freezer in winter and make this warm cobbler to enjoy summer's sweetness.
—**LORI DANIELS** BEVERLY, WV

PREP: 25 MIN. • **BAKE:** 30 MIN. • **MAKES:** 9 SERVINGS

- 3 **cups fresh or frozen blackberries**
- 1 **cup sugar**
- ¼ **teaspoon ground cinnamon**
- 3 **tablespoons cornstarch**
- 1 **cup cold water**
- 1 **tablespoon butter**

BISCUIT TOPPING
- 1½ **cups all-purpose flour**
- 1 **tablespoon sugar**
- 1½ **teaspoons baking powder**
- ½ **teaspoon salt**
- ½ **cup cold butter, cubed**
- ½ **cup 2% milk**
     Whipped topping or vanilla ice cream, optional

1. In a large saucepan, combine blackberries, sugar and cinnamon. Cook and stir until the mixture comes to a boil. Combine cornstarch and water until smooth; stir into the fruit mixture. Bring to a boil; cook and stir for 2 minutes or until thickened. Pour into a greased 8-in. square baking dish. Dot with butter.
2. For topping, in a small bowl, combine flour, sugar, baking powder and salt. Cut in butter until the mixture resembles coarse crumbs. Stir in milk just until moistened. Drop by tablespoonfuls onto hot berry mixture.
3. Bake, uncovered, at 350° for 30-35 minutes or until filling is bubbly and topping is golden brown. Serve warm, with whipped topping or ice cream if desired.

Banana Skillet Upside-Down Cake

My grandmother provided me my first cast-iron skillet, and I've been cooking and baking with it ever since. Sometimes I add drained maraschino cherries to this banana skillet dessert and serve it with ice cream on the side.

—TERRI MERRITTS NASHVILLE, TN

PREP: 25 MIN. • **BAKE:** 35 MIN.
MAKES: 10 SERVINGS

- 1 package (14 ounces) banana quick bread and muffin mix
- ½ cup chopped walnuts
- ¼ cup butter, cubed
- ¾ cup packed brown sugar
- 2 tablespoons lemon juice
- 4 medium bananas, cut into ¼-inch slices
- 2 cups flaked coconut

1. Preheat oven to 375°. Prepare banana bread batter according to package directions; stir in walnuts.
2. In a 10-in. ovenproof skillet, melt butter over medium heat; stir in brown sugar until dissolved. Add lemon juice; cook and stir 2-3 minutes longer or until slightly thickened. Remove from heat. Arrange bananas in a single layer over brown sugar mixture; sprinkle with coconut.
3. Spoon the prepared batter over coconut. Bake 35-40 minutes or until dark golden and a toothpick inserted in the center comes out clean. Cool 5 minutes before inverting onto a serving plate. Serve warm.

Coconut-Pecan German Chocolate Pie

This pie combines the ingredients that everyone loves in its classic cake cousin. It's so silky and smooth, you won't be able to put your fork down.

—ANNA JONES COPPELL, TX

PREP: 50 MIN. + CHILLING
BAKE: 35 MIN. + CHILLING
MAKES: 8 SERVINGS

- 1¼ cups all-purpose flour
- ¼ teaspoon salt
- 6 tablespoons cold lard
- 3 to 4 tablespoons ice water

FILLING
- 4 ounces German sweet chocolate, chopped
- 2 ounces unsweetened chocolate, chopped
- 1 can (14 ounces) sweetened condensed milk
- 4 egg yolks
- 1 teaspoon vanilla extract
- 1 cup chopped pecans

TOPPING
- ½ cup packed brown sugar
- ½ cup heavy whipping cream
- ¼ cup butter, cubed
- 2 large egg yolks
- 1 cup flaked coconut
- 1 teaspoon vanilla extract
- ¼ cup chopped pecans

1. In a small bowl, mix flour and salt; cut in lard until crumbly. Gradually add ice water, tossing with a fork until dough holds together when pressed.

Shape into a disk; wrap in plastic wrap. Refrigerate 30 minutes or overnight.
2. Preheat oven to 400°. On a lightly floured surface, roll the dough to a ⅛-in.-thick circle; transfer to a 9-in. pie plate. Trim pastry to ½ in. beyond rim of plate; flute edge. Line unpricked pastry with a double thickness of foil. Fill with pie weights, dried beans or uncooked rice.
3. Bake 11-13 minutes or until bottom is lightly browned. Remove foil and weights; bake 6-8 minutes longer or until light brown. Cool on a wire rack. Reduce oven setting to 350°.
4. In a microwave, melt chocolates in a large bowl; stir until smooth. Cool slightly. Whisk in milk, egg yolks and vanilla; stir in pecans. Pour into crust. Bake 16-19 minutes or until set. Cool 1 hour on a wire rack.
5. Meanwhile, in a small heavy saucepan, combine the brown sugar, cream and butter. Bring to a boil over medium heat, stirring to dissolve sugar. Remove from heat.
6. In a small bowl, whisk a small amount of hot mixture into egg yolks; return all to pan, whisking constantly. Cook 2-3 minutes or until mixture thickens and a thermometer reads 160°, stirring constantly. Remove from heat. Stir in coconut and vanilla; cool 10 minutes.
7. Pour over the filling; sprinkle with pecans. Refrigerate the pie 4 hours or until it is cold.

Caramel-Apple Skillet Buckle

My grandmother used to make a version of this for me when I was a little girl. She would make it using fresh apples from her tree in the backyard. I have adapted her recipe because I love the combination of apple, pecans and caramel.

—EMILY HOBBS SPRINGFIELD, MO

PREP: 35 MIN. • **BAKE:** 1 HOUR + STANDING
MAKES: 12 SERVINGS

- ½ cup butter, softened
- ¾ cup sugar
- 2 large eggs
- 1 teaspoon vanilla extract
- 2 cups all-purpose flour
- 2½ teaspoons baking powder
- 1¾ teaspoons ground cinnamon
- ½ teaspoon ground ginger
- ¼ teaspoon salt
- 1½ cups buttermilk

TOPPING
- ⅔ cup packed brown sugar
- ½ cup all-purpose flour
- ¼ cup cold butter
- ¾ cup finely chopped pecans
- ½ cup old-fashioned oats
- 6 cups thinly sliced peeled Gala or other sweet apples (about 6 medium)
- 18 caramels, unwrapped
- 1 tablespoon buttermilk
  Vanilla ice cream, optional

1. Preheat the oven to 350°. In a large bowl, cream butter and sugar until light and fluffy. Add the eggs, one at a time, beating well after each addition. Beat in vanilla. In another bowl, whisk the flour, baking powder, cinnamon, ginger and salt; add to the creamed mixture alternately with buttermilk, beating well after each addition. Pour into a greased 12-in. ovenproof skillet.
2. For topping, in a small bowl, mix brown sugar and flour; cut in butter until crumbly. Stir in the pecans and oats; sprinkle over batter. Top with apples. Bake 60-70 minutes or until the apples are golden brown. Cool in pan on a wire rack.
3. In a microwave, melt caramels with buttermilk; stir until smooth. Drizzle over the cake. Let stand until set. If desired, serve with ice cream.

Berry White Ice Pops

Kids and adults will love these ice pops speckled with colorful mixed berries for a nice cold treat.

—SHARON GUINTA STAMFORD, CT

PREP: 10 MIN. + FREEZING
MAKES: 10 POPS

- 1¾ cups whole milk, divided
- 1 to 2 tablespoons honey
- ¼ teaspoon vanilla extract
- 1½ cups fresh raspberries
- 1 cup fresh blueberries
- 10 freezer pop molds or 10 paper cups (3 ounces each) and wooden pop sticks

1. In a microwave, warm ¼ cup milk; stir in honey until blended. Stir in remaining 1½ cups milk and vanilla.
2. Divide berries among molds; cover with milk mixture. Top molds with holders. If using cups, top with foil and insert sticks through foil. Freeze until firm.

> **YOGURT POPS**
>
> For a refreshing summer treat, push a wooden pop stick through the foil cover of a small yogurt container. (Be sure to remove the plastic lid first if there is one.) Pop it in the freezer until it's frozen, then remove the plastic container and enjoy your frosty fruit pop!
>
> —DIANNE M. LAKEMOOR, IL

PEANUT BUTTER LOVE

What takes a dessert from delicious to over-the-top good? Answer: peanut butter!
You deserve to treat yourself with these decadent delights.

Peanut Butter Cup Trifle

The billowing layers of the trifle are a nice contrast to the peanut butter cups. You can add a little extra decoration with chocolate jimmies, too.

—CHRIS NELSON DECATUR, AR

START TO FINISH: 20 MIN.
MAKES: 12 SERVINGS

- 4 **cups cold 2% milk**
- 2 **packages (3.9 ounces each) instant chocolate pudding mix**
- 1 **prepared angel food cake (8 to 10 ounces), cut into 1-inch cubes**
- 1 **carton (12 ounces) frozen whipped topping, thawed**
- 2 **packages (8 ounces each) Reese's mini peanut butter cups**

In a large bowl, whisk the milk and the pudding mixes for 2 minutes. Let the mixture stand for 2 minutes or until soft-set. In a 3-qt. trifle bowl or glass bowl, layer half of cake cubes, pudding, whipped topping and peanut butter cups. Repeat layers. Refrigerate until serving.

Peanut Butter Chocolate Dessert

For me, the ideal dessert combines chocolate and peanut butter. So when I came up with this rich treat, it quickly became my all-time favorite. It's a cinch to whip together because it doesn't require any baking.

—DEBBIE PRICE LA RUE, OH

PREP: 20 MIN. + CHILLING
MAKES: 12-16 SERVINGS

- 20 **chocolate cream-filled chocolate sandwich cookies, divided**
- 2 **tablespoons butter, softened**
- 1 **package (8 ounces) cream cheese, softened**
- ½ **cup peanut butter**
- 1½ **cups confectioners' sugar, divided**
- 1 **carton (16 ounces) frozen whipped topping, thawed, divided**
- 15 **miniature peanut butter cups, chopped**
- 1 **cup cold milk**
- 1 **package (3.9 ounces) instant chocolate fudge pudding mix**

1. Crush 16 cookies; toss with butter. Press into an ungreased 9-in. square dish; set aside.
2. In a large bowl, beat cream cheese, peanut butter and 1 cup confectioners' sugar until smooth. Fold in half of the whipped topping. Spread over crust. Sprinkle with peanut butter cups.
3. In another large bowl, beat the milk, pudding mix and remaining confectioners' sugar on low speed for 2 minutes. Let stand for 2 minutes or until soft-set. Fold in remaining whipped topping.
4. Spread over peanut butter cups. Crush remaining cookies; sprinkle over the top. Cover and chill for at least 3 hours.

Contest Winner

Chocolate & Peanut Butter Mousse Cheesecake

It'll take a bit of time to make this no-bake cheesecake with chocolate, peanut butter mousse and a silky ganache, but it is well worth the effort.

—JANON FURRER PRESCOTT, AZ

PREP: 50 MIN. + CHILLING
MAKES: 16 SERVINGS

- 1½ cups chocolate wafer crumbs (about 24 wafers)
- ¼ cup butter, melted

MOUSSE LAYERS

- 1¼ cups heavy whipping cream
- ¾ cup creamy peanut butter
- 5 ounces cream cheese, softened
- 2 tablespoons butter, softened
- 1¼ cups confectioners' sugar
- 5 ounces bittersweet chocolate, chopped
- 1 milk chocolate candy bar (3½ ounces), chopped
- ⅓ cup sugar
- ¼ cup 2% milk
- 1 teaspoon vanilla extract

GANACHE

- 6 ounces bittersweet chocolate, chopped
- ⅔ cup heavy whipping cream
- 1 teaspoon vanilla extract

1. In a small bowl, mix wafer crumbs and butter. Press onto the bottom of a greased 9-in. springform pan.

2. In another bowl, beat cream until stiff peaks form. In a large bowl, beat the peanut butter, cream cheese and butter until mixture is smooth. Beat in the confectioners' sugar. Fold in half of the whipped cream. Spread evenly over crust. Refrigerate while preparing the next layer.

3. Place the bittersweet and milk chocolates in a small bowl. In a small saucepan, combine sugar and milk; bring just to a boil, stirring constantly. Pour over the chocolate; stir with a whisk until smooth. Stir in vanilla. Cool to room temperature, stirring occasionally. Fold in the remaining whipped cream. Spread evenly over the peanut butter layer. Freeze 2 hours or until firm.

4. For ganache, place chocolate in a small bowl. In a small saucepan, bring cream just to a boil. Pour over chocolate; whisk until smooth. Stir in vanilla. Cool to room temperature or until the ganache thickens to a spreading consistency, stirring occasionally. Spread over cheesecake. Refrigerate for 1 hour or until set. Remove rim from the pan.

FREEZE OPTION *Wrap individual portions of cheesecake in plastic wrap and place in a resealable plastic freezer bag. Seal bag and freeze for future use. To use, thaw completely in the refrigerator.*

Contest Winner

Peanut Butter Popcorn Balls

Friends and family are always happy to see these popcorn balls. I love making them just as much as eating them!

—BETTY CLAYCOMB ALVERTON, PA

PREP: 20 MIN. + STANDING
MAKES: 10 POPCORN BALLS

- 5 cups popped popcorn
- 1 cup dry roasted peanuts
- ½ cup sugar
- ½ cup light corn syrup
- ½ cup chunky peanut butter
- ½ teaspoon vanilla extract
- 10 lollipop sticks

1. Place popcorn and peanuts in a large bowl; set aside. In a large heavy saucepan over medium heat, bring sugar and corn syrup to a rolling boil, stirring occasionally. Remove from the heat; stir in peanut butter and vanilla. Quickly pour over popcorn mixture and mix well.

2. When cool enough to handle, quickly shape into ten 2½-in. balls; insert a lollipop stick into each ball. Let stand at room temperature until firm; wrap in plastic wrap.

Berried Treasure Angel Food Cake

My husband grills anything and everything, even dessert! With his encouragement, I came up with this easy recipe that takes just a few minutes to prepare yet always impresses dinner guests.

—ANITA ARCHIBALD AURORA, ON

START TO FINISH: 25 MIN.
MAKES: 4 SERVINGS

- 8 slices angel food cake (1½ inches thick)
- ¼ cup butter, softened
- ½ cup heavy whipping cream
- ¼ teaspoon almond extract
- ¼ cup almond cake and pastry filling
- ½ cup fresh blueberries
- ½ cup fresh raspberries
- ½ cup sliced fresh strawberries
- ¼ cup mixed nuts, coarsely chopped
  Confectioners' sugar

1. Using a 1½-in. round cookie cutter, cut out the centers of half of the cake slices (discard removed cake or save for another use). Spread butter over both sides of cake slices. Grill, covered, over medium heat or broil 4 in. from the heat 1-2 minutes on each side or until toasted.

2. In a small bowl, beat cream until it begins to thicken. Add the extract; beat until soft peaks form.

3. To serve, stack one solid and one cutout slice of cake on each dessert plate, placing outer edges on opposite sides for a more even thickness. Spoon almond filling into holes; top with the whipped cream, berries and nuts. Dust with confectioners' sugar.

Mini Lemon Cheesecake Tarts

Dainty and light, these tiny tarts feature two of my favorite things: lemon and cheesecake. And all in one yummy bite! They look lovely topped with fresh raspberries, but sliced strawberries are just as pretty and sweet.

—GWYN BRANDT HIBBING, MN

PREP: 35 MIN. + CHILLING
BAKE: 20 MIN. + COOLING
MAKES: 2 DOZEN

- 8 ounces cream cheese, softened, divided
- ½ cup plus 2 teaspoons butter, softened, divided
- ¼ teaspoon grated lemon peel
- 1 cup all-purpose flour
- ½ cup plus ⅓ cup sugar, divided
- 1 teaspoon plus 2 tablespoons lemon juice, divided
- ½ teaspoon vanilla extract
- 1 large egg, lightly beaten
- 4 teaspoons cornstarch
- ⅓ cup water
- 2 drops yellow food coloring
  Fresh raspberries

1. In a small bowl, beat 3 ounces cream cheese, ½ cup butter and lemon peel until blended. Gradually add flour, mix well. Refrigerate, covered, 1 hour or until firm.

2. Preheat the oven to 325°. Shape dough into 1-in. balls; press onto the bottom and up the sides of 24 ungreased mini muffin cups.

3. For filling, in a small bowl, beat ½ cup sugar and the remaining cream cheese until smooth. Beat in 1 teaspoon lemon juice and vanilla. Add egg; beat on low speed just until blended. Fill cups half full with cream cheese mixture. Bake 18-22 minutes or until set. Carefully run a knife around tarts to loosen from pan. Cool in pans on wire racks.

4. Meanwhile, in a saucepan, combine the cornstarch and remaining sugar; whisk in water. Bring to boil, stirring constantly; cook and stir 1-2 minutes or until thickened. Remove from the heat; gently stir in food coloring and remaining lemon juice and butter. Cool to room temperature.

5. Remove cooled tarts from pans. Spoon on the topping; top with raspberries. Store in an airtight container in the refrigerator.

Contest Winner

Cinnamon-Pear Rustic Tart

I was lucky enough to spend the holidays with my husband's family in Montana. I loved the rustic simplicity of each dish we tasted, especially this pear tart my mother-in-law made.
—LEAH WALDO JAMAICA PLAIN, MA

PREP: 45 MIN. + CHILLING • **BAKE:** 45 MIN.
MAKES: 8 SERVINGS

- 2½ cups all-purpose flour
- 1 teaspoon salt
- 1 cup cold butter, cubed
- 8 to 10 tablespoons ice water

FILLING

- 2 tablespoons butter
- 8 medium ripe pears, peeled and thinly sliced
- 1½ teaspoons ground cinnamon
- ⅓ cup apple cider or juice
- ¼ cup packed brown sugar
- 1 teaspoon vanilla extract
- 1 tablespoon coarse sugar

1. In a large bowl, mix flour and salt; cut in butter until crumbly. Gradually add ice water, tossing with a fork until dough holds together when pressed. Shape into a disk; wrap in plastic wrap. Refrigerate 30 minutes or overnight.
2. Preheat oven to 375°. In a large skillet, heat butter over medium-high heat. Add the pears and cinnamon; cook and stir 2-3 minutes or until tender. Stir in cider and brown sugar. Bring to a boil; cook and stir until thickened, 8-10 minutes. Stir in vanilla; cool slightly.
3. On a lightly floured surface, roll dough into a 14-in. circle. Transfer to a parchment paper-lined baking sheet.
4. Spoon filling over pastry to within 2 in. of edge. Fold the pastry edge over filling, pleating as you go and leaving an opening in center. Brush folded pastry with water; sprinkle with the coarse sugar. Bake until crust is golden and filling is bubbly, 45-50 minutes. Transfer tart to a wire rack to cool.

Gingerbread & Pumpkin Cream Trifle

We wait for these flavors all year long. Stack up the layers in a big trifle bowl, or make minis for everybody at the table.
—AMY GEISER FAIRLAWN, OH

PREP: 45 MIN. + CHILLING
MAKES: 10 SERVINGS

- 1 package (14½ ounces) gingerbread cake/cookie mix
- 1 package (3 ounces) cook-and-serve vanilla pudding mix
- ¼ cup packed brown sugar
- 1⅔ cups canned pumpkin pie mix
- 1 carton (8 ounces) frozen whipped topping, thawed
  Optional toppings: caramel topping, toasted pecans and gingersnap cookies

1. Prepare and bake gingerbread cake according to package directions. Cool completely on a wire rack.
2. Meanwhile, prepare pudding mix according to package directions; stir in brown sugar and pie mix. Transfer to a bowl; refrigerate, covered, 30 minutes.
3. Cut or break the gingerbread into ¾-in. pieces. In ten 12-oz. glasses or a 3-qt. trifle bowl, layer half of each of the following: cake, pumpkin mixture and whipped topping. Repeat layers. Refrigerate, covered, 4 hours or overnight. Top as desired.

Oregon's Best Marionberry Pie

I believe Oregon Marionberries make about the best berry pie in the world. And when you add some cream cheese and flavorings, you'll be making the best even better!

—FRANCES BENTHIN SCIO, OR

PREP: 30 MIN. • **BAKE:** 65 MIN. + COOLING • **MAKES:** 8 SERVINGS

- 2 cups all-purpose flour
- 1 tablespoon sugar
- 1 teaspoon salt
- ½ cup cold butter, cubed
- 5 tablespoons shortening
- 4 tablespoons ice water
- 2 tablespoons lemon juice

FILLING
- 1 cup plus 1 teaspoon sugar, divided
- 2 tablespoons plus 2 teaspoons quick-cooking tapioca
- 1 tablespoon lemon juice
- 4 cups fresh Marionberries or blackberries
- 1 package (8 ounces) cream cheese, softened
- ½ cup confectioners' sugar
- ½ teaspoon almond extract
- ½ teaspoon vanilla extract
- 1 tablespoon heavy whipping cream

1. In a large bowl, mix flour, sugar and salt; cut in butter and shortening until crumbly. Gradually add ice water and lemon juice, tossing with a fork until dough holds together when pressed. Divide dough in half. Shape each into a disk; wrap in plastic wrap. Refrigerate 10 minutes.

2. Meanwhile, in a large bowl, mix 1 cup sugar, tapioca and lemon juice. Add berries; toss to coat. Let stand 15 minutes. Preheat oven to 425°. On a lightly floured surface, roll one half of dough to a ⅛-in.-thick circle; transfer to a 9-in. pie plate. Trim pastry to ½ in. beyond rim of plate.

3. In a small bowl, beat the cream cheese, confectioners' sugar and extracts; spread mixture over prepared crust. Top with berry mixture.

4. Roll out remaining dough to a ⅛-in.-thick circle; cut into ½-in.-wide strips. Arrange over filling in a lattice pattern. Trim and seal strips to edge of bottom pastry; flute edge. Brush lattice strips with cream; sprinkle with the remaining sugar.

5. Bake 15 minutes. Reduce oven setting to 350°; bake 50-60 minutes longer or until crust is golden brown and filling is bubbly. (Cover the edges with foil during the last 15 minutes to prevent overbrowning if necessary.) Cool on a wire rack.

Baked Apple Dumplings

These versatile dumplings can be made with peaches or mixed berries in place of apples, and drizzled with hot caramel sauce instead of icing. Add vanilla custard or ice cream, and it's the perfect dessert.

—EVANGELINE BRADFORD ERLANGER, KY

PREP: 35 MIN. • **BAKE:** 15 MIN. • **MAKES:** 1½ DOZEN

- ½ cup sugar
- 3 tablespoons dry bread crumbs
- 4½ teaspoons ground cinnamon
    Dash ground nutmeg
- 1 package (17.3 ounces) frozen puff pastry, thawed
- 1 large egg, beaten
- 2¼ cups chopped peeled tart apples

STREUSEL
- ⅓ cup chopped pecans, toasted
- ⅓ cup packed brown sugar
- ⅓ cup all-purpose flour
- 2 tablespoons plus 1½ teaspoons butter, melted

ICING
- 1 cup confectioners' sugar
- 2 tablespoons 2% milk
- 1 teaspoon vanilla extract

1. In a small bowl, combine sugar, bread crumbs, cinnamon and nutmeg. On a lightly floured surface, roll pastry into two 12-in. squares. Cut each sheet into nine 4-in. squares.

2. Brush squares with egg. Place 1 teaspoon sugar mixture in the center of a square; top with 2 tablespoons chopped apple and 1 teaspoon sugar mixture. Gently bring up the corners of pastry to center; pinch edges to seal. Repeat with remaining pastry, crumb mixture and apples. Place on greased baking sheets.

3. In a small bowl, combine the streusel ingredients. Brush remaining egg over dumplings; press streusel over tops.

4. Bake at 400° for 14-18 minutes or until golden brown. Place pans on wire racks. Combine icing ingredients; drizzle over dumplings.

Lemon Chiffon Cake

My dad loved this cake. Mom revamped the original recipe to include lemons. When I make it now, my family is thrilled!

—TRISHA KAMMERS CLARKSTON, WA

PREP: 30 MIN. • **BAKE:** 50 MIN. + COOLING • **MAKES:** 16 SERVINGS

- 7 large eggs, separated
- 2 cups all-purpose flour
- 1½ cups sugar
- 3 teaspoons baking powder
- 1 teaspoon salt
- ¾ cup water
- ½ cup canola oil
- 4 teaspoons grated lemon peel
- 2 teaspoons vanilla extract
- ½ teaspoon cream of tartar

FROSTING
- ⅓ cup butter, softened
- 3 cups confectioners' sugar
- 4½ teaspoons grated lemon peel
- ¼ cup lemon juice
    Dash salt
    Additional grated lemon peel

1. Place the egg whites in a large bowl; let stand at room temperature 30 minutes. Meanwhile, preheat oven to 325°.

2. Sift flour, sugar, baking powder and salt together twice; place in another large bowl. In a small bowl, whisk egg yolks, water, oil, lemon peel and vanilla until smooth. Add to flour mixture; beat until well blended.

3. Add cream of tartar to egg whites; with clean beaters, beat on medium speed just until stiff but not dry. Fold a fourth of the whites into batter, then fold in remaining whites.

4. Gently spoon batter into an ungreased 10-in. tube pan. Cut through batter with a knife to remove air pockets. Bake on lowest oven rack 50-55 minutes or until the top springs back when lightly touched. Immediately invert pan; cool completely in pan, about 1 hour.

5. Run a knife around sides and center tube of pan. Remove cake to a serving plate.

6. In a small bowl, combine frosting ingredients; beat until smooth. Spread over cake. Top with additional grated lemon peel if desired.

Strawberry-Hazelnut Meringue Shortcakes

In early summer, the strawberry farms in our area open to the public for picking. These shortcakes really show off the big, juicy berries of our harvest.

—BARBARA ESTABROOK RHINELANDER, WI

PREP: 25 MIN. • **BAKE:** 45 MIN. + COOLING
MAKES: 8 SERVINGS

- 2 large egg whites
- ½ cup sugar
- ¼ cup finely chopped hazelnuts
- 6 cups fresh strawberries, hulled and sliced
- 4 cups low-fat frozen yogurt

1. Place egg whites in a small bowl; let stand at room temperature 30 minutes.
2. Preheat oven to 250°. Beat the egg whites on medium speed until foamy. Gradually add sugar, 1 tablespoon at a time, beating on high after each addition until sugar is dissolved. Continue beating until stiff glossy peaks form.
3. Drop the meringue into eight mounds on a parchment paper-lined baking sheet. With the back of a spoon, shape into 3-in. cups. Sprinkle with hazelnuts. Bake 45-50 minutes or until set and dry. Turn off oven (do not open oven door); leave meringues in oven 1 hour. Remove from oven; cool completely on baking sheets. Remove meringues from paper.
4. Place 3 cups of strawberries in a large bowl; mash slightly. Stir in the remaining strawberries. Just before serving, top meringues with frozen yogurt and strawberries.

Autumn Cupcakes

These yummy pumpkin cupcakes are draped in cream cheese frosting and drizzled with a homemade salted caramel sauce. They're sweet and so tasty.

—WENDY RUSCH TREGO, WI

PREP: 30 MIN. • **BAKE:** 20 MIN. + COOLING
MAKES: 2 DOZEN

- 2 cups sugar
- 1 can (15 ounces) solid-pack pumpkin
- 4 large eggs
- ¾ cup canola oil
- 1 teaspoon vanilla extract
- 2 cups all-purpose flour
- 2 teaspoons baking soda
- 2 teaspoons pumpkin pie spice
- 1 teaspoon salt
- 1 teaspoon baking powder

SAUCE
- ½ cup packed brown sugar
- 6 tablespoons heavy whipping cream
- ¼ cup butter, cubed
- ⅛ teaspoon salt
- ½ teaspoon vanilla extract

FROSTING
- 1 package (8 ounces) cream cheese, softened
- 1 cup butter, softened
- 1 teaspoon vanilla extract
- 3 cups confectioners' sugar

1. Preheat the oven to 350°. Line 24 muffin cups with paper liners. In a large bowl, beat sugar, pumpkin, eggs, oil and vanilla until well blended. In another bowl, whisk the flour, baking soda, pie spice, salt and baking powder; gradually beat into the pumpkin mixture.
2. Fill the prepared cups two-thirds full. Bake 20-22 minutes or until a toothpick inserted in center comes out clean. Cool in pans 10 minutes before removing to wire racks to cool completely.
3. For sauce, in a small, heavy saucepan, combine brown sugar, cream, butter and salt; bring to boil. Reduce the heat; cook and stir 2-3 minutes or until thickened. Remove from heat; stir in vanilla. Cool to room temperature.
4. Meanwhile, in a large bowl, beat cream cheese, butter and vanilla until blended. Gradually beat in the confectioners' sugar until smooth. Frost cupcakes; drizzle with sauce.

It's-It Ice Cream Sandwiches

You'll discover why the treat is so popular in San Francisco. It's snack heaven: ice cream, oatmeal cookies and a touch of chocolate. If you like, swap out the vanilla for your favorite flavor, such as chocolate, caramel or cherry.

—JACYN SIEBERT SAN FRANCISCO, CA

PREP: 40 MIN. + FREEZING
BAKE: 15 MIN./BATCH + COOLING
MAKES: 7 SERVINGS

- ½ cup butter, softened
- ¾ cup packed brown sugar
- ¼ cup sugar
- 1 large egg
- ½ teaspoon vanilla extract
- ¾ cup all-purpose flour
- ½ teaspoon baking soda
- ½ teaspoon ground cinnamon
- ¼ teaspoon baking powder
- ¼ teaspoon salt
- 1½ cups quick-cooking oats
- ¼ cup chopped raisins, optional

ASSEMBLY
- 3 cups vanilla ice cream
- 1 bottle (7¼ ounces) chocolate hard-shell ice cream topping

1. Preheat oven to 350°. In a large bowl, cream the butter and sugars until light and fluffy. Beat in egg and vanilla. In another bowl, whisk the flour, baking soda, cinnamon, baking powder and salt; gradually beat into creamed mixture. Stir in oats and, if desired, raisins.

2. Shape into fourteen 1¼-in. balls; place 2½ in. apart on ungreased baking sheets. Bake 11-13 minutes or until golden brown. Cool on pans for 3 minutes. Remove the balls to wire racks to cool completely.

3. To assemble ice cream sandwiches, place ⅓ cup ice cream on the bottom of a cookie. Top with a second cookie, pressing gently to flatten ice cream. Repeat with the remaining cookies and ice cream. Place on a baking sheet; freeze until firm.

4. Remove the ice cream sandwiches from the freezer. Working over a small bowl, drizzle the chocolate topping over half of each sandwich, allowing excess to drip off.

5. Place on a waxed paper-lined baking sheet; freeze until serving. Wrap individually in plastic wrap for longer storage.

Contest Winner

Butterscotch-Pecan Bread Pudding

Fans of bread pudding will absolutely adore this treat. Toppings like whipped cream and a butterscotch drizzle help make the dessert irresistible.

—LISA VARNER EL PASO, TX

PREP: 15 MIN. • **COOK:** 3 HOURS
MAKES: 8 SERVINGS

- 9 cups cubed day-old white bread (about 8 slices)
- ½ cup chopped pecans
- ½ cup butterscotch chips
- 4 large eggs
- 2 cups half-and-half cream
- ½ cup packed brown sugar
- ½ cup butter, melted
- 1 teaspoon vanilla extract
  Whipped cream and butterscotch ice cream topping

1. Place the bread, pecans and butterscotch chips in a greased 4-qt. slow cooker. In a big bowl, whisk eggs, cream, brown sugar, melted butter and vanilla until they are blended. Pour over the bread mixture; stir gently to combine.

2. Cook, covered, on low 3-4 hours or until a knife inserted in center comes out clean. Serve warm with whipped cream and butterscotch topping.

Lemon-Blueberry Pound Cake

Pair a slice of this moist cake with a scoop of vanilla ice cream. It's a staple at our family barbecues.
—**REBECCA LITTLE** PARK RIDGE, IL

PREP: 25 MIN. • **BAKE:** 55 MIN. + COOLING • **MAKES:** 12 SERVINGS

- ⅓ cup butter, softened
- 4 ounces cream cheese, softened
- 2 cups sugar
- 3 large eggs
- 1 large egg white
- 1 tablespoon grated lemon peel
- 2 teaspoons vanilla extract
- 2 cups fresh or frozen unsweetened blueberries
- 3 cups all-purpose flour, divided
- 1 teaspoon baking powder
- ½ teaspoon baking soda
- ½ teaspoon salt
- 1 cup (8 ounces) lemon yogurt

GLAZE
- 1¼ cups confectioners' sugar
- 2 tablespoons lemon juice

1. Preheat oven to 350°. Grease and flour a 10-in. fluted tube pan. In a large bowl, cream butter, cream cheese and sugar until blended. Add eggs and egg white, one at a time, beating well after each addition. Beat in the lemon peel and vanilla.

2. Toss blueberries with 2 tablespoons flour. In another bowl, mix the remaining flour with baking powder, baking soda and salt; add to the creamed mixture alternately with yogurt, beating after each addition just until combined. Fold in blueberry mixture.

3. Transfer the batter to prepared pan. Bake 55-60 minutes or until a toothpick inserted in the center comes out clean. Cool in the pan for 10 minutes before removing to wire rack; cool completely.

4. In a small bowl, mix confectioners' sugar and lemon juice until smooth. Drizzle over cake.

NOTE *For easier removal of cake, use solid shortening when greasing a fluted or plain tube pan.*

Chocolate Lover's Pudding

I first made this dish when my husband asked me, "Why don't you ever make chocolate pudding?" It's not too rich, but it has an amazing chocolate flavor. I love preparing this homemade delight!
—**CHARIS O'CONNELL** MOHNTON, PA

START TO FINISH: 30 MIN. • **MAKES:** 6 SERVINGS

- ½ cup sugar, divided
- 3 cups 2% milk
- 3 tablespoons cornstarch
- ¼ teaspoon salt
- 2 large egg yolks, beaten
- ⅓ cup baking cocoa
- 2 ounces semisweet chocolate, chopped
- 1 tablespoon butter
- 2 teaspoons vanilla extract
  Fresh raspberries, optional

1. In a large heavy saucepan, combine ¼ cup sugar and milk. Bring just to a boil, stirring occasionally. Meanwhile, in a large bowl, combine cornstarch, salt and remaining sugar; whisk in egg yolks until smooth.

2. Slowly pour hot milk mixture in a thin stream into egg yolk mixture, whisking constantly. Whisk in cocoa. Return the mixture to the saucepan and bring to a boil, stirring constantly until thickened, about 1 minute. Immediately remove from the heat.

3. Stir in chocolate, butter and vanilla until melted. Whisk until completely smooth. Cool for 15 minutes, stirring occasionally. Transfer to dessert dishes. Serve warm or refrigerate, covered, 1 hour. Just before serving, top with raspberries if desired.

Contest Winner

Gingersnap Crumb Pear Pie

This basic recipe was one my grandmother used for making crumble pies from fresh fruit. She simply substituted oats, gingersnaps or vanilla wafers depending on the fruit. Pear was always my favorite. I added the ginger and caramel to give it a new twist.

—FAY MORELAND WICHITA FALLS, TX

PREP: 35 MIN. + CHILLING • **BAKE:** 1 HOUR 20 MINUTES + COOLING
MAKES: 8 SERVINGS

    Pastry for single-crust pie (9 inches)

TOPPING
- 1 **cup crushed gingersnap cookies (about 16 cookies)**
- ¼ **cup all-purpose flour**
- ¼ **cup packed brown sugar**
- **Pinch salt**
- ½ **cup cold butter, cubed**

FILLING
- ⅔ **cup sugar**
- ⅓ **cup all-purpose flour**
- ½ **teaspoon ground ginger**
- ¼ **teaspoon salt**
- 2½ **pounds ripe pears (about 4 medium), peeled and thinly sliced**
- 1 **tablespoon lemon juice**
- 1 **teaspoon vanilla extract**
- **Hot caramel ice cream topping, optional**

1. On a lightly floured surface, roll pastry dough to a ⅛-in.-thick circle; transfer to a 9-in. pie plate. Trim and flute edge. Refrigerate 30 minutes. Preheat oven to 400°.

2. Line unpricked pastry with a double thickness of foil. Fill with pie weights, dried beans or uncooked rice. Bake 15-20 minutes or until the edges are light golden brown. Remove foil and weights; bake 3-6 minutes longer or until bottom is golden brown. Cool on a wire rack. Reduce oven setting to 350°.

3. For topping, in a food processor, combine the crushed cookies, flour, brown sugar and salt. Add the butter; pulse until crumbly.

4. For filling, in a large bowl, mix sugar, flour, ginger and salt. Add pears, lemon juice and vanilla; toss gently to combine. Transfer to crust; cover with topping.

5. Place pie on a baking sheet; bake 60-70 minutes longer or until topping is lightly browned and pears are tender. Cover loosely with foil during the last 15 minutes if needed to prevent overbrowning. Cool on a wire rack at least 1 hour before serving. If desired, drizzle with caramel topping.

PASTRY FOR SINGLE-CRUST PIE (9 INCHES): *Combine 1¼ cups all-purpose flour and ¼ teaspoon salt; cut in ½ cup cold butter until crumbly. Gradually add 3-5 tablespoons ice water, tossing with a fork until dough holds together when pressed. Wrap in plastic wrap and refrigerate 1 hour.*

NOTE *Let pie weights cool before storing. Beans and rice may be reused for pie weights, but not for cooking.*

Nutella-Stuffed Strawberries

Gourmet strawberries are pricey to order but easy to make. We serve strawberries with hazelnut spread as a crowd-pleasing appetizer or dessert.

—DARLENE BRENDEN SALEM, OR

PREP: 15 MIN. + CHILLING • **MAKES:** 1 DOZEN

- 12 **large fresh strawberries**
- ¼ **cup Nutella**
- 1 **cup milk chocolate chips, melted**
- ¼ **cup chopped hazelnuts**
- **Confectioners' sugar**

1. Remove stems from strawberries. Using a paring knife, cut out centers; pipe Nutella into strawberries.

2. Insert a toothpick into the side of each strawberry. Holding toothpick, quickly dip stem end of strawberry into melted chocolate; allow excess to drip off. Sprinkle with hazelnuts; place strawberries on a waxed paper-lined baking sheet, point side up. Remove toothpicks; refrigerate strawberries until set. Just before serving, dust with confectioners' sugar.

Substitutions & Equivalents

EQUIVALENT MEASURES

3 teaspoons	= 1 tablespoon		16 tablespoons	= 1 cup
4 tablespoons	= ¼ cup		2 cups	= 1 pint
5⅓ tablespoons	= ⅓ cup		4 cups	= 1 quart
8 tablespoons	= ½ cup		4 quarts	= 1 gallon

FOOD EQUIVALENTS

GRAINS

Macaroni	1 cup (3½ ounces) uncooked	=	2½ cups cooked
Noodles, Medium	3 cups (4 ounces) uncooked	=	4 cups cooked
Popcorn	⅓ - ½ cup unpopped	=	8 cups popped
Rice, Long Grain	1 cup uncooked	=	3 cups cooked
Rice, Quick-Cooking	1 cup uncooked	=	2 cups cooked
Spaghetti	8 ounces uncooked	=	4 cups cooked

CRUMBS

Bread	1 slice	=	¾ cup soft crumbs, ¼ cup fine dry crumbs
Graham Crackers	7 squares	=	½ cup finely crushed
Buttery Round Crackers	12 crackers	=	½ cup finely crushed
Saltine Crackers	14 crackers	=	½ cup finely crushed

FRUITS

Bananas	1 medium	=	⅓ cup mashed
Lemons	1 medium	=	3 tablespoons juice, 2 teaspoons grated peel
Limes	1 medium	=	2 tablespoons juice, 1½ teaspoons grated peel
Oranges	1 medium	=	¼ -⅓ cup juice, 4 teaspoons grated peel

VEGETABLES

Cabbage	1 head	= 5 cups shredded		Green Pepper	1 large	= 1 cup chopped
Carrots	1 pound	= 3 cups shredded		Mushrooms	½ pound	= 3 cups sliced
Celery	1 rib	= ½ cup chopped		Onions	1 medium	= ½ cup chopped
Corn	1 ear fresh	= ⅔ cup kernels		Potatoes	3 medium	= 2 cups cubed

NUTS

Almonds	1 pound	= 3 cups chopped		Pecan Halves	1 pound	= 4½ cups chopped
Ground Nuts	3¾ ounces	= 1 cup		Walnuts	1 pound	= 3¾ cups chopped

EASY SUBSTITUTIONS

When you need...		Use...
Baking Powder	1 teaspoon	½ teaspoon cream of tartar + ¼ teaspoon baking soda
Buttermilk	1 cup	1 tablespoon lemon juice or vinegar + enough milk to measure 1 cup (let stand 5 minutes before using)
Cornstarch	1 tablespoon	2 tablespoons all-purpose flour
Honey	1 cup	1¼ cups sugar + ¼ cup water
Half-and-Half Cream	1 cup	1 tablespoon melted butter + enough whole milk to measure 1 cup
Onion	1 small, chopped (⅓ cup)	1 teaspoon onion powder or 1 tablespoon dried minced onion
Tomato Juice	1 cup	½ cup tomato sauce + ½ cup water
Tomato Sauce	2 cups	¾ cup tomato paste + 1 cup water
Unsweetened Chocolate	1 square (1 ounce)	3 tablespoons baking cocoa + 1 tablespoon shortening or oil
Whole Milk	1 cup	½ cup evaporated milk + ½ cup water

Cooking Terms

Here's a quick reference for some of the most common cooking terms used in recipes:

BASTE To moisten food with melted butter, pan drippings, marinades or other liquid to add more flavor and juiciness.

BEAT A rapid movement to combine ingredients using a fork, spoon, wire whisk or electric mixer.

BLEND To combine ingredients until *just* mixed.

BOIL To heat liquids until bubbles form that cannot be "stirred down." In the case of water, the temperature will reach 212°.

BONE To remove all meat from the bone before cooking.

CREAM To beat ingredients together to a smooth consistency, usually in the case of butter and sugar for baking.

DASH A small amount of seasoning, less than $\frac{1}{8}$ teaspoon. If using a shaker, a dash would comprise a quick flip of the container.

DREDGE To coat foods with flour or other dry ingredients. Most often done with pot roasts and stew meat before browning.

FOLD To incorporate several ingredients by careful and gentle turning with a spatula. Used generally with beaten egg whites or whipped cream when mixing into the rest of the ingredients to keep the batter light.

JULIENNE To cut foods into long thin strips much like matchsticks. Used most often for salads and stir-fry dishes.

MINCE To cut into very fine pieces. Used often for garlic or fresh herbs.

PARBOIL To cook partially. Usually used in the case of chicken, sausages and vegetables.

PARTIALLY SET Describes the consistency of gelatin after it has been chilled for a short amount of time. Mixture should resemble the consistency of egg whites.

PUREE To process foods to a smooth mixture. Can be prepared in an electric blender, food processor, food mill or sieve.

SAUTE To fry quickly in a small amount of fat, stirring almost constantly. Most often done with onions, mushrooms and other chopped vegetables.

SCORE To cut slits partway through the outer surface of foods. Often used with ham or flank steak.

STIR-FRY To cook meats and/or vegetables with a constant stirring motion in a small amount of oil in a wok or skillet over high heat.

GENERAL RECIPE INDEX

ALPHABETICAL RECIPE INDEX